D1459258

BIG-HEARTED MAN

Kate Boydell

BIG-HEARTED MAN

Copyright © 2003 Kate Boydell

All rights reserved. Apart from any fair dealing for the purposes of research or private study, or criticism or review, as permitted under the Copyright, Designs and Patents Act 1988, this publication may only be reproduced, stored or transmitted, in any form or by any means, with the prior permission in writing of the publishers, or in the case of reprographic reproduction in accordance with the terms of licences issued by the Copyright Licensing Agency. Enquiries concerning reproduction outside those terms should be sent to the publishers.

The rights of Kate Boydell to be identified as the author of this work have been asserted by her in accordance with the Copyright Designs and Patents Act, 1988.

Matador
12 Manor Walk, Coventry Road, Market Harborough, Leics LE16 9BP, UK
Tel: (+44) 1858 468828 / 469898   Email: books@troubador.co.uk   Web: www.troubador.co.uk/matador

The Love Song of J. Alfred Prufrock
by T. S. Eliot
is reproduced by permission of Faber and Faber Ltd

ISBN
1 899293 34 5 (PB)
1 899293 39 6 (HB)

Some of the names and places mentioned in this book have been altered to avoid potential embarrassment.

Typesetting: Troubador Publishing Ltd, Market Harborough, UK
Printed and bound by WS Bookwell Ltd, Finland

Matador is an imprint of Troubador Publishing Ltd

For Rosie and Alice, my joy and my life.

Come, my Way, my Truth, my Life:
Such a Way, as gives us breath:
Such a Truth, as ends all strife:
Such a Life, as killeth death.

Come, my Light, my Feast, my Strength:
Such a Light, as shows a feast:
Such a Feast, as mends in length:
Such a Strength, as makes a guest.

Come, my Joy, my Love, my Heart:
Such a Joy, as none can move:
Such a Love, as none can part:
Such a Heart, as joys in love.

'The Call' by George Herbert

PART ONE

Some people glide down the neoprene road of life on silken casters, feeling hardly a bump or rattle along the way.

Charlie had been given different directions and ended up on a rutted farm track atop a unicycle with a slow puncture. His journey was never going to be an easy one - but it would be a challenge. And he didn't just face up to that challenge - he pedalled at it full tilt.

I was destined to be the girl who ran alongside him, holding onto his jumper and slowing him down just enough to allow him to keep his balance. But had I known then what I know now, would I have changed anything? Would I have turned my back on him and chosen an easier path? Would I have let go of his jumper and watched as he cycled unsteadily into the distance?

No, I would not. Once I had met Charlie, I knew that whatever happened he was mine - and mine forever.

Chapter One

True love is something that most women aspire to, yet few are lucky enough ever to attain. You can waste endless hours in the back row of a multiplex, necking with the man of your dreams to romantic films by Nora Ephron – but you might still emerge blinking into the sunlight with little more than a bad case of stubble rash and a deep loathing of Tom Hanks. Falling in love is not an exact science – there are books that tell you 'How to' but they never tell you 'Where to' because nobody really knows. You can spend a lifetime searching lonely hearts ads and the lily-strewn margins of fishponds; you can kiss a thousand princes and still end up married to a gigantic, warty toad.

It was January 1988; I was twenty-three years old and although I had kissed a few frogs, I had yet to meet a prince. My social diary was as empty as an 'it' girl's biscuit tin, but I doggedly held onto the belief that somewhere in Devon lurked the man of my dreams.

They say that you cannot look for love – that love has to find you, but I didn't just want it to find me, I wanted it to hit me like a speeding prop forward and carry me off into the stands. I watched and waited but little did I know that true love had already found me – in fact, true love walked past me almost every day.

I was working at that time as a freelance sound recordist and was regularly employed by Television South West, the local Independent television company based in Plymouth. When I arrived each morning I invariably ended up sitting in reception, waiting to be collected by whichever cameraman I had been booked to work with. I always arrived early and to pass the time I used to watch shoes.

Shoes can tell you a lot about a man and it's much less obvious to stare at a man's shoes than it is to stare at his face. Any man can smarten up an old suit with a good pair of shoes, but he can never disguise bad taste in footwear by putting on an Armani suit and hoping that nobody will notice the crinkly crocodile snouts poking out beneath his turn-ups.

I sat and watched as people passed by and on the whole the selection of footwear on offer left a little to be desired. The engineers who walked past me displayed a worrying preference for sandals – summer and winter. Clarks Trekkers were fairly popular too, and tended to be worn by big boy scouts who combined the chunky utility look with a bunch of keys attached to a belt loop. When I saw a pair of burgundy slip-ons, I didn't even need to look up to see what their owner looked like. I knew he would be a middle manager, wearing a shiny, double-breasted suit, with huge lop-sided shoulder pads. I also knew that there would be a hilarious cartoon character lurking somewhere in the deep recesses of his undergarments.

It was hopeless. Weeks went by without a glimpse of decent leather and then I saw them; they were brown leather brogues, often muddy but definitely not from a high street chain – these were handmade shoes. I also noted that the right shoe had a built-up heel and that its owner had a bit of a lop-sided gait – but there was a kind of positive confidence about the way he walked – a spring in his step which only added to my curiosity.

That was it; I was smitten. I had fallen in love with his shoes, but I still needed more clues to his character – I needed to shake his hand.

In the course of my job I was lucky enough to meet people from a variety of different backgrounds. I might be introduced to a foundry worker one day and a prince the next, I never really knew and it didn't really matter because I generally forgot their names as soon as we had exchanged introductions. I had a problem with names; the words came into my head and were then filed by a very absent-minded librarian in the wool shop of my brain. The wool shop is a place that I never visit, and so the names remained there, nestled forever in a dusty corner amongst the balls of lime-green angora.

But whilst I forgot people's names I always remembered their handshake. After shoes, I think it is the hands that give the biggest clues to a man's character.

Picture the scene; you are at a party and you are introduced to an attractive and more important, single man. He looks into your eyes and places into your hand something cold, clammy and very very limp. You don't know whether to shake it or give it the kiss of life, but you have, in that instant, made a full character assessment based on his lifeless digits. A limp handshake says: 'I am dull, humourless and weak-willed. I still live with my parents. I love the feel of a polyester shirt and smell it gives off after I've had it on for a few days. I still have a model railway in the attic, and I think that my trains are called Hornby because I get an erection just thinking about them.'

At the other end of the scale is crushing. A man should never squeeze a woman's hand too hard, it's unnecessary and it hurts. A man who crushes your hand says ' I'm a manly man's man. I have a centre parting – down my spine. I love contact sports and I know five ways to kill, using only a rolled-up newspaper. I like brief, vigorous sex – but the woman I'm with would probably have more fun with my rolled up newspaper.

Firm is what you need. Firm says 'I'm a decent chap with no unspeakable personal habits. I love women and understand how to please them. I know that a G spot is not an abbreviated term for an oral hygiene spray. I'm confident about myself without being too cocky. I can cook, but I don't wear a ridiculous pinny with breasts on it. In short, I am a man who is definitely worth more than a handshake'.

Firm is good. We like firm.

Feet and hands – if you get those right, everything in between should be just dandy.

I must have sat in that reception area on and off for nearly a year, watching the man in the brogues come and go. He appeared each morning as bright and glorious as a shaft of sunlight breaking through a thundercloud on a summer's day. I grew to love his voice, his laugh and the confident sound of his footsteps as he left the building. I loved to watch him, study him, absorb every detail. He was handsome and swarthy with a strong jaw, straight white teeth and bright, intelligent eyes – his was the sort of face you just wanted to cup gently in your hands and cover with soft kisses. He was always dressed in country clothes and sometimes he wore big leather lace-up boots; often there was a girl with him – too often for my liking. As he walked into the foyer he would always stop and have a word with Polly, the receptionist. Most people seemed to be in too much of a hurry to say 'hello' – but not the man in the brogues. And as he was leaving he would say good morning to Derek, the security guard, 'Alright Charles' Derek would say, and off he would go, out of the sliding doors and out of my life once more.

Love hadn't hit me; love hadn't swept me off my feet. Love limped past me wearing a tweed jacket and a smile.

Love didn't even know I existed.

I wanted so much to talk to him. Why couldn't he just stop and ask me the time or pause and look at me just once I wondered? There seemed to be only two options left open to me. Firstly I could use a trip wire – but I decided that

Charlie, with his puppy, Vicky, at Chagford Show, 1987

it might be a little obvious. Second, I could faint at his feet – but I didn't do fainting. I had to face the fact that I was never going to get to talk to him unless fate took a hand. And then one day it did. Lucy threw up.

Lucy was a staff sound recordist. On that fateful January day she called in sick and I was asked to replace her at short notice. I arrived and took up my usual position in reception, waiting for a glimpse of the brogues and was happy when I saw them – but instead of walking past as they always did, they stopped right in front of me.

'Hello, I'm Charlie' came the now-familiar voice; 'I'm the researcher on the business programme.'

He placed his hand in mine. It was strong and broad and then he squeezed – firmly and assuredly but not too hard. My brain was shouting 'Firm! We have firmness here! We have the shoes, we have the grip – jump, jump, jump!'
And then Charlie snapped my brain back into gear by saying,

'We've got a few minutes to wait, so can I get you a cup of tea?'

We walked into the canteen and he went off to get me a cup of Earl Grey. This was my big chance. I had him all to myself and I thought I delivered my opening line of, 'Yes, please.' in a subtle, yet seductive sort of way. I was excited and apprehensive. I hadn't been struck by a thunderbolt, I was just happy to have the undivided attention of the fantasy object of my affections after all this time.

He came back with the tea and started talking. I have no idea what he said, because to this day I can only remember one thing – his eyes. Charlie wasn't saying anything special to me – it was all in his gaze. It was a look of such intensity that I found it almost impossible to meet it for more than a few seconds. He wasn't looking me up and down in a 'phwaaar' kinds of way – his eyes were staring straight into mine, fixed and unwavering. Every girl knows the difference between a casual glance and a full on, 'I want you,' stare. Charlie's stare said, 'I want you – on the counter by the Wagon Wheels – right now.'

I knew then and there that he had seen something that no other man had seen before, something was shining back at me out of his eyes, and the more he stared, the more I wanted him to stare. I tried to remain composed, and as we chatted I made a quick visual assessment. I guessed he was in his mid to late twenties. He had a decent-sized nose (always a good sign) and a wonderfully kind, sexy mouth. He was a few inches taller than me and looked fit and lean. But it was his voice that had the greatest effect upon me. He had the sort of voice that any telesales operator would have given up his commission for. It was deep and mesmeric, with all the confidence but none of the twitishness that can come from a public school education. When he spoke you could tell his words came straight from the heart. There was no artifice about Charlie, his honesty and integrity were immediately apparent and I knew at that moment, that before me, perched on a stool, sat the man of my dreams.

I wanted him to see me at my best that day and I had to convince him that he couldn't live without me. I wanted to be funny; I wanted to be confident. I wanted to be coy, to be a vamp, to be coquettish. I wanted him to see that I was

Sound recording on location for T.S.W.

witty and intelligent. I wanted him to see all of those things in me, but I was a sound recordist, not a supermodel – wearing headphones and an anorak, not Dolce and Gabanna.

It is commonly acknowledged that being a sound recordist is the least cool occupation in television. Nobody takes the slightest interest in what a sound recordist thinks – and why should they? Sound isn't sexy. You are always left trailing after the dashing cameraman like some acoustic afterthought. The only time anybody listens to you is when you have to tell them to shut up, and if that's not bad enough, you have to walk around all day wearing a pair of nerdy headphones.

It really is impossible to look anything but sad in a pair of headphones; they mess up your hair and you can hear nothing except from the direction that your gun mic is pointing, so you are always isolated. It is quite a weird sensation, and after a few years it makes you as mad as a monkey with eight legs.

I hadn't always been a sound recordist, I never really wanted to be one – it was all question of necessity.

Chapter Two

I was born in 1964, the third of four daughters, and from a very young age I developed a fascination for all things mechanical. Before I learned to walk I would crawl around the kitchen, looking for things to unscrew; and as I grew older so my passion for tinkering increased. I loved Meccano and anything that could be taken to bits and put back again – this included our rocking horse, which didn't actually rock but bounced up and down on four springs attached to a metal frame. I must have only been about four years old but I somehow managed to undo the nuts which held the springs in place, and when one of my sisters came in for a canter, the rocking horse collapsed and she ended up being dumped rather unceremoniously on the play room floor.

Luckily my parents indulged me in my strange choice of playthings. They encouraged me to build weird and wonderful machines and never made me feel that just because I was a girl, I couldn't ask for a train set or a trumpet for my birthday. I was brought up to have confidence in myself; my parents tried always to show pride, and not disapproval, and in that way I was able to develop the individuality and strength of character that I would come to rely on in later life.

I was never a violent child, but guns and weaponry always fascinated me. I still have a photograph of my father taking his four little girls to the sweet shop on a cold Northumbrian morning. There is nothing remarkable about the picture; Jane and Sara, my older sisters, walked, and I rode in the front of the pram, protecting Joanna, my younger sister, from monsters with a large plastic machine gun.

When I was six I asked Father Christmas for a fishing rod, which caused a few raised eyebrows because neither he nor any of his little elfin helpers had any interest in fishing. Soon I was reading *The Angling Times* whilst my sisters read *Jackie*, although I must say that the problem page of *The Angling Times* didn't have quite the same appeal as 'Dear Jackie'. Advice on disgorging hooks and how to keep your maggots warm was never really going to be much help in guiding a young girl through the trials of adolescence, but somehow I managed to learn enough from my sisters to get me through, whilst having the added bonus of always knowing how to warm up a cold maggot.

I discovered the delights of the internal combustion engine from the television. Before the advent of full time transmission, BBC 2 used to show public information films, which I savoured as if they were Disney films. They weren't really meant for children; they were the televisual equivalent of expanding foam – cheap, banal and designed to fill dead air time – but I didn't know that,

I thought they were fascinating and I can still clearly remember them.

There was one about a man in Thailand who went to buy a new outboard motor for his canoe, and another one about a science show in Stuttgart, but that one never really held my attention for long – too many Germans in sandals. My favourite by far was an instructional film on how a car engine worked. It showed the engine in cross-section and demonstrated the process of combustion, using coloured lights to illustrate each stage. This film must have stayed in my sub-conscious, because I was soon able to clean the spark plugs on my father's car and service his lawnmower having had no instruction whatsoever.

My father was a highly regarded journalist at that time and not at all inter-ested in practicalities. If a plug needed changing it would be my mother or me who would fix it. Mechanical objects were a complete mystery to daddy and it was all he could do to fill up the car with petrol. He worked extremely hard dur-ing the week and would spend much of the weekend gardening with my moth-er or cursing the lawnmower. Other people had boring machines called Atco or Suffolk Punch, but ours was very grand, ours was called a Fucking Flymo.

My mother is an intensely practical and loving woman who taught me to believe that nothing in life is impossible, and that if you have the will and the determination you can do anything that you set your mind to. The only excep-tion to that rule in my case was knitting.

I went to quite a few schools during the course of my education; my father

The Dobson girls – from left, Joanna, Sara, Jane and Kate

worked for the B.B.C. and we had to move every time he got promoted – which turned out to be quite often. Most of the schools were fine, but there was one that was notable for the misery it caused me. I was a relatively bright student and very well behaved, but for some reason I was never chosen to be a prefect. Whilst my friends were inside guarding doors, or chatting in the prefects' room, I was left outside. I spent every solitary break-time kicking a stone around the playground perimeter, or sitting on a bench on my own. My only consolation during that time of loneliness was that although I was unhappy, I knew I would never be sad enough to sit in the cloakroom doing crochet with the misfit girls. There was a group of them who spent many a happy hour with an old cotton reel with some nails in it, making long tubes of wool. Why? How many scarves can a hamster wear for God's sake?

And when the girls were sufficiently experienced they would progress to the crochet hooks, and then there was no end to their creative talents. It seemed to make them happy, although to this day I cannot understand why.

I must have been mentally scarred by the experience, because now when I try and imagine what Hell must be like, I don't see myself being thrown into a burning pit full of writhing bodies suffering all kinds of unspeakable torments. What I see is a little shop, which I enter to the sound of a jangly bell, to be greeted by the sight of shelves of multicoloured lambswool and acrylic mohair. The walls are lined with are pictures of men in patterned cardigans looking thoughtful, and hideous babies in powder pink crocheted romper suits. The woman behind the counter is called Doreen, and when I walk up to her she shakes my hand limply and says, 'We are all one big happy family here, so make yourself at home.' She gives me my uniform of purple crimpelene A-line skirt, and brown and orange jumper with bat-wing sleeves – and then I realise that I will be working with Doreen in her wool shop until the end of time.
Now that is my idea of eternal damnation.

Apart from my irrational fear of Fairisle, and periods of loneliness at school, my childhood was a happy one. I completed my education in the summer of 1982, but having finished my A levels I found myself on the horns of a dilemma. I had grown up with a love of mechanical things but when I had to decide what to do with my life I was completely stumped. What I really wanted was a job that entailed being outdoors, that was not nine to five and that utilised all the practical skills that I had been developing since the age of three. I tried to follow in my father's footsteps and become a journalist, but failed the entrance exam to the N.U.J. course at Portsmouth Polytechnic.

Despite this obvious failure I was never made to feel like I'd let my father down. There seemed to be no easy solution to my predicament; my parents had done everything they could to help me and so, in desperation, my father suggested a course in shorthand and typing and in desperation I took his advice. I enrolled at a college in Southampton on a course which to me sounded about as much fun as having cocktail sticks jammed under my fingernails. But the week before I was due to start out on the road to Pitman purgatory, I got a lucky break, which would help to shape the rest of my life.

We had been expecting a visit from a director who was an old friend of my father. His son had just begun a career as a wildlife cameraman and wanted a garden location within the New Forest. Our house fitted the bill perfectly. It was a large Victorian vicarage, right in the heart of the forest, with stunning gardens filled with specimen azaleas and rhododendrons. The main bedroom had French doors leading out onto a balcony that overlooked the lawns, and from there you could look straight out onto beech woods and the heathland beyond.

My father was at that time head of BBC South, and had little to do with location filming on the whole, but when he did it usually involved great big green outside broadcast trucks. This was what I was expecting to trundle over the cattle grid that day, so as you can imagine I was a little disappointed when two Volvo estate cars came gingerly up the drive. Out of the first Volvo stepped John King, the director, and his son Simon, who would later become a very well known wildlife cameraman. The other Volvo held the crew, or to be more precise a man called David and his camera.

They set up the camera and started to film. I hovered about in cool yet eager sort of way, trying not to get in the way but desperate to see what the cameraman was doing. When the shoot was over, John, the director, came up to me and asked if I wanted to come along and watch the rest of the day's filming. I was in the cameraman's car with my seatbelt done up almost before he had time to finish his sentence.

It was a glorious autumn day and as we drove along I chatted about my interests and my impending secretarial sentence. When we arrived at the next location I helped David unload his gear, and as we talked, he showed me how to load film into the camera and how the check for hairs in the gate. (As the film runs past the aperture of the camera or 'gate', tiny strips of emulsion are sometimes shaved off. These appear on the exposed film as wiggly hairs, usually at the bottom of frame, and if they are not removed they can ruin an entire roll of film.)

I carried the tripod and generally made myself as useful as possible for the rest of the afternoon. After the shoot David drove me back home, and as we pulled over the cattle grid he asked if I would be interested in training as his camera assistant. I tried to appear nonchalant as I bit his hand off, and then ran into the house to tell my parents the good news.

I was eighteen years old and about to train for a job that only a handful of girls did at that time. But I knew it was exactly the right job for me. I had started my secretarial course, and in my spare time I would get on my moped and ride over to David's house. I sat in his living room with my shorthand notepad and he would dictate to me everything that he knew about filming. I learned about film stock, lenses, tripods and all the technical aspects of using a film camera. I would then trudge off to my college course and whilst the other students were typing what our teacher had dictated, I was typing up the notes I had made at David's house so that I could memorise them for the next time I saw him.

I was taken out on news stories, which in those days were all shot on film, and at some stage during the shoot David would get the reporter to ask me a question about a particular aspect of filming. I was expected to know the

answer, and in that way I learned the job inside out. It was physically very demanding and involved carrying all the gear for the cameraman, sometimes over very long distances An assistant is responsible for loading the camera magazines with rolls of 16mm film. This is done blind, in a black bag – which was literally that, a bag made of lightproof black cloth with elasticated sleeves. This was the most important job of a camera assistant; if you cocked it up and exposed the film to light, it would fog and destroy all the cameraman's hard work. It was a job that required great manual dexterity and it had to be done at speed – anything over a minute was too slow.
It would soon become second nature to me.

I carried on with my apprenticeship for some months, until I became an accomplished camera assistant and was able to graduate from helping out on simple news stories, to working on documentaries. During this time I was lucky enough to fly over to Germany on board a Hercules transport plane, to film Operation Lionheart. We stayed for a week as guests the Army Air Corps, and for me it was like having real Action Men to play with. We were flown about in Lynx and Gazelle helicopters, by pilots who made Tom Cruise seem rather fey. I learned the procedure for loading an air-to-air missile on board a Lynx, (the men thought I might find that useful in later life). I had the best time. I was only eighteen years old and I was living a dream.

I met up with my some of my old college friends in a pub a few months later. They were all full of stories of university life, of getting drunk and going to gigs and doing all the things that students do. As they sat and praised the efficacy of Pernod and black, I quietly sipped my gin and tonic and I realised that my life was now totally removed from theirs. I had forsaken hedonism for realism, I was working for a living, whilst they were clearly having the time of their lives – but I had no regrets. I know must have seem so straight to them and I suppose that I was; after all I was still a virgin, I'd never smoked a spliff or got drunk to the point of passing out. But swapping a mortarboard for a clapperboard was the best thing I ever did. I left them in the pub to enjoy the rest of their evening and drove home to pack for the next day's shoot, knowing full well that I would probably see them again.

I had to travel up to Stratford Upon Avon the next day to film a theatre company. It was a shoot that required two crews; the other crew had come from Birmingham and we worked in tandem throughout the day. The filming went well and when it was time to pack up, the cameraman from the opposition came up to me and asked for my business card. I didn't have anything like that, as I had only ever worked for David, so I gave him my phone number and thought no more about it.

I was at home a couple of months later when the phone rang. It was Jim Knights, the cameraman who had asked for my number, and who also happened to be head of a facilities house called Magpie Films. They were very well known within the industry, so much so in fact that the BBC allowed them to base themselves rather incongruously in a Portakabin in the car park of the Pebble Mill Studios.

Jim wanted me to come up the next morning for a shoot, so naturally I said I would be there. I drove up early the next morning from Hampshire with some trepidation because I knew that I would be closely watched, not only because I was new, but also because I was a female assistant, which in those days was something of a rarity.

To my great relief the day went without a hitch. I had a great time and when I got back Jim came out of the Portakabin to greet me, beaming from ear to ear and clutching all sorts of Magpie goodies. He gave me a leather wallet, a key ring and a pen and told me that I had done really well, which made me feel a bit like a runner-up on Crackerjack. He seemed genuinely delighted with my performance and said that he had lots more work if I wanted it. I said I did – and that was the start of the best four years any girl could possibly have had.

My first impression of Jim was that he was a bit of a 'geezer'. He wore Farrah slacks and a chunky gold identity bracelet and he ended every sentence with 'mate'- but he had an amazing talent for charming people and was a very gifted cameraman. We had a brief chat about what was expected of me and then he introduced me to the rest of the boys and left me to it.

Life at Magpie could have been very difficult for me. After all, I was going to be the only female in a crew room of sixteen men. If I had upset the dynamics of that close-knit group then I would not have been asked back. As I saw it there were three ways for me to approach working with the Magpie males. Firstly, I could try to become like them. I could wear Doc Marten's, get a crew cut, swear loudly and more often than the roughest rigger and talk about football and cars until the men begged me to change the subject to knitting. Secondly, I could adopt the girlie approach. I could wear tight, revealing clothes and lots of make-up. I could flirt whenever possible, make lots of suggestive remarks to individuals in the group, and be really vulgar at every opportunity. Thirdly, I could do my job and do it well; expect no special treatment but act like a lady at all times. I chose the third approach.

Butch girls are a novelty at first but most men like to have a real woman around, one that won't object to having the door opened for her. It makes a man feel good to act like gentleman once in a while. On the other hand, being overtly girlie and flirtatious may amuse the men for a while, but if it means that you don't pull your weight then they will soon get tired of you. Also, toying with men that you work very closely with is asking for trouble. Word gets around and soon any credibility that you might have had will evaporate like cheap perfume. Men may laugh when a girl is really vulgar, but secretly they don't like it one little bit. You can't win a man over by trying to shock him – it just means that you lower yourself in his eyes and he will stop treating you with respect and start treating you with contempt.

I didn't act like some paragon of virtue; I had a dirty mind and an even dirtier laugh but I always knew my limits. I pulled my weight at work but back in the crew room I was allowed to mother the men a little. I made them tea and generally tried to look after them, and they in their turn looked after me. I never needed to use the 'F' word.

Feminism was and still is an anathema to me. Every woman is equipped with the most effective and powerful weapon in the fight for equality – her sex. Men love women – pure and simple, and if you just bypass all the flannel and appeal to their most basic instincts, they become putty in your hands. Be aggressive to a man and he will be aggressive back; be submissive and he will play the caveman and drag you around by your hair. Be smart and sassy; let the man know that he is allowed to keep his testicles and not only will he respect you – he will look after you.

I worked hard at Magpie but I loved every minute of it, loading the car each morning with big silver boxes and driving off to exotic locations like Stoke On Trent and Walsall. I travelled in the company of men who had an amazing outlook on life and a collective sense of humour that made even the grimmest job bearable. They weren't going to get rich working for Jim, but they were going to enjoy themselves. I worked on every programme from Playschool to Panorama and I was also taken along on a number of undercover operations.

We made several documentaries about the miner's strike, filming covertly for much of the time and trying to avoid the wrath of the striking miners. Mike Wilke, who was one of the Directors of Magpie, later chose me to assist him on a shoot he had been asked to do in Belfast. He had become my mentor, and he chose to impart words of wisdom to me about the art of camerawork. Physically he was the total opposite of Jim, he was stocky and bearded and eschewed Farrah slacks for baggy cords and desert boots, but he was equally funny, and the days that I spent in his company never seemed long enough.

The Belfast job was for a documentary about Supergrasses, which would go on to achieve a certain notoriety after Margaret Thatcher tried to ban it. We filmed on the Falls Road and interviewed a tearful mother in the infamous Divis Flats, about her son, who had been killed by a plastic bullet during the 'Troubles'. We drove through staunch Protestant housing estates which were marked out by their distinctive red, white, and blue kerbstones, and secretly filmed the wife of man who was in prison for terrorist offences too numerous to mention. An army helicopter hovered over the house for the whole time we were there – but then we did look rather suspicious, trooping into the house of a known Protestant terrorist, laden with silver boxes. We did take the precaution of leaving the tripod case in the car, just in case the soldiers thought it was some sort of enormous bazooka, and when the filming was over we all but came out of the house waving a white flag.

I returned to England feeling as if I had just witnessed something incredible – it was living history and I had helped commit it to film. It was extremely dangerous work, but thrilling at the same time and I felt privileged to have been asked to do it. Mike never said, 'Oh, Kate's a girl, so she can't go out on any dangerous jobs.' He knew I could do the job and I made sure that I didn't let him down. I loved my job and my colleagues and would have stayed at Magpie – but times were changing. A dark cloud was looming on the horizon and its name was video.

There was always a kind of romanticism associated with a film camera. It had something to do with way a simple mechanical object could create such breathtaking images. It was as if the camera had given life to the film, a frame at a time, 25 frames a second. The film camera was a thing of beauty in itself, especially the Arriflex SR2. It's German, it's beautifully engineered, it is the Mercedes Benz of film cameras, and I knew it inside out. There were other makes of course, but it was the Arri that did it for me.

But the Betacam, a Japanese invention that was the first professional video camera to carry its own recorder, heralded the dawn of the new age. It was big, bulky and very ugly. The pictures it produced were instant – but had no soul. Even the most glorious sunset would appear harsh and clinical on the screen. The Betacam sat on your shoulder but stuck out by over a foot at the back, which made it a serious danger to unwary members of the public. I have been present at many smart functions where some hapless mayoress has ended up with 15 minutes of pain and not 15 minutes of fame, as a direct result of mis-timed whip-pan.

My job started to become rather dull. There is no satisfaction and no skill involved in simply plonking a tape into a camera. My clapperboard, which had seen a lot of action – literally, was now redundant and I knew that in time I would be too. I had been offered the chance to go and live in the States and so I resigned from the job I loved.

I consider myself very fortunate to have experienced a working life of such richness and diversity and I still think about it with wonderment. The friend-ships that were formed all those years ago are still just as strong today, even though we may not see each other for years at a time. They were my brothers and still are.

As far as romance was concerned, my experience with men was somewhat limited by my job. I was rarely at home for long; I lived out of a suitcase for a large part of the time and when I got home all I wanted to do was veg out. Most people meet a partner through work, but I had made it a rule right from the start never to get involved with any of my male colleagues. I had seen the result of enough overnight dalliances to know that my hard-earned reputation would lie in tatters if I ever got caught up with another crewmember.

The situation seemed rather hopeless. My mother was tearing her hair out. My sisters had all left home and between them had amassed quite a respectable tally of boyfriends. I was definitely lagging behind. This was nothing new how-ever, and one day my mother came up with a cunning plan. She told me that I should go to a pub and it was there, she decided, that I would meet a nice young man. I had to tell her gently but firmly that I was not about to find the man of my dreams by sitting alone looking like some desperate hayseed hooker, in a dis-mal lounge bar filled with horse brasses and men in cardigans. The next bright idea involved the Young Farmers. (I had actually always fancied marrying a farmer – but one with clean fingernails and a farm manager to do all the hard work.) I decided for the sake of a quiet life that I would give it a try, and so I found myself sitting alone one evening in a pub full of ruddy-cheeked rustics. I eventually plucked up the courage to speak, but I never got to find out anything about them because they all wanted to ask me about my job in television, rather than talk about farming. Later in the evening they started to disappear in groups of two or three, out of the bar and into the loos. When they reappeared a few minutes later, they were giggling like a bunch of schoolgirls. I found out later that they had abandoned their traditional tool of merriment – the flagon of scrumpy, for the joys of amphetamines. So much for innocent rural pleasures, but at least I had discovered where the saying 'speed the plough' came from.

My romantic prospects seemed bleak indeed and my mother was unremitting in her quest to find me a man – any man, however unsuitable. One day I stopped her in the middle of a particularly lengthy diatribe and said. 'I'm not going to go out with any old saddo just for the sake of getting out of the house for a few hours. I don't mind being single because I know it won't be forever. I know that somewhere out there is the man for me – the man I am destined to be with and it is only a matter of time before I meet him'. I believed in destiny. It was something I always held onto when I thought I would never meet a man. I never wanted the ordinary, I wanted the extraordinary – but needless to say my mother was not convinced.

My romantic stoicism was gained during my formative years. I had watched as each of my three sisters brought home a variety of young men, some of whom were perfectly nice and some of whom were designed to promote premature ageing in any responsible parent. A revolting boyfriend is like a stealth bomber in the arsenal of any girl who wishes to embark on a teenage rebellion. The parental radar remains oblivious to the threat until their sweet and innocent daughter comes walking in through the door with a fellow who makes Cro-Magnon Man look like Noel Coward – and by then it's too late. Girl power is all very well – you can get a tattoo, but if you really want to upset your father, turning up with a bad boy on your arm is so much more effective.

I never had a teenage rebellion – watching my sisters go through theirs and dealing with the resulting fallout at home was enough for me. I didn't see the point in it all, so I sat on the sidelines and kept score. But I knew exactly what I wanted and what I didn't want; my last boyfriend had demonstrated that appearances can be deceptive and I had made up my mind from that moment onwards to be rather more selective in my choice of men. He was a perfectly nice chap and an amazing dancer, which is a rare and wonderful thing in a man, but our timing was all wrong.

 I met him at a New Year's Eve party; we danced all night, had a big snog and then started going out shortly afterwards. I had the expectation of spending every weekend dancing the night away at the local night club with a boy whom I had lusted after at school, but who'd never given me a second glance. I wasn't nearly glamorous enough or popular enough to catch his eye in those days, but he was a man now and he was all mine – mine to parade before the admiring gaze of all my old school mates; mine to do with what I wished.
I wished to dance...

When I turned up at his house on the occasion of our first date I had a big shock – he opened the door and I looked down and saw that his leg was in plaster from hip to ankle. He noticed my look of horror and told me that he'd broken it playing rugby and that it would be several weeks before we could hit the dance floor. I was a little disappointed to say the least, but determined to make the best of it.

He welcomed me in and we sat and talked for a while – then he got out a Freeman's catalogue and began to flick through it. I was taken off guard for a moment. I couldn't really believe that one of the coolest boys in my year was now pouring over page upon page of questionable casual wear like a middle-aged agoraphobic – but he was.

Eventually we moved away from clothing and onto the subject of music; I could have forgiven the fondness for patterned jumpers but when he told me that his two favourite singers were Cliff Richard and Michael Jackson, I knew I had made a serious mistake. His mother appeared a short while later and we all sat down for a formal tea, complete with hostess trolley and lace doilies. I made polite conversation over tinned ham and sausage rolls and then made my excuses and left.

I thought he was what I wanted but he wasn't; he was just a school girl's fantasy object and I had moved on since then. I had been around, I was more mature and worldly-wise; I knew that my perfect man would wear country clothes and proper shoes. He would have impeccable manners and a public school education. He would love rugby and hate football and he would know enough about the world for me never to become bored with his company. And most important of all, he would be funny enough to make me laugh out loud. I knew that the chances of him owning his own castle were pretty slim but I still lived in hope.

My job continued to keep me busy and I was still living out of a suitcase for a large part of the time, but I did have a couple of boyfriends in the meantime. I knew they weren't right – I was just filling in time and learning new tricks at that stage. But my life was about to change. Soon after my twenty- first birthday I was given the opportunity to go and live in Seattle for six months, and I jumped at the chance.

I had been offered a room in the house of an American couple called Jerry and Betsy Greenway, whom my parents had met whilst staying at the Mermaid Hotel in Rye. They had invited us to stay with them in Seattle the previous summer and we had cruised with them in their boat, up to the San Juan Islands, where we trolled for salmon and spotted pods of killer whales swimming in the calm waters around our boat. I found it to be the most idyllic holiday of my life and I totally fell in love with Seattle and all that it had to offer. My only love at that time was fishing and Seattle had more than enough of that to satisfy the most voracious demands of any angler.

Jerry was a keen fisherman, and he and Betsy were more than happy to have me to stay for as long as I wished, but finding casual work at that time was very difficult, as the U.S. government were clamping down hard on people who didn't have a green card. I figured that it might not be easy for me to find a job and so I decided to finance my trip by selling my car and spending the proceeds on antique fishing tackle and golf clubs.

On board *Breakwater*, with my parents Terry and Eileen, during our trip to the
San Juan Islands with Jerry and Betsy Greenway

I had begun to collect vintage tackle a few months earlier, and had struck
up a friendship with a young antiques dealer in Stratford upon Avon. I went to
see him and he agreed to sell me a quantity of his stock. I paid him trade price
for everything and came home with fantastic selection of rods, reels cartridge
bags, gun cases and golf clubs. It had to be said that working in a bar would have
been a much easier option, but I could see that there could be a market for vintage tackle overseas. The people that I had met in Seattle all seemed to fish and
they also loved English antiques, so combining the two seemed like a great way
to make a living – and so it turned out to be.

When I arrived I sorted out my stock and then set about printing up a catalogue using Betsy's typewriter and photocopier. I illustrated the catalogue with
old woodcuts of fishing tackle that I had found in a reference book, and then all
that remained was for me to ask Jerry to put the word around with his friends and
wait for them to call. And they did call. I didn't print any prices in my catalogue
– choosing instead to watch for their car pulling up the driveway. If my prospective customer drove a Mercedes then I would price the items accordingly; it was
a simple plan but it worked very well and my best sale was to a rich lawyer who
happily paid $380 for a rod, which had cost me the princely sum of £24.

I made a good living and I fished and skied to my heart's content, but after six months I became so homesick that I decided to return home. I was starved of Marmite, pork pies and irony – but nearly a stone heavier nonetheless. When my sister Jane came to collect me from the airport she was visibly startled, and from that moment onwards referred to me not as Kate, but as 'Bulky'.

My parents had moved house whilst I was away in – sneaky, but I soon tracked them down. They had retired to Devon, to a small village, which was only a few miles from the place where I was born. I arrived home needing to find a job and so I picked the name of a film company out of the yellow pages and rang them up to see if they had any work. They took me on – but I was in for a rude awakening because the cameraman who owned the company would turn out to be the most vile and verbally abusive man I had ever worked with. In contrast, my home life was tuning out to be positively idyllic. The house my parents now lived in was stunning; it was my dream house – a perfect country estate in miniature on the banks of a river teeming with sea trout and salmon and I couldn't have been happier there.

Soon after settling in I discovered that my mother's unrelenting search for a man had borne fruit. To my astonishment she had managed to find a suitable candidate who lived in the same village. I casually bumped into him one day and to my surprise I found him to be rather attractive. Against my better judgement I chose to ignore the fact that his preferred choice of footwear was the flip-flop and we began to go out together.

Big mistake.

I soon realised that he was about as exciting as a long weekend in a geriatric ward, but somehow the relationship dragged on for six months. My father, especially, was mystified that I was stepping out with such a dull man; he knew that I deserved better, but decided not to interfere. I terminated the relationship at the end of 1987 – a Christmas I would never forget.

The all-too familiar smell of mothballs wafted into the sitting room, heralding the arrival of my boyfriend. He greeted me with a musty kiss, removed his tartan car coat and handed me my gifts. As I pulled back the wrapping paper I discovered that he had chosen to give me the stunningly romantic offering of an otter's paw mounted on a wooden plaque. As you can imagine I was utterly speechless, but worse was to come when he handed me another package, which contained the otter's tail with a brass ring attached to one end. He chose to finish with a flourish and gave me a final parcel containing another mounted paw. I sat and looked at his gifts in stunned disbelief. All I could think of was what had happened to the rest of the otter? Was he saving it for my birthday? Had he fashioned it into a pyjama case or a novelty hot water bottle cosy?

I was too afraid to ask.

Most women balk at the thought of being given a kitchen gadget for Christmas – but not me. I would have loved a Magimix, or a fully-limbed furry mammal for that matter – instead of which I got a cross between the two – Tarka in a blender.

I was not happy. He looked at me and I looked at him and we both knew that it was over.

After we had split up, I was left with the distinct impression that I would never get to meet the man of my dreams. I tried to bury myself in my work but that wasn't so easy because I hated my job. I had encountered unpleasant men before. When I was at Magpie I was sometimes hired out to assist other cameramen – some were perfectly nice but others were not. Good cameramen are, as rule, very nice blokes. Bad cameramen tend to make up for their lack of ability by blaming everybody else, starting with the person closest to them – namely the assistant.

As I had feared, the amount of film work was steadily contracting and video was now the industry standard. Kevin, the man I had started working for in Plymouth, decided to train me up as his sound recordist. And that meant that not only was I still the closest person to him, I was now attached by a cable – so there was no way of escaping his splenetic venom. At Magpie, unpleasant jobs were always those that involved working for people outside the company, but now my working life was one long nightmare, punctuated by Elysian trips up the road to TSW. It was there I escaped Kevin's aural battering – it was there that I got to see the man in brogues.

Chapter Three

It was January 1988, I had been single for nearly two months and I found myself working on location with a fellow who more than fulfilled every criterion that I had set for my perfect man. The shoot in Cornwall was going well – technically, if not emotionally. I only had a couple of chances to get to speak to the dashing young researcher but he must have made an impression on me because I could instantly recall his name. For once it had been kept out of the wool shop of my brain by the absent minded librarian and had instead been taken straight to the romance section. He was called Charlie – Charlie Boydell – a name to conjure with if ever there was one.

I liked his name; I liked him – but I hadn't had the chance to make an impression because our only exchanges came when I had to tell him to be quiet during an interview because he was making too much noise on his mobile. Things weren't going as well as I'd hoped but at least I had the lunch hour to make my mark.

The crew stopped at a really seedy pub, one that Charlie had chosen – so he was very embarrassed when we walked to find a totally deserted bar. Charlie had moved from being a reporter on the farming programme to being a researcher for the current affairs department. He prided himself on his thoroughness and had even gone as far as getting a photocopy of the pub menu so that we didn't have to waste time waiting to order. What his research didn't reveal was that this was possibly one of the nastiest-looking pubs in the whole of the county and that the only available item on the menu was a toasted sandwich. We were in too much of a hurry to look for anywhere else to eat, so we sat down and awaited our food.

I was sitting right next to Charlie and so got a chance to really study him. I wanted to make sure there were no massive flaws that I might have missed earlier. And to my great dismay I found one – a truly gigantic one.
Charlie was a smoker.

I had always detested cigarette smoking. My father was a heavy smoker and also an asthmatic, so he used to have one drag on his cigarette, followed by a puff of his inhaler. I always felt as if I was witnessing his slow demise, one cigarette at a time. I hated him smoking so much that I used to put on a smog mask every time he lit up, but he carried on regardless. When Charlie lit up I simply moved away a little, which surprised him. He asked if I disliked smoking and I told him that I did – mainly because of what I had seen it do to my father. Charlie sort of shrugged his shoulders a little and then turned to me and said,

21

My 7 1/2 lb sea trout, taken from Thornham Pool on the river Erme, September 1987

'I'll give up when I fall in love.' I learned later that as Charlie drove home that night, he wound down the window of his car and threw out his last packet of Marlboro.

He never smoked again.

I had secretly discovered by judicious use of my directional microphone, that Charlie lived in a village that boasted the two best pubs in Devon. The Ship and The Anchor were names that were familiar to me, but it was only when Charlie mentioned Ugborough that I realised that he lived in the next village down the valley – I had lucked-out at last.

I managed to drop into a subsequent conversation the fact that I lived just down the road and shortly after that Charlie said, 'You must come over to The Anchor sometime for a drink.' About half an hour later he said, 'Look, if you're passing the village tonight just call in. If the light is on in my cottage I'll be at home, if not I'll be in the pub.' When the shoot was over and we were unloading the gear back at base, Charlie wandered into the crew room and said, 'Don't forget to call in tonight if you're passing, it would be great to see you,' in a casual but pleading sort of way. And then he told me where he lived and repeated the instructions about the light. I drove home but it didn't feel as if my wheels touched the tarmac for the entire journey. I raced indoors and yelled to my dad 'I've got a date, I've got a date.' Not that I was desperate or anything...well actually, I was pretty desperate; I had just broken up with a man who had showered me with mammalian body parts. My luck had to improve.

I was showered and changed and out of the door by 7.45pm and knocking on Charlie's door on the dot of 8.00pm. He opened the door and looked slightly surprised to see me – I think I had played it so cool that he had given up hope. He stood in the doorway holding a plate, bearing what appeared to be leftover lamb in some kind of gravy. I was struck by the complete lack of vegetables on the plate and decided that what he needed was sprouts, carrots, potatoes, and somebody to take care of him.

He welcomed me into the sitting room of Wood Cottage. It is always a nerve-wracking moment for a girl so see a bachelor pad for the first time and if I had walked into a sea of black leather and black ash I would probably have turned on my heels and run screaming down the road. Thankfully, the room I walked into was small and beamed, with a huge stone fireplace flanked by row upon row of books. There were antique prints on the walls, a Turkish rug by the fire and an old Pembroke table in one corner. I fell in love with that room at first sight.

Charlie had intended to take me to his local, but we started talking and carried on until the early hours of the morning. I had to get back home but I was enthralled by this man, this gentle, wonderful man. I wanted to hold his hands. They were strong and characterful – not the hands of an idle man but hands that could wield an axe just as easily as a fountain pen. When I went upstairs to the bathroom, I noticed he had a badger bristle shaving brush and a wooden bowl filled with Trumper's rose shaving soap. Everything I saw in that cottage told me that Charlie was a man of quality – a gentleman. He was only 27, but he had the style and bearing of a man many years older. That was it for me. I wanted to rush downstairs, I wanted to kiss his mouth and tell him that he was the total embodiment of all I had ever dreamed of – but how could I? We had only just met.

I left his mouth unkissed and drove home. But I loved him. I loved him there and then and I could hardly bear to leave him.

Charlie rang the next morning, as I knew he would, and asked if I wanted to go shooting the next day and stay for lunch. I tried to be nonchalant when I replied – but in reality I was desperate to see him again. I arrived the next morning to find Charlie chopping wood in the alleyway that ran alongside his cottage. I kissed him for the first time, just on the cheek, and he looked at me and said, 'You're dressed in exactly the right clothes.' As luck would have it I had decided that my black leather catsuit might be a little unsuitable for shooting and opted instead for jeans and a red moleskin shirt – not very exciting but he seemed to like it.

We walked to the house of a friend of Charlie's and set up the trap in his field. Luckily, I had just recently been taught to shoot clay pigeons by a friend, and so I wasn't a complete novice. We had a great morning; I managed to hit a good few clays and then we adjourned to Charlie's local pub to have a drink before lunch.

Charlie had only recently moved to Ugborough. Up to that point he had been renting a cottage up on Dartmoor, but had decided to find a house that was closer to Plymouth. It was a wise move as he had chosen one of the prettiest villages in the area.

Ugborough is situated in the heart of the South Hams, midway between Dartmoor and the coast. Its central feature is a fine square bordered by the slate-hung houses so typical of the area. The square is dominated by St. Peter's, the biggest parish church in Devon. It stands at the top of the square and its imposing granite tower features a large, black clock face with gold numerals. The clock is an ancient timepiece, which in those days ran on Devon time – not slow, just very relaxed. It often broke down, and when it did it was always mended directly (pronounced 'd'recly'). You get used to the time difference when you move to the West country, especially when you something needs fixing. If you try and pin a local tradesman down to a specific time, you will invariably get the same response, 'Us'll be along d'recly.' Which can mean straight away or more often next week – it makes no difference anyway, the job always gets done and if you are in too much of a hurry to wait for local labour you shouldn't have moved down in the first place.

Charlie had bought a cottage right on the square by the church, and from there he could see Ugborough's two greatest assets, the Ship and the Anchor. Charlie's cottage was closest to the Ship but he chose the Anchor as his local. The Anchor was a very old, very traditional Devon pub. The four-ale public bar was as small and dark as a mole's under stair cupboard, serving in-comers with Bass and locals with lager. It had a low, heavily beamed ceiling, and the feeling of claustrophobia was heightened by the unbroken line of boilersuited-beefcake around the bar.

The local boys, pronounced 'bays' were not boys at all, but gurt strapping men ranging in age from early twenties to late fifties. They always stood by the bar and in doing so formed an almost impenetrable wall of muscle which only that most hardy of tourists would dare to breech. These were big men in every sense of the word; the oldest was Trevor, who had a white beard and looked like Father Christmas in overalls. He sold turf and was a man of few words, but when Trevor spoke everybody listened. George was a bit younger than Trevor. He was always bare-chested, which became apparent as the buttons on his overalls popped open after each successive pint. Anson was a farmer who had a sense of humour as dry as the local cider. Rangy and bearded, he was never seen without his Breton sailor's cap, which he would lift up to scratch his head whenever he was asked a tricky question. Chap, a softly spoken man in his thirties, was the quietest of the boys. He was well read and could talk with authority on a wide range of subjects. He, in common with many of the men, was a bachelor, and he made a living by farming with his mother on the edge of the moor. Ilkey was the log man and also a bachelor. He sold wood, felled trees and talked with an accent so thick that on occasion even the locals had trouble understanding him. After he'd had a few pints he became almost totally unintelligible, but nobody seemed to care at that stage – everyone knew what he meant.

And then there were the Long brothers. They came from a family who had farmed in the village for generations and their reputation was fearsome. If you upset any one of them you might as well pack your bags and leave. Rodgey was the eldest of the three brothers; he was the local plumber and the only one who was married. He was aged about forty, and shared the same stocky, muscular build as his brothers. Jim was the middle brother; he was divorced and a builder by trade. He was barrel-chested and bearded and enjoyed a reputation as the local ladies-man. He was a great storyteller – very charming and funny and it was easy to understand why he was never short of female company. He used to disappear for weeks on end and Charlie soon discovered that he had a habit of taking himself off to Jamaica when things began to get a little too complicated at home.

The youngest and toughest of the three brothers was Tim (as in inTIMidate) who looked as if he had been chiselled out of a solid lump of Dartmoor granite. He was not especially tall, but he had an air of brooding menace about him. He didn't look for trouble but if one of the young lads annoyed him, he would just look at him and give a low growl, which was generally all that was needed to make his point. He had muscles in his forearms like twisted steel cables and when young lads caught a glimpse of them, they generally thought twice about upsetting him. Forearmed was forewarned where Tim was concerned.

These were not men to be taken lightly. These were horny-handed sons of red Devon soil. Upset any one of them and at best you would walk out of the pub knowing that you would not be made welcome in future, and at worst you would crawl out, picking up your teeth on the way. They took no nonsense, but were some of the most honest and generous men you could ever wish to meet. It took a while to gain their respect and not everybody got it, but once you had it, you had it for life. And when Charlie first walked into the Anchor one thing was certain – he didn't have it.

Things got off to a bad start when he arrived at the bar wearing little round glasses and carrying a book under his arm. He bought his pint and as he walked to the back of the room the boys at the bar took one look and made an instant assessment of the newcomer.

He was a communist.

Charlie was hardly a communist – he was just lonely. He was, by nature a very gregarious man. He hated being on his own, in fact it made him positively miserable, which is why he chose to sit in the public bar of the Anchor – he didn't know anybody but at least he wasn't alone. The locals didn't see any of this, what they saw was a specky wierdo who preferred reading to having a laugh with them at the bar. They also took great exception to him leaving half of his plate of gammon, egg and chips behind when he left one night. That incident might appear trivial to you or me, but to men who had been working hard all day, all that good food going to waste was positively criminal.

The deadlock had been broken one night when Charlie had struck up a conversation with Nigel, who worked part-time behind the bar. He had been lucky enough to choose the funniest and most approachable of all the locals and once Charlie got talking, Nigel realised that he wasn't a bookish leftie at all; he was the new farming reporter for Television South West and he was a stand-up guy.

Nigel was Charlie's introduction into village society. He was in his early twenties and was big and soft and hugely entertaining. Born and bred in Ugborough, he lived opposite the Anchor with his childhood sweetheart, Angie. He was as good-natured a man as Charlie had ever met, with a quick wit and a talent for self-deprecation that was shared by all of the men at the bar. Nigel made sure that everyone knew that Charlie was all right, and one night as he was leaving, Charlie received the ultimate compliment from Jim Long.

'Rush along steady,' he said. This was a farewell that was reserved for only a chosen few and it meant that Charlie was an Anchor boy at last.

By the time I met Charlie he was a regular face in the Anchor. When I walked in to the public bar by his side I was given an enthusiastic reception by the other locals – which consisted of shy nods, grunts, and a lot of winks in Charlie's direction. Charlie had a couple of pints of Bass and I had a large gin and tonic in preparation for the rigours of a bachelor's Sunday lunch.

I didn't know what to expect when we got back to the cottage, but fortunately I had no need to worry because Charlie turned out to be an excellent cook. We had local roast pork, freshly supplied by a doctor friend of Charlie's, who bred pigs as a hobby. It was quite the most delicious food I had ever tasted but then I was so smitten that Charlie could have made me beans on toast and it would still have tasted like ambrosia.

From that moment on I saw Charlie at every possible opportunity. I was completely and utterly intoxicated by him and I could think about nothing else, day and night. I remember him saying on the day we met that he was fed up with eating Tesco's ocean pie, but it wasn't that he couldn't cook, it was just that he had no interest in cooking for himself. So I decided to cook for him. I would prepare a hot meal before I left home each evening, and then drive to his house with it in a wicker basket. I just wanted to look after him; I wanted to make him happy.

Exactly a week after our first meeting, Charlie invited me to supper with an English couple who had come over from Portugal. They were old family friends and often stayed with him on their way up country .We sat down to supper in Charlie's kitchen, and had just finished the first course when the front door burst open. There stood Penny, Charlie's ex girlfriend, looking somewhat surprised at finding the assembled company sitting round the kitchen table. Penny was unaware of my existence until that moment. Charlie had told me all about her; he said that she could be a little volatile at times and so we thought it best if we kept our relationship a secret for the time being. She and Charlie had split up a couple of months before, but she was still totally unprepared to see me that night. Charlie managed to shoot me one look, imploring forgiveness, before getting up to face his ex.

John, the man sitting opposite me, just looked at me and put his napkin over his head. It was all too embarrassing for words. Charlie managed to get Penny outside; where she proceeded shriek at him, battering him all the while about the head and body. He came back inside looking a little shell-shocked and we finished the meal.

Eventually John and Sheila went up to bed, leaving Charlie and me alone at last; and it was then that Charlie made love to me. He used only words but those words were as soft and tender as the most delicate of caresses. He talked about his hopes and his dreams and he asked me about my own dreams for the future. I told him that I wanted to have a farm one day, with a duck pond, a Gloucester Old Spot and a house cow. Nothing more than that; no designer labels or expensive jewellery – those things wouldn't make me happy; but ducks – now ducks would make me happy.

Charlie didn't seem at all surprised, he just looked at me and said, 'All I want is a farm of my own. I want to be able to stand at the back door and look down and see five sets of wellington boots, descending in size, sitting on the steps below me.'

We sat in silence for a moment. It all seemed too perfect – we wanted the same things and we wanted each other, but then Charlie began to tell me about the reality of his future. He told me that he had to wear a built-up shoe because he had shattered his leg in a motorcycle accident a few years before. He said that his hip often troubled him in the wintertime but apart from that he was fully recovered. But then came the news that I was totally unprepared for. Charlie walked off into the kitchen, and as he did so he told me that when he reached his forties he would need to have one of his heart valves replaced. I was momentarily stunned by what he'd said. Charlie looked so young and so fit that I found it hard to imagine that he had anything wrong with his heart – after all there were no outward signs that he was anything other than a normal, healthy twenty- seven year old man. But he seemed so matter-of-fact about it that my worries were soon allayed. He had a leaky heart valve, so what? So did Roger Black and he still managed to become an Olympic runner.

The operation was many years away but Charlie said that he couldn't just ignore his condition. He told me that he was reminded of it every time he thought about his father, Tony, who had died of a heart attack at the age of forty one.

When Charlie told me about his father's death it was obvious that he was still profoundly affected by it. Tony had died in Paris, on his way back from a business trip to South America. It was sudden and unexpected – one day Charlie was waving his daddy off at Heathrow and the next he was sitting on his mother's bed, silently listening as she explained that daddy would never be coming home. Charlie said he was devastated by the news, but he was only seven at the time and his mother had thought it best that he didn't attend the funeral. He told me that because he didn't see for himself that his father was actually dead, he never really believed that he had died at all. He said,

'I used to think my daddy was a secret agent and that he didn't come home because he was away on a covert mission. Sometimes I thought I saw him out of the train window on my way home from school or on the top deck of a bus as it passed me in the street.'

Charlie lay himself completely open to me that night and as I listened to him, sitting before me with the dying embers of the fire reflecting in his eyes, I knew that he was the man that I wanted to spend the rest of my life with. His confessions hadn't put me off – they had emboldened me. I could forget about the leaking valve because I couldn't see it – all I could see at that moment was a man with a good heart.

We kissed goodnight at 3.00am and I drove back home knowing exactly what I had to do next. My father was making a pot of tea when I came downstairs the following morning and I walked straight up to him and said, 'I've met the man I'm going to marry.'

That was a pretty bold statement to make to my dad, as he hadn't even met Charlie at that stage, but I knew I was going to marry Charlie and telling my dad seemed the right thing to do.

Charlie had been invited to shoot at a friend's estate near Dartmouth the following weekend. He couldn't take me because the invitation was a long - standing one, so we had arranged to meet at my parents' place that evening. The whole house was buzzing with anticipation. My parents and my eldest sister were all lined up in the kitchen ready to assess this new man in my life. At last the doorbell rang and I went to answer it, only to be shoulder-barged out of the way by my mother, who then raced up the hall and flung the door wide open. There stood Charlie, still dressed in his shooting gear, holding a brace of pheasant like some love-struck caveman. My mother was standing in the doorway but Charlie looked right through her. He didn't see her – his eyes were searching for me and me only. I kissed him and told him how proud I was of his marksmanship and he then recovered his senses enough to introduce himself to my mother and the rest of the family. To my great relief he seemed to make a good impression, especially on my father. They had a lot common; they were both television journalists and were also both very honourable men. Charlie managed to score extra Brownie points by giving my mother one of the pheasants. It was a token of good will but my mother seemed to remain somewhat sceptical.

In the weeks that followed, Charlie and I continued our courtship. We never got to work together again after our first meeting, so he would leave notes for me on my car windscreen, telling me what time he would be home, or asking if he could come and pick me up from my parents' house. I had wanted to leap into bed with him on our first evening together but something made us both act with restraint. It was almost as though we both realised that we were committing to each other. We didn't want to rush it. There was something very sensual about the anticipation of making love – it was something to be savoured.

We spent our evenings by the fire, listening to Ella Fitzgerald records.

Sometimes we did nothing but kiss – all evening. And sometimes we just sat at either ends of the sofa, staring at each other. It sounds so soppy and pathetic, after all we were both young, vibrant people and should have been at each other like crazed weasels, but we were both aware that there was a very powerful bond being formed between us.

It was a bit like being in a Barbara Cartland novel – only with less face powder. But after a couple of weeks I got bored with putting Charlie off – restraint is all very well but I was a lusty Devon maid, not Mother Teresa. I decided to sneak my overnight bag into the cottage one evening and surprise Charlie; he was totally unaware of my cunning plan but I will never forget the look of pure delight on his face when I reached behind the sofa and pulled out the bag. Ironically it happened to be the first ever Comic Relief night – pretty apt really because by the following morning I was deliriously happy. I hadn't given money to charity – I had given myself to Charlie.

Chapter Four

Valentine's Day was fast approaching and Charlie had chosen the weekend on which it fell to introduce me to his family; he had also planned a dinner party at which I would meet all of his closest friends. It was a daunting prospect.

Charlie's mother, Jane, lived in Godalming, with her second husband, John. I travelled down on the less than auspicious evening of Friday the 13th, after what had been a particularly vile day at work. Charlie obviously adored his mother and so it was essential that I made the right impression on her when I arrived. I walked into the house and was introduced to Jane (or 'Tiny' as she was known) for the first time. She was immaculately turned-out, utterly charming and thankfully not the least bit intimidating.

Jane may have been vertically challenged – but in terms of verbosity she was undefeated. If you lost sight of her, you always knew where she was by her voice, which was like a shrill horn blaring out in the fog of her family. Jane was a mighty atom, a miniature marvel – she looked and spoke just like the Queen and I virtually curtsied the first time I saw her. She had not had an easy life; having been left to bring up three children on her own after Tony had died. The early years had been an enormous struggle for her, but she was a very determined woman. Her children had obviously grown up in a warm and loving family atmosphere and as a result had all developed into talented and well-adjusted adults.

Over the course of the weekend I talked at length to Jane; she told me that Charlie's determination and sense of duty had begun soon after his father died. He had seen his mother struggling to get a bucket of coal one day and took it from her, saying, 'I'm going to get the coal for you Mummy, because I'm the man of the house now.'

Charlie had a particular fascination for anything connected with the First World War and devoured books on the subject. According to Jane, his interest began when he was just a boy, and at a time when most children of his age were reading about Desperate Dan downing cow pies, Charlie was reading about desperate men, drowning in a sea of mud at Passchendaele. One day Jane found him crawling over the top of the sofa; and when she asked what he was doing he simply looked up and replied 'I'm stuck in a bomb crater in no-man's land and I'm trying to get back to my trench.' He was seven years old.

Charlie's interest was apparently sparked by tales of his Grandpa Charles, who was the youngest ever Captain in the Royal Flying Corps. He was a courageous flyer who was decorated with the M.C., D.F.C., and Croix de Guerre. He was once chosen to drop a wreath at the funeral of the famous German air ace

Immleman, a man who was held in very high regard by the British pilots. Charles managed to deliver the tribute, skimming the treetops and dropping the wreath a few hundred yards away from a group of rather startled mourners. They were so taken aback at the audacity of the young pilot that they allowed him to leave – but not before they had peppered his plane with bullet holes.

If there was ever a reincarnation of brave and dashing Grandpa Charles, it was Charlie. I discovered that he went through his childhood with his finger firmly Sellotaped to the self-destruct button. He was struck by lightening at the age of 10, but was saved by his new rubberised raincoat and wellington boots. The lightening lit up the hood of his mac, but he escaped unscathed. He loved being outdoors and when he wasn't riding his tricycle down the slide he was building camps. One-day he went to a friend's house and built a particularly fine example at the bottom of his garden, which happened to run alongside a railway cutting. When the camp was completed they decided to raise a pirate flag and not having a skull and crossbones to hand, they improvised using a red tea cloth. Unfortunately for the boys, a train driver mistook the pirate flag for a stop signal and it brought the almost whole of the Wimbledon underground system to a virtual standstill.

For Edward, Charlie's younger brother, life was not without incident. He got used to being turned out of his pram by his brutal sibling on an almost daily basis. Charlie soon got bored with that game and decided to smother him instead. Edward was rescued by his mother but Charlie was undeterred. He didn't stop – he just switched tactics. What Charlie really wanted was to experiment on live animals and Edward was the closest approximation to a white mouse that he could find. One night at bath time he held his little brother underwater. Edward was struggling beneath the Matey bubbles for so long that he saw his life flash before him. He was only two and a half at the time, so he was actually able to review his life several times over, and was only saved from a warm watery grave in the nick of time by his ever-vigilant mother. Charlie soon turned his attentions to his infant sister Victoria, who still bears the scars of a suicidal journey in a toy car chauffeured by Demon Hill. He ended up crashing the car at the bottom of a steep driveway, and Victoria ended up in hospital having a load of loose chippings removed from her face.

But Jane was at pains to tell me that his reckless nature was always tempered with an acute sense of responsibility for his brother and sister. As he grew older, Charlie took on a more paternal role, albeit a rather unconventional one. He taught Victoria about poetry and he showed her how to smoke a joint for the first time. When he went on holiday to Scotland with a group of friends, Victoria was allowed to come along. She enjoyed being made to feel like an adult, rather than a gauche kid sister and she knew that although Charlie was not a totally conventional role model, he was one who would always be there to show pride in her achievements.

Charlie and Eddie had apparently been through a rough patch during their teens but had both matured enough to regain the closeness that they had enjoyed as children. Charlie had stopped trying to kill Eddie, which I think he was grateful for, and I was about to get to meet him at last. If there was ever a time when I would need all my skills of charm and diplomacy, then surely this was it. I would soon be introduced not only to Edward and Victoria, but also to eighteen of Charlie's closest friends. These were people whom he had known since he was a small boy. They had seen him with many girls since then, and I was determined to show them that I was not just another notch on Charlie's bedpost.

It started well enough. Eddie arrived fresh from football practice, said 'Hello' and promptly dropped his tracksuit-bottoms. He wanted to change and obviously thought I wouldn't mind if he did so in front of me. I didn't mind at all, in fact I was very flattered that he should grace me with the sight of his fine, muscular legs. I liked him immediately, he was very similar to Charlie in a lot of ways; he was good-looking and very charming – but he didn't interest me for I only ever had eyes for his older brother.

Other guests soon began to arrive and I could see each couple sizing me up as they greeted me at the door. They had all heard Charlie speak of me in glowing terms and were obviously keen to see for themselves what the mystery woman looked like. I was not a classic English rose in that I didn't float about in a diaphanous dress, wearing a big straw hat and a winsome smile – but Charlie wouldn't have wanted that. He liked the fact that I wore jeans for the majority of the time because they showed off my long legs and what he regarded to be my greatest asset (Charlie was a bottom-man). I loved to get dressed up whenever we went out together and he knew that when I walked into a room, people would invariably do a double-take and say, 'God, is that Kate, I didn't recognise her in a dress.'

Charlie had taken me shopping soon after we met in order to get one essential, which had been missing from my wardrobe – namely the 'little black dress'. We trawled all over London and eventually I found a dress that looked promising. I disappeared into the changing room and walked out a few minutes later to what I can only describe as a standing ovation. Charlie had a wicked grin on his face and to begin with I couldn't understand why. But when he took me over to a mirror and stood beside me, it became obvious that he was paying me the finest compliment that a man can pay to a woman. I virtually ran to the cash desk to pay for the wondrous garment, which from that moment onwards became known as 'stiffy' dress. I wore it on many occasions and I can honestly say that it never failed to live up to its name.

Charlie loved that dress and he loved me. He and I were made for each other. We wore the golden glow of a couple that had everything to live for and nothing to lose. I knew exactly what I was taking on when I fell in love with Charlie. Admittedly, a man with a wonky leg and a dickey heart doesn't sound like the catch of the century – as I learned to my cost when I tried to describe him to a colleague one day. Despite my best efforts to paint Charlie as I saw him, the burly lighting man who was driving us to our next location just turned to me and said, 'So, you're telling me that he's got a heart condition and a limp? What on earth do you see in him?' But how could I explain what I saw? I couldn't possibly explain that physical imperfections were immaterial to me – that I had seen the future and that the future was Charlie.

Jane seemed to know how I felt, which is why I believe she chose to tell me so much about him so soon after our first meeting. She wasn't trying to put me off; she was just preparing me for what might lie ahead. Charlie's finger was evidently still on the self-destruct button, but it seemed that after he'd met me he had released the pressure a little. He wasn't a fool; he knew that smoking with a heart condition was an act of gross stupidity, but until I came along he didn't see any reason to stop. I had provided him with a reason, but at the same time I knew that I was now charged with his wellbeing. If Charlie was going to take care of me then I would have to take care of him, pedalling unsteadily as he was along the rutted farm track of his life.

I had no doubts; I took a firm grasp of his jumper and walked with him. We had begun our journey.

I had made up my mind, but I had yet to prove to all of his dearest friends that I was truly the girl for him. When all the guest had arrived and the formal greetings were dispensed-with, it was time to sit down for dinner – and to my horror I realised that I would not be sitting next to Charlie. He had seated me next to an old friend of his from university days who went by the name of Fat Alex. Alex wasn't fat at all – just a little more compact than most people and he was a laugh-riot.

Alex and Charlie could have stepped straight form the pages of a P.G. Woodhouse novel. They were men of another age – an age where manners and dress were always correct and dinner was a meal you dressed for in the evening and not a snack in the middle of the day. Alex proved to be the perfect dinner companion. I had a blast and managed to survive the meal without upsetting anybody.

Charlie's sister Victoria (or Pixie, as the family called her) had arrived fashionably late as usual. She was a stunningly attractive girl, with very dark hair and flawless skin. Men always flocked around her but she wasn't interested in them – she loved women.

She sidled up to me later in the evening and asked me what I thought about her brother. I was totally honest with her and told her that I loved him and that if he asked me to marry me that night, I would have no hesitation in saying 'yes'. I told her not to repeat what I had said to Charlie, as we had been going out together for only month and he might think I was a little desperate. She promised not to breathe a word to her big brother and I believed her. In the early hours of the morning I found the two of them sitting at the bottom of the stairs, deep in conversation and left them to it. Charlie was totally intoxicated by love and alcohol and slurred to Pixie, 'Do you know, I could easily ask Katie to marry me tonight.' Apparently, Victoria then turned to him and said; 'Funny you should say that, because Katie said exactly the same thing to me earlier.'

If I had know what she had said I think I would died of embarrassment, but first I would have gone up to my future sister-in-law and punched her hard in the mouth. Every girl knows that it is absolutely imperative not to mention the 'M' word during the early stages of a relationship. Even though I knew that I would marry Charlie, I did not want him to know. I wanted to keep him guessing. I wanted to maintain the upper hand but since Pixie's gross indiscretion I had no ace up my sleeve. Charlie had seen all my cards – it was a done deal.

By 2 a.m. we had waved goodbye to the last of the guests and by that stage Charlie was completely lashed. He had given me a gold signet ring earlier in the evening and had told me how much he loved me; then he went around telling everyone else how much he loved me and then he told me he loved me all over again. When we got into bed, he held me close to him and somehow managed to recite this poem. The poem, by Andrew Marvell, would prove to be strangely prophetic.

To His Coy Mistress

Had we but World enough, and Time,
This coyness Lady were no crime.
We would sit down, and think which way
To walk and pass our long Loves Day.
Thou by the Indian Ganges side
Should'st Rubies find: I by the Tide
Of Humber would complain. I would
Love you ten years before the Flood:
And you should if you please refuse
Till the conversion of the Jews.
My vegetable Love should grow
Vaster than empires, and more slow.
An hundred years should go to praise
Thine eyes, and on thy Forehead Gaze;
Two hundred to adore each Breast:
But thirty thousand to the rest.
An Age at least to every part,
And the last Age should show your Heart.
For Lady you deserve this State;
Nor would I love at lower rate.

But at my back I always hear
Time's winged Chariot hurrying near:
And yonder all before us lie
Deserts of vast Eternity.
Thy beauty shall no more be found;
Nor, in thy marble vault, shall sound
My echoing Song: then Worms shall try
That long preserv'd Virginity:
And your quaint honour turn to dust;

And into ashes all my Lust.
The Grave's a fine and private place,
But none I think do there embrace.

Now therefore, while the youthful hue
Sits on thy skin like morning dew,
And while thy willing soul transpires
At every pore with instant Fires,
Now let us sport us while we may;
And now, like am'rous birds of prey,
Rather at once our Time devour,
Than languish in his slow-chapt power.
Let us roll all our Strength, and all
Our sweetness up into one Ball:
And tear our Pleasures with rough strife,
Through the Iron gates of Life.
Thus, though we cannot make our Sun
Stand still, yet we will make him run.

Chapter Five

Charlie didn't hear Time's winged chariot at his back, what he heard was Time's sixteen-wheel juggernaught thundering up behind him. Charlie was like a hedgehog on the dual carriageway of Fate, and it was whilst he was at school that he first felt the tarmac begin to tremble.

After their father had died, Charlie and his brother were sent Bradfield School courtesy of their Uncle Peter. Jane could not afford to pay for the boys' education and so Peter had very generously taken it upon himself to put them through school. He had, however, absolutely no control over what his rather unruly nephew got up to whilst he was away in the wilds of Berkshire.

Charlie was one of a number of boys at the school who had lost a father at an early age and they were all imbued with the same air of maturity that set them apart from the other boys. Charlie was also regarded as one of the toughest boys in his year. He captained the rugby first XV and was also an extremely aggressive defensive player on the football pitch. He was very fit indeed and did at least 100 push-ups every night, followed by a five mile run the next morning. He led the college cadet force – but their manoeuvres did not always have a military motive. He once led them on a daring night raid to plunder the sixth-form wine cellars, which proved to be highly effective. Charlie managed to escape being found out but was later caught committing a far more heinous crime.

One night, a local girls' school provided a number of dancing partners for the school disco. Charlie was caught showing one of the girls the finer points of romantic fiction in the school library. He achieved instant hero status and also a severe reprimand from his housemaster. He took his punishment, but was also at pains to point out that two boys who had been caught together a few weeks before, had escaped with nothing more than a few pages of Latin text and a slap on the wrist.

Charlie's carefree school life altered irrevocably when he was 18. He had suffered a severe bout of glandular fever, from which he took a very long time to recover. He became listless and lethargic and was eventually sent to see the school doctor, who discovered that Charlie had a heart murmur. It was decided that he should be sent to see a local heart consultant for a more thorough examination. Charlie and his mother walked into the doctor's examining room to be greeted with the words, 'Your father died of a heart attack at the age of forty one, didn't he?' The kindly physician then took Charlie's blood pressure and carried on with his sympathetic diagnosis by telling Charlie that he would have to

Charlie on the Bradfield assault course, 1978

stop playing rugby, football and any sport or activity which would require a lot of physical exertion.

It would have been kinder to take Charlie outside and shoot him.

Jane raised herself up to her full height of 4ft 11 inches, looked the Hippocratic oaf straight in the eye and said, 'Don't tell me what he can't do, just tell me what he can do.'

But for Charlie, the damage was already done.

Charlie was a pupil at public school where social standing was attained by physical prowess. Nobody idolised the swotty boys, but if you became captain of games, as Charlie had done, then you were afforded hero status. Charlie was proud of his sporting achievements and to be told that he would no longer be able to play all the games that he loved was totally and utterly devastating to him.

The social swallow dive that Charlie was about to take would prove to be much more debilitating than the ailment itself. He had, by some miracle, been able to live a very active life, whilst having frighteningly high blood pressure. When it was properly measured, it was found to go as high as 240/40 during exercise- and to put that in perspective, a normal reading would be around 140/80. More tests followed and it soon became clear that Charlie had a congenital defect in his heart – he had been born with a bicuspid aortic valve.

The main pumping chamber of the heart is called the left ventricle. It is equipped with two non-return valves, which basically means that blood can only flow through them in one direction. One, called the mitral valve, is pushed open as blood flows into the ventricle and is forced shut by the pressure of blood within the chamber. When the ventricle contracts, it forces the blood out through the aortic valve, which then snaps shut due to the pressure of the blood which it has just released into the aorta. The top of the aortic valve resembles a Mercedes badge, with three flaps, or cusps, which are opened and closed by pressure of blood alone. Charlie had been born with two of the three cusps fused together, which meant that they did not form a tight seal, and so the pressure of blood flowing through his heart was never equal to that of a normal heart. His condition is shared by about 1 per cent of the population and was not life threatening in any way. In fact, once he was given drugs to reduce his blood pressure he was able to resume a perfectly normal life – normal except for the fact that he now knew that what had killed his father might also kill him.

When at last he recovered from the news that he had a heart defect, Charlie started to get on with his life again. He concentrated on sailing at school, which was something that he really loved. Charlie had wanted to join Her Majesty's Royal Navy since he was a small boy and was always happiest when he was afloat. He had already been on a naval cadet course and was due to enrol as an officer cadet at the Britannia Royal Naval College at Dartmouth.

He was a gifted scholar and had excelled at maths and physics at Bradfield, so the entrance exam would not be a problem to him. There was to be a written test, which would be followed by a full physical examination and various fitness tests. Charlie sat his entrance exam but failed his physics paper, which was something he should have sailed through. His mother always believed that he failed it on purpose, to prevent the further humiliation of being told that he was unfit to go to sea. Charlie knew that they would not let him continue with the course once his heart condition had been detected and at least there was some dignity in getting out before that happened.

Being unable to serve on one of Her Majesty's ships would be the greatest disappointment that Charlie would ever have to suffer. It was something that would haunt him for the rest of his life and he would never really get over it. He loved the sea and he wanted to serve his country, but that ambition had been denied him. Charlie's hopes for the future had been dashed; he felt he had nothing to look forward to and he started to become a very disillusioned young man.

The loss of his father, the discovery of his heart defect and the news that he would never go to sea – individually those events would be enough to make Charlie depressed, but together they proved to be of life-altering significance. He began to tell friends that he would die young, like his father, but said that he believed it would happen before he got the chance to become a father himself. It was almost as though he was preparing himself for yet another crushing disappointment. He desperately wanted to have a family but he just could not allow himself the luxury of believing that such a dream might one day become a reality.

Charlie only had to look at his family history to know that the odds were stacked against him. His father and grandfather had died of heart failure and Charlie was well aware that his own heart was malformed. There was only one course of action as he saw it, and that was to 'give it large'. He would live life full on – regardless of the consequences.

He decided to take a degree in English at Bedford College, University of London. Before the course started he spent his time with his cousin Nick, fitting out a shop for a friend's catering company and doing a bit of dispatch riding on the side. Charlie and Nick were very close, they had grown up together and it was Nick's father Steve who became Charlie's role model as he matured into adulthood. Charlie idolised Steve. He was the sort of man who could mend a boiler and cook Sunday lunch simultaneously, and it was by following his uncle's example that Charlie learned many of the skills that would serve him so well in later life.

Charlie and Nick were a wild pair in their late teens and early twenties. They spent their time riding around on matching B.S.A. motorcycles and smoking anything they could lay their hands on. They had built the bikes themselves, having bought two boxes of bits from a man in Birmingham for £250. They assembled the engines on an oak dining table in their granny's flat, but she had moved to a nursing home by that stage so thankfully she was none the wiser.

The flat was situated just at the bottom of Wimbledon Hill, in a prime location but with one major drawback, namely that the other tenants were all

Charlie on Nick's BSA

over sixty and didn't take too kindly to living near a flat full of rowdy testos-
terone-laden bikers. The boys in black leather fought a war of attrition with the
blue rinsed ladies below. Their flat was an oasis of abandonment in a desert of
decorum. The ladies were always blaming Charlie and his friends for various
misdemeanours and in most cases they were totally innocent of the charges –
but they always found a way of getting their own back.

    One lady would always bring her shopping trolley back from Sainsbury's
and then leave it outside Charlie's flat, so that he got the blame. He got a little
tired of this and decided one day to teach her a lesson. He tied a length of button thread to the lift cage and secured it to the trolley. He then attached a
bungee cord to the other end of the trolley and stretched it until it could be
attached to the old lady's door. Then he rang her bell, and when she opened her
door, the button cord snapped, the bungee cord twanged and the trolley was
hurled forward, catching her just above the knees. She was a little bruised but
otherwise unharmed, and she never ever brought her trolley home again.

    Charlie lived those days in a haze of parties, biking and girls. He and Nick
were living rent-free in a large flat when all their friends were still living at home.
Charlie's best friend Tom was the next to move in and he would soon be followed by several other likely lads who wanted to swap cocoa and crumpets for
crumpet and an endless supply of big, fat, spliffs. It was a time of excess; and
even a couple of policemen who had been called out one night to stop a particularly noisy gathering, had the good sense to stay on and party until the early
hours.

    The boys were getting a student grant, which they managed to supplement
by working for a catering company called 'The Running Buffet'. It was perhaps
not the wisest decision to employ them as wine waiters, but it did mean that
they were never short of a drink to offer the many visitors who turned up at
their door. Charlie even managed to get a job working at Blitz, the fabulously
trendy club that was to become birthplace of the New Romantic Movement.
Charlie occasionally worked behind the bar and at that time he was totally
unaware that George, the funny-looking bloke who checked the coats was about
to be discovered, and would go on to front a band called Culture Club.

    It was a joyous time for Charlie; he was young, he was handsome, he had
Cannabis growing in his cupboards and girls coming out of his ears – in short,
he had it all. I have no doubt that he would have carried on with his full-on,
hedonistic lifestyle and entered adulthood with the same kamikaze attitude –
but everything was about to change.

    A few months later, Charlie went off on his motorbike to see a friend in
Norfolk for the weekend. He was on his way back home to London, when he
saw a car that had stopped in the opposite lane and was indicating to turn right.
He dropped down a gear and flashed the driver so that she could turn. She did-
n't seem to see him so he slowed down further and flashed her again. She
remained stationary, so Charlie assumed she had stalled and accelerated to get
past her. She chose that moment to turn right and Charlie slammed into the side
of her car. The force of the impact hurled him 140ft through the air and had he

Charlie's BSA after the crash

gone any further he would have hit a brick wall and been killed instantly.

The bike was a lying in a mangled heap, but when the paramedics arrived they found that Charlie was in a far worse state. What was most apparent to them as they assessed the damage was that although Charlie was lying facedown, the heel of his right leg was sticking into the ground. His right femur (thighbone) had been snapped and rotated 180 degrees by the force of the impact. The shinbones of his right leg were shattered and he had broken bones in his right foot and elbow. He had a total of eleven fractures on his right side, and was only alive because his leg, rather than his head, had borne the main force of the impact.

The angels had been watching over Charlie on that cold February morning, because the vehicle which had been travelling immediately behind his bike just happened to be a bus full of nurses. They were able to tend to him before the paramedics arrived and when Charlie decided that a kiss might take his mind off the pain a little, a pretty young staff nurse was only too willing to oblige.

Charlie was quickly taken to the Royal Norfolk and Norwich Hospital where the casualty staff began the slow process of removing his clothing. He had been asked to take a friends' motorcycle leathers back to London with him and the easiest way to transport them was to wear them on top of his own. The nurse taking care of Charlie had to cut through six layers of clothing before she got to his leg and it was clear to her that although he was badly injured, had Charlie been wearing anything less, he would almost certainly have lost his leg.

The police got in touch with Jane and she then had to endure a tortuous four-hour journey before she got to see her son. It gave her time to come to terms with what had happened, but despite that she was totally unprepared for the shock of finally seeing her poor broken boy. He was lying on a trolley, waiting to go into theatre and when she went over to him he looked up at her and said, 'You've been waiting a long time for this, haven't you Ma?'

He was right of course. Jane had seen Charlie come close to death on many occasions. He was always going to be a man who took risks, but he had often said that if he had an accident on his B.S.A., then it would be caused by somebody else's careless driving and not his own. He was to be proved right, but neither he nor any of his family could have predicted just how much damage the resulting accident would cause him.

The brilliant surgeon who operated on Charlie had managed to rebuild his elbow by wiring all the fragments of broken bone together. It was a difficult operation – but was simple in comparison to the task of piecing together the remains of his shattered leg. His fractured tibia and fibula were held together with metal plates, which were screwed across the fractures. This would give the bones time to knit together until they were strong enough for the plates and screws to be removed. His thighbone was a rather more difficult proposition. Rather than being snapped cleanly in two, the bone had been twisted until it shattered – leaving two splintered stumps which would never knit together cleanly. All the surgeon could do was immobilise the leg and hope that the bone would eventually re-form into something resembling a thigh.

Charlie would spend three long months in traction. He was a long way from home but his friends and family made sure that he had visitors every day. When he wasn't being entertained by his friends, he would amuse himself by firing his spud gun at the fat bloke on the opposite side of the ward whilst he was sleeping. The boy in the next bed would often assist Charlie with his target practice by holding up his temperature chart, so that Charlie could get the pellet to ricochet across the room. It was a childish game but it kept them amused during their long confinement.

Charlie also spent many weeks perfecting the ultimate painkiller. This involved mixing different combinations of the painkilling tablets that he had been given, with malt whiskey. The effect was immediate and long lasting and although the young nurses on the ward knew exactly what was going on, they always turned a blind eye because Charlie was such a total charmer.

One of the nurses had a particular fondness for Charlie and in the evenings she would wheel his bed into a side ward so that they could watch Kenny Everett on television together. She was not alone in her affection for Charlie however, there seemed to be no shortage of female admirers for the young Mr. Boydell. There was an almost magnetic attraction about this man in traction and as he would later confess to his sister, the plaster cast did not get in the way when it came to pleasures of the flesh. On one memorable occasion, a girl to whom I will only refer to as Ann. L. Gesia, decided to draw the curtains around Charlie's bed and then took it upon herself to provide him with a rather more satisfying form of pain relief. Having his leg suspended above his head may have caused Charlie some discomfort – but it certainly never cramped his style.

The days in hospital passed slowly, but eventually Charlie was told that he was sufficiently well recovered to return home. He had just had more surgery to remove the pins from his leg – allowing him to come off traction for the first time, and was learning to stand upright again. The hospital had given him a wheelchair to use because he'd only been out of bed for three days and didn't really have the strength to support himself.

Charlie was extremely thin and gaunt and the muscular physique that he had once been so proud of had wasted away to nothing. He was certainly not ready to use his crutches – yet he refused to get into the wheelchair. He told his mother that he was going to walk out of hospital and that is exactly what he did. It was terribly difficult for him, but he was so determined that he somehow managed to get to the car unaided. Jane knew from past experience that if her son decided that he was going to do something, then he would do it – regardless of whether it was physically possible or not. He may not have had any strength left in his legs, but his strength of will was undiminished and it was that which got him to the car.

Charlie had a lot to think about as he was driven back to Wimbledon. The doctors had been very frank during their last consultation with him. They told him that he had lost an inch of bone from his right thigh and that he would be left with a permanent and pronounced limp. This would, in turn, affect his hip, which had already suffered damage as a result of the accident – his leg had been wrapped around his head when the nurses first found him. The doctors told Charlie that the combination of traumas inflicted on his leg and hip would result in him being confined to a wheelchair by the age of 30.

It was a long journey home.

Charlie insisted on being taken straight back to his flat, despite his mother's insistence that he would not be able to manage on his own whilst he was still getting used to his crutches. He was too stubborn to ask for her help and so he was left alone for the first time in three months. He started to make himself a cup of coffee, and got as far as putting the kettle on the stove before he realised that it was physically impossible for him to carry a kettle full of boiling water and use his crutches at the same time. He broke down and wept – he was so angry at the senselessness of it all. Why had that stupid woman not seen him? Why had he ended up with a shattered leg on top of a dodgy heart – hadn't he suffered enough? What the hell was the point of it all?

His mother decided to send him to see a physiatrist after he snapped his fountain pen in two one day. But as Charlie sat in the learned shrink's office, he came to the rapid conclusion that the bloke sitting opposite him was barking mad. He got up and walked out, happy in the knowledge that although he may have been a little odd, he would soon get better, unlike the fruitcake that he'd left sitting behind the desk.

There was not getting away from the fact that Charlie was a broken man, and it was clear that if he stayed in that flat, he would never regain the mental strength that had carried him through all the traumas of his life thus far. He needed to rest and he needed time to heal himself, both mentally and physically. Nick knew what he needed. He needed to be driven up over Holden Hill and be greeted by a sight that would make his heart glad. He needed to see the most beautiful county in all England laid out before him, bathed in golden sunlight, with its lush green hills rolling down to the sea. He needed to rest and recuperate and he needed to do it in Devon.

Nick knew Devon well; his parents had lived there for a while, and it was on their drive that Charlie had crashed his pedal-car all those years ago. Nick knew a family who were willing to have Charlie to stay for as long as he needed, and so it was that Charlie's love affair with Dartmoor began.

Charlie stayed in a thatched Devon longhouse near the village of Chagford. It was a fair trek to reach the village and its isolation made it attractive to the type of people who sought total anonymity. The inhabitants of Chagford were a collection of quirky and sometimes distinctly odd people – but that's what gave the place its immense charm.

The houses that surrounded the village were not immediately obvious, but were often stunningly beautiful. They lay in the soft folds of the hills, hidden from view; and their rough cob walls and thatched roofs only added to the impression that they had not been built, but had simply risen up out of the red Devon soil.

Charlie was immediately captivated by the area; he loved being there and the combination of fresh air and long walks helped to clear his mind and strengthen his frail legs. Gradually his wounds healed and he began to regain some of the mobility that he had lost during his three months in traction. It was a long, slow process but eventually he felt sufficiently well to return to the flat. He was still very weak, so an old friend of the family called Anne Palmer gave him a course of intensive physiotherapy. She had coached the demure ladies of England Lacrosse team and so she knew what she was doing when it came to treating serious injury.

Charlie and his family had spent many happy holidays at the Palmers' cottage in Cornwall, and it was there that Anne took him for a bit of water torture. Charlie was made to walk up and down the beach through the waves, and after a while the salt water and the pummelling of the surf began to restore the suppleness to his leg. Once he was walking properly again his life got back pretty much to normal. He spent an extra year at university and finished his English degree and then got a job as a researcher and picture editor for the publishers Buchan and Enright, before leaving to join Cassel's. It was a perfect job for Charlie, combining his love of the English language with an opportunity to work on books about the war. He should have been totally fulfilled, but there was something gnawing away at him. He could not forget his time in Devon, and when Nick decided to leave college and move down to the West country, Charlie was provided with the impetus he needed. He made a very big decision. He would leave the safety of the flat, he would leave his friends and family and he would resign from his job. He packed up all of his things, took one last look down Wimbledon High Street and left.

It was a new beginning. Gone were the days of black leather and BSAs – he was about to enter a world where the pace of life was altogether slower and where the loud, brash colours of London would be replaced by the muted, agrarian shades of grassland and granite. Charlie always said he was drawn to Devon by an invisible length of baler twine, and as he left the M5 and travelled west along the A30, he started to get a very peculiar urge – he felt the need, the need for tweed.

Chapter Six

Charlie may have been somewhat idiosyncratic in his choice of clothing, but he did have the knack of knowing how to be properly dressed for any occasion. If he went to a wedding it would be in a beautifully tailored morning suit, bought from a second hand shop that specialised in quality clothes for gentlemen. If he went to a black tie dinner, it would be in a dinner jacket of similar quality – bought from the same shop. Consequently, despite the fact that most of his clothes were fairly elderly, they were so well made that you would never have guessed that he had not bought them from a bespoke tailor.

Now that Charlie was in Devon, he had to tone down his metropolitan wardrobe and adopt a more rusticated style. He took a trip to 'The Farmers Friend' in Exeter, and bought the basics of his new wardrobe, complete with tweed jacket and the ubiquitous button-fly corduroy trousers. Once he had blended into his surroundings he could begin to think about the reality of living in a place where there were no big publishing houses, or catering companies to work for. It was farming, farming or farming.

Far from being dejected at the prospect of having to do manual labour, Charlie was in his element. He had always loved being outdoors and thanks to the time he spent on his stepbrother Clive's farm, he was very handy when it came to anything involving tractors or livestock. He soon got a job working for a local farmer and also managed to utilise his skills in catering by working behind the bar of the local pub. It was a long way from the Blitz club, but the likes of Boy George and Steve Strange seemed rather dull in comparison to some of the bucolic regulars at the Sandy Park Inn.

When Charlie talked of his past, the funniest stories were all connected to the Sandy Park and it was obvious that that period in his life had a profound and long-lasting effect on him. The most notable thing about the Sandy Park was its landlord, James Douglas. According to Charlie, he was a character who had to be experienced to be believed. James had only recently taken over the running of the pub, with his partner Marion, and once he was behind the bar, life at the Sandy Park would never be the same again.

Charlie said that James had an almost pathological hatred of tourists and made it his business to make life as uncomfortable for them as possible. You would have thought that it would have been in his interests to encourage their custom – but that was far from the case. The locals drank enough beer to keep the pub running at a handsome profit and once they got to know the new land-lord, they made sure that news of his reputation was spread far and wide.

James Douglas, in relaxed pose

Charlie had the enviable job of being paid to observe the daily tirades of a man who became known in the British press as 'Mr. Toad – the most unpleasant landlord in the country'. The news programme 'Nationwide' even came down film an item about him, and I can vividly remember watching it, although at the time I was not to know that the young man behind the bar would one day become my husband.

James would wake up in the morning, pull on his battered cords and army boots, button up his shirt and stagger downstairs to open up for business. Some days he would decide to leave the door locked and people would have to climb in through the window if they wanted a drink. At other times he would place a sign outside the pub banning anyone driving a Ford Sierra from entering the car park. And on the outside wall of the pub was a small notice, bearing the legend 'Tourists will be served last, charged extra, and will be made to sit outside (unless it's sunny).'

If you were the sort of person who tended to wear a leather jacket and slip-on shoes then you would be told in no uncertain terms that your custom was not welcome. But there were some lucky tourists who slipped through the rigorous selection process and eventually made it to the safety of the bar. What they did-n't realise as they stood at the counter, trying to find the non-existent selection of premium lagers, was that they would have been better-off turning on their trainer-clad heels and sprinting out of the pub. By the time the sardonic Mr. Douglas had asked them for their order, their fate was already sealed.

Tourists had a habit of ordering crisps with their drinks and when one of them did so, James would pause momentarily and ask the seemingly incongru-ous question, 'Large or small?' They invariably answered, 'Small.' and at that point James would reach for a perfectly standard bag of crisps, place it on the bar and bring the palm of his hand down smartly on the bag. He would them pick up the packet of pulverised potato pieces and give it to the hapless fellow,

Charlie riding Magnus – taken just before he set out for a day's hunting
with the Mid Devon

saying, 'There you are, sir – small crisps.'

He also kept a newspaper behind the bar and if a lone male drinker happened to walk in and sit at the bar, he would be offered a chance to read up on
the day's events. The paper was always folded in half and when the poor man
opened it out, what everyone else in the pub but him would know, was that he
was reading a copy of Gay News. And if James ever had to serve a man he really disliked, he would draw the pint, place it on the counter and say with a smile,
'Here's your beer, sir. Hope it fucking chokes you.'

Charlie enjoyed working for James so much that it hardly seemed like work
at all. He relished being a barman as it gave him access to two of the things he
loved most at that time – beer and people. He was constantly amazed at how
James could get away with insulting so many people on such a regular basis. The
two men had a lot of respect for each other and Charlie soon realised the behind
the bombastic front that James presented to the world, there lurked the brain
of a brilliant man. James would have completed the Telegraph crossword in the
time it took Charlie to sort out the bar and open up for business. He was a most
amazing fellow – an intolerant, intelligent, inelegant individual, who was loved
and loathed in equal measure. Charlie never tired of telling me stories about
James's antics and I never tired of hearing them. Sadly, James died a few years
ago, but no one who met him would ever forget him.

Charlie's work brought him into contact with a local farmer's daughter
called Sarah, the and true to form, the new farm hand soon made his intentions

clear, and it was not long before they started going out together. Sarah was a keen horsewoman; in fact most of the people that Charlie got to know in Chagford seemed to ride one type of animal or another. Charlie had been told in no uncertain terms that he would be risking his life if he was ever foolish enough to get on a motorbike again, so he though he would play it safe and decided to take up fox hunting instead. Charlie saw himself as a latter-day Siegfreid Sassoon and was soon to be seen out on the hunting field as perfectly attired as always.

He got himself all the kit, including a great big whip. His boots, of course were new, hand made and highly polished and when he was all dressed up he cut quite a dash. He managed to borrow a huge brute of a horse called Magnus and once he was in the saddle it was hard to tell that he hadn't been riding all his life. Being on horseback gave him an incredible feeling of freedom. Nobody noticed his limp when he was mounted, and he quickly became a fearless and well-respected member of the Mid Devon Hunt.

Being in an isolated part of the country didn't put a stop to his hedonistic ways. The wild parties that he had hosted in Wimbledon simply de-camped and moved down to the Westcountry. Charlie's cottage became an unofficial country club for all of his oldest friends – although they must have been a little shocked at some of the antics that went on in sleepy old Chagford. But it wasn't just the wild side of life that Charlie loved – it was the peace and simplicity of it all. On one occasion he was driving a friend to Exeter station so he could catch his train back to up to London. As Charlie drove down the narrow lanes on the outskirts of Chagford he met Nick, who was walking back to the cottage after a day's rabbit shooting. Nick was strolling along in the late-afternoon sunlight with a gun under his arm and a brace of rabbits slung over his shoulder. It was a sight that made Charlie truly appreciate why he had left London in the first place; for here he was in God's county, with nothing to worry about for the rest of the day except getting back in time to skin the rabbits, and making sure there was enough wood to light the Rayburn.

Life was great for Charlie at that time; he'd found a place where he felt happy and fulfilled; he had embraced a way of life that was totally alien to him. Yet to see him out hunting and working on the farm, you would have thought that he had never wanted to do anything else. But fate was about step in and land yet another surprise at the feet of Mr. Boydell. One of the regulars in the Sandy Park was a man called Ron Bendell. He liked Charlie, and would often ask about his life and his ambitions for the future. Charlie would always fob Ron off by saying that he was happy working behind the bar and enjoying all the benefits of being a farm labourer. But one day Ron said, 'Come on, Charlie, what is it that you really want to do with your life?' Charlie paused and said, 'Well, what I really want is to be a writer.' So Ron told him that he should get off his backside and apply to a local paper, to see if they would give him a job as a cub reporter. Ron was the presenter of the farming programme on T.S.W., he could see that Charlie had an agile mind and it upset him to see all that grey matter being wasted on pulling pints.

Charlie told me that it was a major turning point in his life when he took

Charlie taking a rest during a ride out on Dartmoor

Ron's advice and applied for a job as a journalist at *The Western Times and Gazette*. He was taken on as the district reporter for Okehampton. It was a large patch but was so sparsely populated that he was pretty much left to his own devices. The paper was happy just as long as Charlie phoned in his copy each day.

It was clear from they way that he talked about, that he loved his job at that time. His responsibilities included attending local Parish council meetings, writing up the results of all the local flower shows and fetes and also producing the odd feature piece now and then. He soon devised a way to carry out his duties as district reporter and exercise Magnus at the same time. If the job was within hacking distance, he would mount up and ride to whichever parish meeting he had to attend and once it was over he would ride into Chagford and tie Magnus up outside the pub. He would then go inside and order a pint, write up his copy and then phone it into the paper. That done, he would make a few more calls to set up work for the following day and then take Magnus back to his stable for a bag of oats and a good rub down. What followed for Charlie was pretty similar – only without the bag.

Charlie was soon promoted to the position of farming reporter and managed to produce some fairly respectable articles for his paper. They had decided to send him on a course to Cardiff, to help him improve his skills as a journalist – it would mean being away from home for eleven weeks but he knew that it would be in his best interests to go. He found some digs with a decidedly odd landlady, who insisted in serving a gigantic meal every evening on the dot of 5.00 p.m. He spent a week learning the finer points of journalistic law and then caught the first train back to Chagford so that he could be home in time to hunt the next morning.

The story goes that he went for a drink afterwards and bumped in to Ron Bendell at the bar. Ron was an incredibly genial fellow; but that evening he seemed to be much more animated that normal. He asked Charlie if he had ever considered a career in television. Charlie told him that he couldn't consider anything until he'd completed his course, but added that if there was anything going after that, then naturally he would be interested. Ron told him that there was a position open as his researcher on the Farming programme and asked if that would persuade Charlie to leave the paper. Charlie said that he was committed to finishing the course – to which Ron replied, 'Too late, I've forged your signature on the application form – you start on Monday.'

Charlie started working for Ron during the glory days of commercial television. The work was easy, the pay was good and life was just one long succession of filming and farm teas. Charlie loved working for Ron; they got on very well together and Ron was soon teaching Charlie all the tricks of being a television journalist and in the best journalistic tradition, showed him all the places to get a drink when the pubs were shut.

Ron was an exceptionally gifted journalist but he always gave the impression of being rather more relaxed about the job than was absolutely necessary. On an average day he would finish a shoot at lunchtime and then retire to the pub for a few pints of Special Brew. When he came out he would have completed the script for the item he had just filmed. It would be partly in his head and partly scrawled on an old beer mat, but the words would be perfect and the item would invariably be a televisual gem. With Ron's help, Charlie quickly progressed to doing small film reports and was soon presenting *Farming News* alongside his mentor. It was during that time that I first saw Charlie – or rather his shoes, as he walked briskly through reception on his way to interview some bullock or other. But I was not a regular viewer of *Farming News*, so I failed to realise that he was a man who was famous enough to have been mobbed in some of the more remote villages of North Devon.

According to Charlie, the years that he spent in the company of Mr. Bendell were the best years of his working life. Ron gave Charlie the chance to have a career in television, he gave him the chance to have a laugh – but he gave him so much more besides. With Ron's help, Charlie had developed into a brilliant researcher and was fast becoming a very good television journalist. He had inherited his mother's ordered way of thinking and he was frighteningly thorough when it came to getting his facts straight. Charlie was soon poached by the head of Current Affairs, who recognised his potential. His promotion also gave him the chance to come into contact with a shy young sound recordist called Kate, the one who was always waiting patiently in reception, looking down at people's shoes...

Ron Bendell and Charlie, taking a break during a *Farming News* outside broadcast

Chapter Seven

It was Valentine's weekend 1988, and my stay in Godalming had passed without a hitch. I had been introduced to all of Charlie's closest friends and there wasn't a single person that I didn't like. More importantly, I found his family to be just as wonderful as he had described. It was a revelation to me. My family seemed to be in a constant state of flux; going through an almost continual cycle of rows, followed by huge diplomatic efforts by various other members of the family. We were all possessed of very strong personalities and this did not make for a particularly harmonious home life. Charlie's family had suffered a loss, which had resulted in them having to pull together, and so to be in a house where everybody got on was a complete joy.

I loved sitting around the dining table with the Boydell family as the verbal sparring got into full flow, but I was rather unprepared for the after dinner game which would become synonymous with our visits to Godalming. The game consisted of trying to find a girl that Charlie had slept with and of whose existence I was unaware. Eddie and Victoria would go through all the possible candidates (which could take a considerable length of time) until they saw me raise an eyebrow and look over a Charlie. He would just give me a wink, which was his way of saying that I was the only one for him. And I knew that I was.

Charlie and I became totally inseparable, but six weeks after our first meeting, I was told that I had to go away for three weeks on a job for Saab. We were to travel around the whole country filming Saab garages for a training film. I didn't really care about the subject matter, all I knew was that I would be apart from my love for an unbearable amount of time. We had lunch together in Plymouth, which was not the most romantic of places at the best of times, and when it came to saying goodbye, we just couldn't. We stood in the middle of Armada Way and kissed and kissed and kissed, but still it wasn't enough. I hated the thought of leaving and Charlie couldn't bear the idea of being without me for almost as long as we had been together. Eventually, I turned and walked away, but I knew that it would be worth the trip just to see Charlie's face when I returned.

We talked on the phone several times a day, and it began to dawn on me that Charlie was not being guarded in the way that a man can be at the start of a relationship. He was being very frank about the way he felt about me and I found it difficult to know what to say in reply. I knew that if I was too gushy then I could blow my chances and scare him off, but at the same time I wanted to let him know that his feelings were fully reciprocated.

He wrote to me after I'd been away for a week.

5 iii 88

Darling Kate,

Thanks for your letter, and for the list of hotels – I do hope you get this!
It's not quite the same without you – for one thing it's too quiet, and
though it's lovely to talk to you on the 'phone for week seven/eight, it does
rather cramp a chap's style.

It's really unusual for me to write – I'm not sure it's very comfortable, I'm
normally typing – much easier to read, eh! Someone once complained
about my writing style – describing it as drunken! Maybe I was when I
wrote what they were trying to read! This time – SOBER!

It's Saturday morning – I've chopped the wood, written to the bank and
lit the fire.

I love you – and I'm looking forward to you coming home – let's work hard
at this, it could be the start of something big (mix through to grubby
laugh!) then cut to figure walking down Ugborough Square, to sit looking
over the south bound carriageway of the A38.

Much love,
C xxx

The weeks dragged on but eventually we finished the filming and at last I was
able to get back to Ugborough. As I drove into the square I could see Charlie
coming out of the cottage to greet me. I barely got the car door open before he
grabbed me and smothered me with kisses. I think if it had been darker, he
would have had me up against the car there and then, but he managed to contain himself until we got inside. And once inside, he let me know just how much
he had missed me; in fact he let me know three times before we even got up the
stairs. Charlie may have been written off by some misguided members of the
medical profession, but I knew that he was a stud muffin, pure and simple.

We worked through the summer and planned to go away at the end of
August, but as our relationship strengthened, so relations with my mother took
a turn for the worse. She had just entered the wacky world of the menopause
and having to cope with that, and the fact that the last of her daughters was
potentially about to leave home, proved to be very difficult for her. I vividly
remember her chasing me down the drive one day as I was about to leave to go
and stay with Charlie, shouting, 'He'll drop you like a stone.' And on another
occasion, we had a row as I was leaving and she slammed the car door on my leg
in a fit of peak. I didn't take too kindly to that gesture and tried my damnedest

to reverse over her as I swept out of the drive.

I decided the best course of action was to persuade mother that Charlie's intentions were entirely honourable. I told her that he would definitely ask me to marry him and I even told her when it would happen. We were about to go on holiday together and I assured my mother that I would have a ring on my finger when we returned.

Charlie and I were going to visit his stepbrother, Clive, who farmed sheep and pigs in the Limousin region of France. It was to be our first proper holiday together and we were really looking forward to it. Clive and his wife Anne were in the process of renovating their farmhouse, so the accommodation was somewhat basic. We slept up in the attic and were up at the crack of dawn each morning to feed the pigs and sheep. It was not the sort of holiday that most girls would have chosen, but I was with Charlie, seeing him doing what he enjoyed most. Charlie was in his element. He may have been born and bred in wildest Wimbledon but he was a country boy at heart. It was always my ambition to buy him a Ferguson T20 tractor. Some men might aspire to a Ferrari or a Porsche, but all Charlie wanted was a field to call his own and a little grey Fergy to ride around on. I was aware that I would be under very close scrutiny for the duration of the holiday; I knew that Charlie would be watching me to see if I was really cut out for a life of farming and I was determined to prove that I was. But

Charlie and Panda the sheepdog puppy, France 1988

I didn't realise quite what I had let myself in for.

Clive and Anne had planned to go away for a much-needed rest, leaving Charlie and me in sole charge of the farm. All went well for a while, but soon we were up to our knees on pig manure, trying to rescue a young sow with an alarming bloody lump protruding from her rear. We went indoors, found a veterinary textbook and discovered that she had a prolapsed anus – all very unpleasant to look at, but easily remedied by a little isolation from the other pigs.

Shortly afterwards, Charlie was nearly crushed to death as he tried to stop a runaway tractor. Clive had an ancient Renault, which would only start if you rolled it down a hill and slammed it into gear. It was parked on the hill behind us, but the slope was so steep that it had begun to creep forward. We both had out backs to it, but by some chance I happened to turn around, only to see it careering down the hill, with its loading forks pointing straight at us. I stood helplessly by, as Charlie launched himself at it. He was knocked to the ground, but luckily the concrete counterweight on the back came off and dragged the runaway tractor to a halt before it could do any damage.

The tractor had only narrowly missed killing us both and totalling the Landrover that we were standing beside. We both stood for a while, unable to believe our luck. It was all very exciting – in a scary kind of way, but was nothing compared with what was to follow...

We had been given instructions by Clive to separate the ram lambs from the rest of the flock, which we somehow managed to do – despite the best efforts of a recalcitrant French sheepdog. The lambs were waiting in their pen, ready for collection by a local farmer, when some men came into the farmyard. They were speaking very fast but Charlie understood enough to know that some of Clive's sows had escaped, and were heading south on the road to Oradour-sur-Veryes. Charlie had to stay behind and deal with the sheep and so I was dispatched to recapture to rogue females and re-fence their field.

Pigs are very wilful creatures and these petulant sows were determined to visit the next village. I think that they must have got bored with pig nuts and decided to try *pain au chocolat* instead, and it was a hell of a job to get the reluctant ladies back to their field. I eventually managed it with the aid of the two French farmers and that accomplished, my next task was to re-fence the part of the field where the pigs had escaped. It was a baking hot day and the air was alive with big, biting flies, which spent the afternoon feasting on my bare arms and legs. Eventually, after a lot of banging and cursing the field was secure. I was just putting the sledgehammer and sheep netting back into the Landrover, when I saw a cloud of dust and heard the engine of a tractor approaching. It was Charlie; he had dispatched the ram lambs and had come to see how I was getting on.

This was it; this was the moment I had been waiting for since January. I may have appeared all hot and sweaty after my labours, but inside I was as cool as a cucumber. I knew I had done everything that was expected of me as the future Mrs. Charles Boydell and as I watched my gentleman farmer jump down from the cab of his tractor, I was certain that he was about to ask the BIG question.

Shopping in the rain, France 1988

Charlie handed me a bottle of chilled Evian water and looked at me. I saw his lips part and I heard those words – it must have been the heat and the flies and the drone of the tractor engine, but what he said sounded suspiciously like, 'Well done Katie, you've just passed test number three.'

Bloody buggering hell. I had just spent two hours being eaten alive in a god-forsaken field in the middle of fucking France. I had bled for Charlie, I had sweated for Charlie – and he had, at that moment, the chance to make my life complete. He chose not to do that. Instead he chose to hold up a verbal score card and pat me on the head and tell me what a good girl I had been. If anyone had ever laboured under a false apprehension, then surely it was I.

Anyway, what I wanted to know was what were the first two tests and how many more would there be? I didn't want to ask Charlie to marry me – I wanted to be asked. I wanted him to get down on bended knee and plight his troth. I was a simple old-fashioned girl and I wanted it to be done right – I wanted it to be done right there in that porcine penitentiary that I had just created. Why couldn't he just ask me the pigging question and put me out of my misery?

As I stood there letting the cold Evian course down my parched throat and trying to hide my ignominy as best I could, a nagging thought came into my head. It was quiet at first, but soon became louder and eventually it screamed, 'MOTHER!'

Oh my God, I was going to have to return home without a ring. What would I say to my mother? I couldn't possibly go back and tell her that she had been right all along. Charlie hadn't dropped me like a stone after all; he'd just delayed the inevitable. I would go home with my head held high, secure in the knowledge that it was only a matter of time before he popped the question. I would go home and eat the humble pie that my mother had so expertly baked for my return. I would eat that pie until I choked on it.

Once I had digested the awful pie, life soon returned to normal. We lived for our weekends. Sunday was always a special day for us; Charlie would cook a roast, and before we sat down to eat it we would stroll across the square to the Anchor and have a drink with the boys. They had quickly accepted me, just as they had done with Charlie and once I had entered the bar I was lucky to get out without being bought a double gin and tonic by each of them in turn. The boys had become part of our lives and we could never envisage a time when we would not be able to wander down for a Sunday lunchtime drink and get locked in with them until we were almost too drunk to navigate our way back home. I was extremely fond of them all – they spoilt me rotten and I knew that if I ever needed anything, I would only have to ask and it would be sorted.

Tim was my favourite. He had a heart of gold and was a big softie where I was concerned. We would often bump into him at local clay shoots; he won every competition we ever saw him enter, but was never too busy to give us advice and encouragement. Charlie was a very good shot, but preferred driven game to clays. I, on the other hand, had become a reasonable shot at little round birds but had yet to distinguish myself with anything feathery.

Charlie and I had been asked along to shoot at the estate where he had shot when we first met. The family who ran the shoot were formidable to say the least, and being with Charlie didn't protect me from the acerbic comments that flew around the table during the shooting lunches. If you were brave enough to enter the family's verbal fray, then you were likely to be shot down as quickly as one of their pheasants.

The eldest son was called Christopher. He had known Charlie for some time and was obviously very fond of him – as was the rest of the family. I knew I had to make a good impression with him, but I never knew whether his taciturn manner was normal, or just reserved for me. My only hope would be to distinguish myself during the shoot. I knew that if I could impress him with my marksmanship, then I might have a chance to break the ice a little.

The day started well, but after a couple of drives I didn't even have a duck to call my own. We moved to a small valley and I was told to take up my position opposite a copse; the birds started to fly over and I fired at a few without success. Suddenly I saw a hen pheasant flying through the trees in front of me, I fired, and the bird dropped out of sight. I was so elated that I shouted at the top of my voice, 'I've just shot my first pheasant.' Not really the done thing, but I was too excited to care.

A man was dispatched to retrieve my trophy but he seemed to take an age to reappear. He didn't bring the bird over to me, in fact he didn't come over to me at all. There seemed to be a lot of hushed whisperings and then they came to tell me the bad news – I had shot an owl. Oh my God, I had just committed the worst possible shooting sin imaginable – I had killed a rare and beautiful creature on the estate of a senior member of the RSPB. It was a nightmare. I had just committed social suicide.

The family made mincemeat of me over lunch, but were gracious enough to forgive me and invited me to shoot again the next year. That year I was positioned just below the copse where the awful owl incident had happened. I was waiting for the beat to start, when I saw a large bird fly out of the trees on the hill above me. At first I thought it might have been a pheasant, but as it got closer I could see that it was a large tawny owl. It dived down, talons extended and I had to duck as it skimmed the top of my head. I don't think that owls usually attack humans, so I can only assume that it was the mate of the owl that I had shot the year before. It must have been waiting for me but I didn't need an enraged bird to remind of my misdemeanour, and I am still trying to live it down to this day.

Chapter Eight

By the autumn of 1988 my job had become unbearable. I could hardly stand to be in the same room as Kevin, but I was not yet confident enough to go it alone and become a freelance sound recordist. My father had told me that it would be foolish to resign without another job to go to, but I couldn't put up with any more abuse.

On Sunday October 15th, I was talking to Charlie about the situation and he said that he thought I should set myself up as an antique dealer, specialising in sporting equipment. I had supported myself for six months in Seattle by selling antique fishing tackle and so it seemed perfectly feasible that I could repeat my success over here. I still had some rods and reels left over from that trip and I had kept in contact with the dealer who had sold me all my stock, so getting another collection together would be easy enough.

Charlie offered to lend me the money to buy a van, but I told him that I couldn't accept his money. I was talking and crying and walking around the kitchen and I just couldn't seem to see a way out of the situation. Charlie told me I had to stop vacillating and make a decision and I told him I couldn't. Then he stopped and looked at me and said, 'Well, will you make just one decision for me?' I said, 'What's that?' and then he said, 'Will you marry me?'

It was such an unexpected question that it took me a few seconds before I could answer. I had envisaged candlelight and a bottle of wine, a gentle preamble before the inevitable proposal. But Charlie had surprised me, he had chosen my lowest point to raise me up and fill me with joy – he knew how to pick his moment. And what could I say in reply? There was only one answer to the question that I had waited so long to hear and that was, 'You'll have to get down on one knee and ask me properly.'

Well, I had waited all that time and I knew he was only going to ask me once, so I thought it only right that he should ask me in the correct manner. And he did what I asked – albeit with a little difficulty. Kneeling had been a problem for Charlie ever since he'd shattered his leg in the motorcycle accident, but once he was down on one knee he got his answer – I said yes.

Then I burst out crying and we stood in the kitchen in our weekend uniform of torn jeans and tatty old jumpers, and held each other. Charlie had finally asked me to be his wife and I was totally elated. He told me that he was trying to hold out until his birthday on October 26th, but events had rather overtaken his carefully laid plans. He had apparently been spurred into action after he had attended a wedding on the day before he proposed to me. He told me that as he sat in the church, watching the happy couple walking down the aisle, he realised that there was no point in waiting any longer. Charlie wanted me to be his wife, and thanks to Victoria's lack of discretion back in February, he knew that I had been waiting for him to ask me THAT question for months – ten long months to be exact. It was inevitable that he would ask me – but nothing could detract from the joy of the actual proposal.

We were expecting a friend to come over for supper, so Charlie 'phoned and put him off, and the we got into the car and drove over to my parent's house to tell them the good news. When we arrived at the house Charlie ran in through the door, all pale and out of breath and my Dad thought there had been some terrible accident. Charlie soon recovered his composure enough to ask my father's permission to marry me and I went next door and told my Mother. My parents seemed genuinely delighted and duly gave his permission, and we cracked open a bottle of bubbly to celebrate.

We arrived home a couple of hours later but were too excited to think about eating and so made our way down to the Anchor for a celebratory drink. It was the last night that the landlords Geoff and Di would be running the pub and the whole place was packed to the gunwales with happily – pissed locals. We told Jim Long the good news and he got up on a table and brought the drunken proceedings to a hushed standstill. He then told the assembled company that we had just got engaged and then there rose the most almighty roar of approval, followed by the first of many toasts.

Celebrating our engagement at a Hunt Ball, November 1988

The whole place was awash with beer by the time we left. People were throwing buckets of it across the bar and everybody was soaking. Charlie was more drunk than I had ever seen him and when we eventually fell through the front door of Wood Cottage, he insisted on phoning everybody he knew to tell them the news. It was 2.00am, and by that time Charlie was so drunk that he could barely speak, but he somehow managed to get the general idea across. It was then left to me to translate what he had said into something resembling English and then apologise to whomever we had called for disturbing them at such an ungodly hour. Charlie actually rang his brother Eddie about four times that night, asking him each time to be his best man, but by the fourth time I think Eddie must have been very tempted to have said 'No!'

I loved Charlie's family as much as my own and considered Eddie and Pixie to be my brother and sister, rather than my future in-laws. I had a real soft spot for Eddie – he was so funny and kind and he and Charlie had a wonderfully close relationship. When I first saw them greet each other with a kiss on both cheeks I was a little surprised, but I soon realised that it was a much more fitting greeting for two brothers than a formal handshake. They were very different when it came to women however. Charlie wore his heart on his sleeve, whereas Eddie was rather more circumspect. But there was no doubt about it – they were both girl-bait.

Charlie wanted to take me to the family jeweller in Burlington Arcade, but first he needed to find the money to buy the ring. I guess we were a typical a yuppie couple in those days, all Filofaxes and Fitou and we both drove G.T.I.s – mine was a Golf and Charlie's was one of the sporty new Peugeot 205s. Charlie realised that he would have to sell his little black bomber in order to realise enough cash to get me the ring that he thought I deserved, and as it turned out we found a rather unconventional way of getting the money.

We went up to the Midlands to visit friends and tell them about our engagement, and on the way home we decided to call in on the antique dealer who had sold me all my old fishing tackle. We arrived at James's house, and over a cup of tea we soon got chatting about the car. James loved a deal, and he was rather taken with Charlie's Peugeot. He had a Landrover, which was something that Charlie both quite fancied acquiring, and so we decided to do a deal. Being a typical antiques dealer, James was reluctant to give us a cheque for the full amount of money that made up the difference between the two vehicles, so we agreed to have part of the sum in goods.

We embarked on a long process of viewing and haggling, but by the time darkness fell we had come to an agreement. James kept the car and we drove off in a Landrover, complete with military chest, Victorian cast-iron hall stand, bearing the relief of a hunter and gun dog, and last but not least a Purdey hammer-action shotgun. It was a bizarre thing to do and the journey back to Devon was long, noisy and very uncomfortable, but it would definitely be something to tell the grandchildren.

We had a great deal of fun in that Landrover, it was not a ponsey four by four; it was a very useful tool. We used to take it over to my parent's house and clear the riverbank of overgrown sycamore trees. Charlie was very handy with a chainsaw and I became quite adept at dragging great hunks of timber out of the river with my trusty workhorse. I loved working alongside Charlie. We never argued about anything, we just enjoyed being together, being outdoors and being useful. Over the course of the winter we managed to amass a substantial wood-pile for my parents and came to realise that although working in television was fun, working on the land was all we really wanted to do. It was a distant dream in those days but we often talked of it. For my own part I knew that I could be with Charlie twenty-four hours a day and not tire of his company. I pictured us together, with a few acres of land and some animals, with three noisy children scuttling down the steps, pulling on their wellies and running off the fields to play. It seemed perfectly feasible in those days, Charlie was very fit and I didn't see any reason why he wouldn't remain so until it came time for his valve replacement. The operation seemed like such a long way off that I never really gave it much thought.

It was lucky for me that I didn't.

After selling his car, Charlie had the necessary funds to take me to London to choose the ring, and after a bit of careful consideration I walked out of the shop with a big smile on my face and five fat diamonds on my finger.

In the winter of 1988 my career was about to change yet again. Two men with whom I had worked on many occasions had offered me a job. Chris Denham was an ex-BBC presenter and Colin Rowe was an experienced camera-man; they had just set up a production company and had been appointed to sup-ply news coverage for the area to the newly launched Sky Television. They had decided to take a gamble and employ me to do all the filming, which would make me the first single camera operator in the Southwest and also the target of a con-siderable amount of scorn from my colleagues. I had no sound recordist, so I was responsible for pictures and sound, and as I often didn't have the luxury of a reporter, I sometimes had to ask the questions too. It was an exciting, ground-breaking job but I was on call 24 hours a day and had all of Cornwall, Devon and Somerset to cover, so I certainly had my work cut out.

Charlie made me sell my beloved Golf GTI, because he did not consider it an appropriate vehicle for a camerawoman. I was soon the rather embarrassed new owner of a Volvo 340, which came equipped with cushions for the rear par-cel shelf and a lovely tartan blanket for my knees. It was the dullest, slowest car in Christendom. In my GTI I felt like a hot chick in a hot hatch, all racy and raunchy, but now I just felt like pulling over in a lay-by, making a cup of Ovaltine, and burying my nose in a Dick Francis.

A few weeks before Christmas, Charlie was invited to his first A.I.D.S. din-ner. This was not some sort of charity event; it was a men-only dinner, hosted by The Anchor Inn Dining Society. Essentially, it was an evening of beer drink-ing, interspersed with steak and kidney pie and speeches. Charlie set off to the pub early in the evening and when it got very late, I went up to bed. I heard him stumble through the door at some ungodly hour of the morning. He came into the bedroom and said in a pissed, little-boy voice, 'Hello Katie, I had a lovely

evening and I've had lots of beer, but I really love you, I do, I reeeeally love you.'
He was so sweet that I couldn't be cross with him, and so I helped him get into
bed and turned off the light.

I was awoken some time later by a loud, retching sound, and switched on
the light to find Charlie sitting on the side of the bed, vomiting onto the carpet.
He managed to say that he was really sorry between retches and I told him to
get to the bathroom whilst I figured out how to clear up the mess. When I came
back upstairs with the cleaning things, Charlie was standing on the window seat,
vomiting out of the window. I managed to get him down and into the safety of
the bathroom and then I had the delightful job of cleaning up the mess. I fell
into bed at about 4am, knowing that I had to be up early for work the next
morning. Charlie was sound asleep when I woke up and so I went to the window and pulled open the curtains. It was only then that I realised that I had
parked my car outside the house the night before. My hateful white Volvo was
now splattered with carrot, beer, pie, and more carrot, and the front of the cottage looked as though it had been given a quick blast with a quantity of organic
pebbledash. I was not amused.

I woke my slumbering inebriate fiancée and told him to get outside and
clean up his mess. I let him know on no uncertain terms that I would not marry
a drunkard and that if he wanted to get so drunk that he had to vomit on his
own carpet, then he would have to find another woman to clean up after him. It
was our first row and I think it put the fear of God into him. I did secretly feel
that if any car deserved to be vomited on, then it was surely mine – but that was
not the point.

Charlie sent me flowers, along with a heartfelt letter begging forgiveness
and took me out that evening to make amends for his delinquent behaviour –
and I forgave him. It was impossible for me to be angry with Charlie for any
length of time. He was the least-annoying person in the whole world. He spent
his every waking moment trying to make me happy. How could I be angry with
a man like that?

Charlie's career was also about to change. His position at TSW was looking less secure by this time. He was not a member of staff and the length of his
contract had been reduced from a year, to six months. That gave him cause for
concern but there was little chance of getting any more television work in the
area, which would mean that we would have to consider moving. One day he got
a phone call from a chap who we knew in the village called Chris Slade, who was
a television presenter for BBC Plymouth. He said he had something to discuss
with Charlie and asked him out to dinner the next evening.

Charlie came back from the dinner and told me that Chris and his partner
Charles Wace had offered him a job. They wanted him to join them as a pro-
ducer for their newly formed production company. Charlie was unsure what to
do; it was a good offer but the company had no real clients to speak of and
Charlie would be their first employee. I told him that although it was a gamble,
it would be a chance to prove just how good he could be. I knew that once he
started work, he would make himself indispensable and if the company took off,

his prospects would be fantastic. He accepted their offer and agreed to start work after our wedding.

Preparations for the big day were moving on apace. Our vicar, The Reverend Peter Leverton, had given us a series of informal talks on the sanctity of marriage and told us what was expected of us as a married couple in the eyes of God. He also, rather surprisingly, talked about the importance of pleasing one another sexually, which I thought was a right-on thing for a vicar to do. In fact by the time we had completed our discussion I felt ready for anything, but I was not ready for what was about to happen to us.

We had both been suffering from flu, but whilst mine had abated, Charlie continued to spike a temperature of 104 degrees. I was worried about him and so I rang our local doctor and asked him to call round. Dr. John Halliday was an incredibly genial fellow with half moon spectacles and a quietly confident air, which immediately put you at your ease. He and Charlie got on very well together; Charlie had regular appointments with John to get his blood pressure checked and to renew the prescription for the beta-blockers that he took to keep his blood pressure under control.

I showed John upstairs and he examined Charlie, took his temperature and told him that he had a virus and that he would just have to sit it out until the fever eased. He called back a few days later to check on Charlie's progress, but by that time Charlie was out of bed and fully occupied with arrangements for the wedding. John left a note to say that he had called and Charlie 'phoned the surgery when he returned home and told John that he was feeling much better. But in truth, he wasn't feeling much better – he still had a fever but he had so much to do that he just ignored it. I wasn't worried because Charlie said that he felt fine – and that would prove to be a very costly mistake to make.

Chapter Nine

When I awoke on the morning of the 20th of May 1989, I saw the sun streaming through my window and knew we were going to be blessed with a fine day for our wedding. It was a glorious spring day – hot and bright with just enough breeze to stop people getting too sticky in all their finery. Everything was ready; the marquee looked fantastic, the gardens looked amazing – although I was looking less than alluring, walking round the kitchen in my nightie, trying to break in my wedding shoes and gargling with salt water at the same time. I didn't feel at all nervous, I just wanted to get started, but I had to get rid of the tickle in my throat before I took my vows – after all, no girl wants to splutter when she says, 'I do.'

My two older sisters were not talking to each other; they had had a huge fight the day before and this had made the atmosphere in our house positively glacial. It didn't affect me too much but my father was obviously greatly upset by the whole thing and was not himself by any means. My youngest sister Joanna was to be my only bridesmaid and she helped me get ready. I was wearing a dress that I had chosen to placate my mother. I really did not like it all – it was a little too flouncey for my tastes – in fact you could have put some fruit in my hair and called me a Pavlova. But I had agreed to have it because it was by far the easiest way of avoiding another row. Joanna finished doing my hair and I walked out of the room to see my father in full morning dress and I don't think I had ever been as proud of him as I was at that moment.

The clocks around the house tick- tocked the time away, my father kept checking his pocket watch and after what seemed like an eternity it was time to leave for the church. I had not wanted to arrive in a big flash car, so Charlie had arranged for me to travel in the rustic comfort of his uncle's Rangerover, which seemed much more appropriate. I think we got there about one minute late and I walked up the steps with my handsome Daddy, knowing that this would be a day that would be burned into my memory for the rest of my life.

The church was brimming with morning-suited men and their beautifully attired companions, and as we stood in the doorway I could see them all turning round to catch their first glimpse of the meringue. We slowly made our way towards the altar, passing a myriad of familiar faces and I could see my love standing with Eddie – waiting, passively waiting. My father brought me to Charlie's side, stood back and in so doing, passed on the responsibility of my care to a man, the only man, who was equipped for such an undertaking.

Charlie looked devastatingly handsome, but he was dripping with sweat.

He had never been prone to excessive perspiration, so I was a little shocked so see rivers of the stuff running off his forehead and dripping onto the stone floor of the church. I put it down to the heat and the excitement the occasion and tried to concentrate on not fluffing my vows.

Peter Leverton had told us to project our voices so that the whole church could hear our responses, and so when we took our vows nobody was in any doubt that we both 'did'. We knelt down to be blessed, finding ourselves at eye-level with our vicar. He was not exactly the tallest of men but he had a towering presence, and when he laid his hands on our heads and spoke to us, I swear I could feel his blessing going right through me. It was a most peculiar sensation; I had never been a deeply religious person but I knew that through him, God was giving me the strength and the faith to survive all that might happen in the years ahead.

Walking back down the aisle with my new husband was a moment of supreme joy. I knew that I would never look as radiant as I did at that moment – it was bliss, pure bliss. I could see all the boys from the Anchor lined up along the back row, looking rather uncomfortable in their Sunday best, and they were peering back at a couple whom they had never seen dressed in anything other than ripped jeans and tatty jumpers.

We walked out onto the top of the church steps, to a cacophony of pealing bells and people shouting, 'Kiss!' And we kissed – for the first time as man and wife, in front of a square filled with happy villagers and curious tourists, smiling in the sunshine of a glorious day. It was truly the happiest day of my life.

Our wedding day

We climbed into the wedding car, which was an old Morgan, owned by John Houston, the doctor whose pork we had eaten on our first Sunday lunch together. John drove us out of the village, through lanes thronging with bluebells and red campion, leaving a trail of confetti for our guest to follow.

The reception was perfectly planned; there was a mountain of champagne and acres of food, which sadly we did not get to taste because we were being ordered around the garden by a rather over zealous lady photographer. Charlie was beginning to look very tired and pale by this stage, but we still had the speeches to get through before he could relax.

Finally, everybody gathered in the marquee and waited for the speeches to begin. When it came to his turn, Charlie did really well. Luckily we had a great audience, many of whom were expert hecklers, so there was laughter all the way through his speech. My father was exceptionally nervous and spent a large part of his speech talking, not about me, but about people who were unknown to most of the audience. He did get onto the subject of his daughter towards the end, but it was clear to me that he was still deeply affected by the row on the previous day.

Edward's turn had now come and he was also visibly nervous, for not only was it the eve of his final Bar exams, but it was also cup final day and he was passionate about football. He managed to overcome his nerves and forget about the small matter of his future career, to deliver the finest Best Man's speech I would ever hear. It was masterful, and at the end the whole marquee was in uproar. Edward played a blinder that day and it obviously focussed his mind, because he would go on to pass his exams and become an extremely successful barrister.

We were to be flown away from the reception by John, a friend of ours from the village. He had been a submariner in the Navy and was known to everyone as 'The Admiral', but had decided to give it all up to become a balloonist. The flight was to be a wedding gift and also a chance for him to try out his skills as a newly qualified pilot.

The wind was quite strong initially, and so, much to our disappointment, John decided that it would not be possible to fly. However, by late afternoon the breeze had dropped and we got the all clear to fly the balloon. We soon had the canopy inflated, although it was hard to keep it under control in the gusty breeze. It was really borderline as to whether we should have been flying at all, but our pilot was keen to carry us from our wedding in style.

John, resplendent in Panama hat and full morning dress, eventually told everyone to stand clear. He put the burners on full, and we took off, watching two hundred captivated people in the field below us, cheering and waving us off into the blistering blue sky. My mother was sitting on the grass in the midst of all the guests. She had collapsed on the ground as she watched the balloon taking off. I think some people must have thought she had drunk a little too much champagne, but she was just totally overcome with emotion.

We went off in the balloon at a hell of a lick, and very soon it became apparent that we would have to look for somewhere to land, or risk being blown out to sea. John managed to skim a pylon, before coming down in a relatively safe-looking field. We landed with an almighty crash and John began to pull on the cord to release the air from the balloon. He pulled and pulled but we carried on being dragged horizontally across the field, before taking off again. John soon realised that in his excitement, he had been pulling the end of the cord that was tied to the basket and not the end that had been attached to the release parachute. We now faced the prospect on crash-landing a second time, so it was vital that John choose a safe field with not too many cowpats to drag us through. He spotted a likely place and we hit the deck yet again – but this time we stayed put. It was such a relief to be out of the basket, but we now had the task of finding the owner of the field so that we call the recovery crew and take the balloon home.

Charlie had spotted a group of people walking just below the field and so John strode out to ask if they knew the local farmer. They told us that it was their field and seemed genuinely delighted when we told them we had just got married. They asked us to join them for a celebratory drink, but added, 'You'll have to be quiet, because our father is upstairs, dying. The whole family has gathered to say goodbye to him but don't let that put you off, we'd love you to join us for a glass of wine.' We were not sure what to do, but the family was insistent, and so we made our way down to a handsome stone manor house and went inside. It had obviously been their father's life work, rescuing the house from dereliction and restoring it to its former glory. We were ushered into the great hall, which had a magnificent hammer beam roof and cavernous fireplace, and were then given some very welcome refreshments. Shortly afterwards, an elderly lady came down a small staircase at one end of the hall; she walked up to us and introduced herself as Kate Bassett. She was the wife of the dying man and told us that he had rallied at the sight of the balloon going past his window. She then handed us an ancient horseshoe, wrapped in white ribbon and told us that it had been dug up during the restoration of the house. She said she wanted us to have it as a symbol of good luck and added that she hoped that we would be as happy in our marriage, as she had been during the 56 years of her own marriage.

We stayed and chatted with the family for a while, but we didn't have to wait long because the recovery team found us almost immediately, which was remarkable in itself because we were out in the middle of nowhere. We loaded the balloon, said our goodbyes and drove off with the feeling that we had just had our marriage blessed for a second time. It was a strange and magical meeting and one that we would never forget.

We got back to Thornham just in time to greet the extra guests who had been invited to the evening party. Charlie and I got up and danced to 'It's Got to be Perfect' by Fairground Attraction and then we carried on dancing until Charlie asked to go and sit down for a breather. I could have easily danced all night, but by ten o'clock Charlie was really flagging. I was a bit annoyed with him because I was still enjoying myself and I was puzzled by his lack of energy, but I said nothing and we decided to leave. Everybody crowded out into balmy night air to say goodbye and after I had told a number of rather startled people that I loved them, we headed off to a nearby hotel for our first night of wedded bliss.

When we got to our room, I ran a bath and we both had a long, hot soak and a glass of champagne. I was eager to consummate the marriage and Charlie seemed willing to oblige me, but after a short while it was clear that he was to exhausted to continue. He rolled over and immediately fell into a deep sleep.

I lay awake, feeling like a bit of a failure. I knew that Charlie had been tired during the day, but I had hoped that he would recover once we got to the hotel. I felt such disappointment – after all your wedding night is supposed to go with a bang and mine had simple fizzled and gone 'phut', like some faulty firecracker. I watched Charlie as he slept, hoping that this would not be some kind of portent for the rest of our marriage. I couldn't understand what was wrong; it was a depressing way to end our wedding day but I simply had no idea that his tiredness was the first outward indication that his body was fighting a serious infection from within. I didn't know that – all I knew, as I lay awake beside him was that I wanted my old Charlie back.

We set off the next day for our honeymoon. Charlie had decided to give me a real treat and take me salmon fishing in Ireland. This was not the kind of honeymoon most brides would have chosen, but Charlie knew that I would much rather spend my honeymoon in chest waders than a skimpy bikini.

We took the ferry over to Dublin, and drove to our first billet, a modest country house in county Wexford. Our hosts sounded a bit formidable in the brochure, so we did not know what to expect – but as it turned out we had no need to worry.

Sir Richard Levigne was not the doughty old buffer we had pictured, but a tall, gently spoken dairy farmer who ran the family shooting lodge as an upmarket B&B. His wife Maria was the last person to be born in Waterford castle – a genuine Irish aristocrat. She was a warm and wonderful woman who seemed totally unaffected by her title or her surroundings. She was also a fantastic cook. We were the only guests staying at the time but that didn't seem to matter to Maria, who appeared from the kitchen throughout the day with a succession of cordon bleu meals. It didn't seem to matter to us either; we rather enjoyed the luxury of eating alone together at the end of the long mahogany dining table in a sumptuous room hung with family portraits and lit only by candlelight.

It was a perfect start to our honeymoon. We were left alone for the most part, but at the same time were made to feel like part of the family. Richard even joined us for dinner on our last evening, sitting between us in his milking overalls, talking with us long into the night about fishing and farming.

We left the Levigne's, vowing to return as soon as we could and carried on through the south of Ireland, drove west round the ring of Kerry and out to Loch Currane. We spent long, lazy days, drifting around the loch in an open boat, soaking up the sun, reading and trolling for salmon. Our afternoons were spent sleeping and making love in the sunshine, and as a result we had to spend part of each evening picking off unwanted ticks, which had attached themselves to us as we cavorted in the heather.

Our last stop was at another beautiful house, owned by an English couple called Merrie and Jeremy Green. They were a real hoot and we ate most of our meals with them in their kitchen, rather than in the formal dining room. We were actually trying to avoid the other guests, who seemed an interesting mix of eccentrics and misfits. We were able to observe to curious carnival of caricatures from a safe distance as it revolved around us, but all too soon it was time to catch the ferry home again.

We had enjoyed the rare privilege of seeing Ireland bathed for a fortnight in brilliant sunshine and we knew that we would be back, if only to remind ourselves what a real pint of Guinness tastes like. It was a memorable trip for so many reasons. We managed to relax totally, and Charlie seemed to recover some of his youthful vigour, although he did need a nap every afternoon, which was not entirely due to the voracious demands of his blushing bride. It was unusual for him to need so much sleep but I decided to put it down to the fact that he was getting over his virus. There was nothing to indicate otherwise, but time was ticking away and unbeknown to me, Charlie was growing weaker with each passing day.

PART TWO

The first year of our married life was to be a time of excitement and of joy. We were two people preparing to take the first steps on a journey that would last the rest of our lives.

The man of my dreams had tuned out to be a slightly battered version of the original concept, and I had forsaken the neoprene road of life for a rutted farm track, but I wouldn't have had it any other way.

My path was strewn with rose petals, my future – imperfect. Misfortune had blunted any spiky character traits that might have kept me at arms length from Charlie – and so I embraced him. I embraced his past, his family and his friends; and he in turn wrapped me in his arms and became my protector. He would guard me from danger; he would love me and look after me, in sickness and in health. We both knew that whatever happened in the future, this first year was sacrosanct, untouchable – safe. There was nothing to stand in our way as we embarked on our journey together. The road ahead was clear; we were coasting happily along.

It was downhill all the way.

Chapter Ten

Charlie was keen to get on with his new job as soon as we returned from our honeymoon, and approached the challenge with typical zeal. He soon settled in at Two Four Productions, and Charles and Chris seemed very happy with his work. But at home all was not well.

Charlie complained of a niggling cough and despite downing gallons of disgusting, sticky brown linctus, the cough refused to go away. At the same time I noticed that he was losing a bit of condition. He seemed to have shrunk and was now on the weedy side of slim. In my wifely wisdom I decided that he ought to lift weights before bed each night to try and recover his fine physique, and even though he was exhausted by bedtime, he wearily did as I asked. I did think that he ought to go and see Dr. John Halliday again, just to make sure that the virus had gone completely, but Charlie insisted that it would not look good if he took time off work so soon after joining the company, and so he ignored my advice.

A few weeks went by and Charlie was showing no signs of improvement. He had lost so much weight by that stage that I had to lend him my belt to stop his trousers falling down. Charlie's new offices were in the same building as mine and I noticed that other people had begun to comment on his sudden weight loss, but still he refused to see a doctor.

Charlie was having physiotherapy on his back and leg at the time from a wonderful lady called Cynthia Wright. She had performed a small miracle by managing to stretch Charlie's damaged leg to such an extent that he no longer needed to wear a built-up shoe. I think it had something to do with relaxing the muscles, which had been bunched-up after the accident. I wasn't exactly sure – all I knew was that Charlie was a different man. He now had the ability to wear any kind of footwear that took his fancy, not just the heavy, cumbersome brogues that I had always seen him in.

One day Charlie returned from his appointment with Cynthia with a bag of liver. It occurred to me that this was a rather unconventional form of treatment for his leg, but apparently Cynthia had said that Charlie looked very anaemic and had told him that he should eat some liver to get the colour back in his cheeks. When I had a look at him I realised that he was not only thin, but also very pale. I repeated my plea for him to visit the doctor, but being a stubborn man he refused to make an appointment, saying he felt fine and telling me not to worry. But by that stage the night sweats were so bad that we could have grown a substantial crop of watercress under our duvet.

A couple of days later Charlie was getting ready for work. He sat down on the edge of the bed to button up his shirt and then suddenly collapsed forward. He was doubled up in pain and crying out to me and at that moment I knew that something was seriously wrong – something that no amount of linctus or liver was going to cure. Charlie was ashen-faced and obviously in considerable discomfort; I called his office to tell them that he would not be coming in to work and then finished getting him dressed, and all the while I was thinking 'What the hell is wrong with him?' I struggled to get Charlie out of the house and into the car and then drove him straight to the doctor. It was a grey, cold morning in July, the sky had an ominous blackness about it, and Charlie said it was a portent and that he knew it meant that we were about to hear bad news.

We arrived at the health centre and took our place in the waiting room. I watched Charlie all the while as he struggled to stay sitting upright; he looked terrible – deathly grey and sweaty and I really thought that he might collapse again at any moment. I held onto his hand and tried to reassure him, but all I could think about was what he had said in the car. He knew something was seriously wrong, but how long had he known?

Eventually we were shown into Dr. Halliday's consulting room. He listened to Charlie's heart and it was clear from his expression that he didn't like what he heard. Then he looked at his fingernails and into his eyes and it seemed to me that he already had a good idea what was wrong with Charlie. He sat back in his chair, looked over the top of his spectacles and said, 'You're very seriously ill, old boy, and we need to get you straight into hospital. I think you've got an infection in your heart called sub acute bacterial endocarditis and we have to get you on some intravenous antibiotics right away.'

Charlie was admitted straight to the cardiac ward of Derriford hospital in Plymouth and after a long and thorough examination, it was found that Dr. Halliday's original assumption had been correct. Charlie had contracted a very virulent form of bacterial infection, which attacks the heart valves, and if left untreated results in complete decimation of the internal tissues of the heart, and eventual death.

The people who most commonly contract bacterial endocarditis are those with leaking heart valves, although it is also possible for someone with a perfectly normal heart to become infected. Bacteria can get into the bloodstream via a number of different routes, but their most common point of entry is through the gums, as a result of dental treatment. In a normal person they are simply flushed through the heart with no ill effects whatsoever, but they are able to settle on the inside of an abnormal heart and that's when all the trouble starts. Once they get established, the little blighters form pea-sized clumps in the inside of the valve and then simply munch their way through all the healthy tissue around them. Charlie had been made aware of the risks of infective endocarditis and had been given full antibiotic cover for any dental treatment that he had needed. But he had had bleeding gums a couple of months before our wedding and that may have been when he became infected.

Charlie was now displaying all the textbook symptoms of the disease in its most advanced state. He had a swollen and very tender spleen, tiny haemorrhages in his eyes and splinter haemorrhages in his fingernails. He was very anaemic and had a high fever, accompanied by severe night sweats. His heart had a pronounced murmur – not so much a 'whooshing' noise, more of a 'Oh Shit, Oh Shit, Oh Shit' noise.

When I found out what was wrong I felt as if I had been slapped across the face. Charlie was dangerously ill; his body had been fighting the infection for at least two months and by now it was clear that he was starting to 'lose the battle'. I failed to understand how he had managed to carry on as normal when he must have felt so bloody awful. Charlie lifted those dumbbells for me night after night, when all he must have wanted to do was collapse with exhaustion. He went off to work every day with his clothes gradually falling off him, determined to prove that he was still up to doing the job he was being paid to do. He had stood beside me at the altar of Ugborough church with a fever raging through his body, watching beads of sweat drip, drip, drip onto the granite floor and had willed himself to stay standing long enough to say 'I do.'

And now, in retrospect it was hardly surprising that he had been so tired on our wedding night, he should have been hooked up to a drip in a hospital bed and not rolling around with me on a faux four-poster.

I should have seen the signs instead of thinking about myself; infective endocarditis is notoriously difficult to spot in its early stages, but even so, I should have bullied him into seeing a doctor as soon as we got back from our honeymoon. I should have noticed how pale and tired he was looking. I should have done so many things; but it was too late, the infection was already well established – the damage had already been done.

I rang Charlie's mother from the hospital and told her the news, and she said she would drive down from Surrey immediately. I told my parents and Chris and Charles and then set about phoning Charlie's friends to tell them what had happened. I can only remember one of the 'phone calls clearly. It was to Chris Sutton-Scott-Tucker, who owned the estate where we shot every year. Although he presented a gruff exterior to the world, I knew that he cared about Charlie and would want to hear what had happened straight away.

When I rang, the whole family was obviously in the middle of lunch. Chris's father Michael answered the phone and there was uproar when the rest of the family found out that Mrs. B. was on the line. I would normally have engaged in a bit of verbal sparring with Michael, but on this occasion I was in no mood for jokes and so just asked to speak to Chris.

Chris realised something was wrong and took the call in another room, away from the family. I told him that Charlie was seriously ill, that his heart was badly infected and that he would be in hospital for as long as it took to bring the infection under control. Chris went very quiet, and then told me that he would be in to visit Charlie as soon as he was feeling up to it. He had never been one for great open shows of affection; after all he was a strapping six-foot farmer, not a touchy-feely new man. But I learned later, that after he'd finished speaking to me, he had sat alone in his father's office and wept.

Back in Derriford, the doctors had done an ultrasound on Charlie's heart and had discovered that his aortic valve was now leaking very badly and that his left ventricle had become enlarged. They also detected the presence of 'vegetation' on the cusps of the valve. The streptococcus bacteria were eating away at the inside of Charlie's heart and it would be a race against time to save what remained. Charlie was put on a drip and given very high doses of penicillin and gentamicin, which were two forms of antibiotic known to be effective in the treatment of streptococcal infection. It was now just a matter of waiting and watching and hoping that Charlie would start to show some signs of recovery. I stayed with him for as long as I could and then went back to our empty cottage, feeling dazed, confused, and very alone.

Slowly, Charlie began to respond to the antibiotics. He had lots of visitors during his stay, which kept his spirits up. His high temperature soon returned to normal and he gradually began to look less anaemic. He started feeling frisky again and would chase me around the bed, until a nurse came in and told him to settle down. It really looked as though he might get away with it and recover without having to undergo any surgery. I was so relieved. It had been a very long two weeks and I was desperate to get Charlie back home so that I could look after him.

I was then asked to go over to the Isles of Scilly on a job for Sky News. Richard Branson was attempting to break the Blue Ribbon record for crossing the Atlantic in a powerboat, and Sky wanted me to film him crossing the finish line. As it turned out, it was a total waste of time. Branson arrived after dark, which was no problem for the BBC and ITN crews, as they were up in helicopters equipped with powerful searchlights. They got great footage of the boat when it finally crossed the finish line out at the Eddystone lighthouse. I, on the other hand had to set out in a tiny fishing boat, knowing that my camera would be totally useless in the dark. I did tell Sky what would happen, but they insisted that I go anyway and the result was a forgone conclusion – unusable pictures.

When I got back, I went straight to the hospital because I was sure that the doctors would be on the verge of sending Charlie home. But I was in for a nasty shock. I had left a man who appeared to be recovering fast – very perky and full of beans. But when I arrived back at Charlie's bedside, he looked as pale and sweaty as when he had first been admitted, and when I bent down to kiss him, he hardly had the energy to kiss me back. His doctor told me that he would have to undergo more tests and that there was a strong possibility that he might have to go to London for open-heart surgery.

Open - heart surgery.

Hearing those words suddenly made me feel very afraid and I went home and prayed for the destruction of every bastard bug in my darling boy's heart. I willed Charlie to get better.

I was at work two days later, when the phone rang. It was the ward sister; she told me that I had to get to the hospital straight away, but would not tell me why. I thrashed my Volvo down to Derriford – there had been an urgency in the Sister's voice that scared the hell out of me. Eventually I got to the hospital. I was crying and shouting and it was typical that I couldn't find anywhere to park my car. Eventually I managed to find a space, and I sprinted across the hospital foyer towards the lifts. The doors opened, and there, in a wheelchair, sat Charlie. He was going down to have yet more tests, and when he saw me he burst out crying. We held each other and cried as he was wheeled off to have more tests. I wouldn't let go of him. I knew that if I let him go they would take him away from me and I wouldn't have the chance to make him well again.

The doctors had been alerted to the fact that there might be a problem when Charlie began to spike a temperature. They listened to his heart, detected a new murmur from his mitral valve and decided to send him down for a repeat echocardiogram, which was where he was going when I found him. When he was examined it was clear that both valves were by then grossly infected.

I held onto Charlie as the technician studied the moving image of his failing heart, as he was wheeled outside, as he was put into the ambulance. And then I had to let him go. We were both still crying, trying to tell each other so many things in a jumble of tears and stifled sobbing. Charlie was only 28, we had been married for six, short weeks and he was about to be taken away from me and driven down to London to have his precious heart cut open. Charlie had given his heart to me and I vowed I would do everything in my power to protect it. There was so much love between us. I imagined that when the surgeon cut into his heart, it would burst apart, spraying Charlie's love all over the operating theatre – drenching everybody. Soaking them in pure, precious emotion.

I am not a medical expert, but I do have an understanding of the heart. This is my understanding.

The Heart

The heart is the most remarkable organ in our body. It is a tireless muscle, which beats continually, day and night, for the whole of ones life. It needs neither rest, nor nourishment, yet it alone is responsible for the survival of every other organ in the body.

But it is not simply a pump; it is the centre of our emotional self. The heart responds to any form of excitement, be it fear or lust, by beating faster. When you are in love, you don't say, 'My liver cleaned my blood a little quicker today.' But instead, 'My heart skipped a beat'. And when you suffer the trauma of losing your love, you don't feel your kidneys failing, you feel that your heart is breaking.

The heart is an organ that dominates every aspect of our lives – and yet we take it for granted. It is possible to survive with only one lung, with only one kidney, and if you lose a chunk of liver, the organ will simply regenerate itself. It is possible to remain alive when all electrical activity in the brain has ceased; the body will continue to function as long as the heart continues to beat, but when the heart stops, every other organ in the body will fail.

To put it in its most basic form, when your heart dies, so do you.

Because of the emotional importance that we place on the heart, any problems that may occur in it take on a far greater significance. Having surgery on your heart is a big deal. Of course it is possible to be given a transplanted heart, but you cannot simply magic one out of a hat if some basic procedure suddenly goes wrong. During an operation, when the heart stops, the show is over. It's like having a big, fat opera diva sitting in your chest, just waiting to hit the high note.

Heart surgery is scary stuff, nobody wants to have it and yet so many of us need it.

Charlie needed it, and he needed it quick.

Chapter Eleven

The ambulance that Charlie was travelling in picked up a police escort at Heston services. The two motorcycle outriders cleared a path through the busy London streets and the ambulance tore through the city with its sirens blaring. They made the journey in double-quick time, jumping 28 red lights before finally reaching The London Hospital in Whitechapel. Charlie was quickly taken to Cotton Ward, and placed in the care of a tiny, tough Irish Sister called Marie.

I travelled down on the train, and got to the hospital a couple of hours later. I had been expecting a high tech place, all scrubbed and shiny, but when I turned the corner out of the marble entrance lobby, I descended into Dickensian gloom. The hospital was a rabbit warren of dingy corridors and out dated wards; it was a long way from Devon, but it was the only option available because at the time Derriford Hospital had no cardiac surgery unit.

Charlie had arrived on a Friday, and after he was admitted he was examined and deemed well enough to wait until the following Monday, when there would be a ward round which would determine when he would have to undergo surgery. He had seem relatively well over the weekend, but when I arrived to see him on the Monday morning he was in a terrible state – alternating between bouts of shivering and hot sweats, when he would throw off his bedclothes and sit in his boxer shorts, panting for breath. That was the most worrying thing to me. At that time I knew very little about the heart, but a doctor had warned me before we left Derriford that if Charlie started to get breathless, it meant that he was in heart failure and in serious trouble.

I called the nurse over and tried to get her to do something, but she said I had to wait until the ward round. Charlie was really gasping for breath by this time and it was a huge relief when I saw the doctors approaching. Charlie saw them coming towards us too, and decided to make a full recovery on the spot. He stopped panting, he sat up – looking for all the world as if he was in rude good health, and proceeded to hold a polite and intelligent conversation with the top man. I didn't know what he was playing at, sitting there looking as if he had just popped in for a quick check up – he was in heart failure for God's sake and I wanted someone other than me to see it. His act was so convincing that the chief surgeon decided that there was no real hurry, and told Charlie that he would operate on the Thursday. I just sat by the bed in stunned silence and thought, 'Fuck – he won't be alive on Thursday, he's dying right here on the bed in front of you, why can't you see it?' I felt totally helpless, but I was damned if I was going to sit back and watch Charlie peg out in front of me.

When the 'big cheese' left, I quickly called Marie, the ward sister, over to the bed and told her that I thought Charlie was in trouble. She saw what I saw and immediately called the surgical registrar away from the ward round; and after I had told him about the breathlessness he re-examined Charlie and realised that there was no time to waste.

Charlie was by this time, gravely ill. Not only was his body trying to fight a serious infection, his heart was also barely functioning. Both his aortic and his mitral valves were leaking badly; the blood was washing back out of his heart as quickly as it was being pumped in, so it was having to pump twice as hard just to keep the blood circulating properly. Michael Marrinan, the surgical registrar, acted swiftly. He immediately pulled a surgeon out of theatre and told the nurses to prep Charlie in a side ward. Everything was happening so fast I hardly had time to think, but my head soon cleared when I saw the surgeon.

Doctor Alan Wood strolled over to Charlie and shook his hand. He towered over the bed. He had such massive hands that I found it hard to imagine them being used to perform something as delicate as heart surgery. He was still dressed in surgical scrubs and looked like the jolly green giant, but I could immediately see that he was a good man by the way he talked to Charlie. He was kind and gentle and funny, and I felt totally confident that he would look after him.

Meanwhile, I had rung Charlie's mother Jane and told her that they were about to operate, but it was a 40-minute journey from Godalming, and I seriously doubted whether she would arrive in time to see her son. Charlie was desperate not to go before he had seen her, and the nurses managed to delay things for a while, but eventually we were told that it was time. They wheeled Charlie out of the ward and it was then that Jane came running up the stairs. She held her dying son's hand and told him that he was going to be fine. It was the grimmest thing I had ever witnessed, this tiny woman, clutching on to the hand of her poor battered boy, desperate not to let it go, but knowing that she had to. She whispered that she loved him, released her grip and let me say goodbye.

What do you say to the love of your life when you know that this might be the last time that you ever see him? I was only twenty-five. I was not equipped. I didn't have the words to express how I felt. I just wanted it all to go away. I wanted to take Charlie back home – I didn't want anyone cutting his chest open. I wanted to love him better, but my love alone wasn't enough to save him now. I told Charlie how much I loved him. I told him that he would be fine and that we would soon be back home in Devon. I knew in my heart that he was going to be all right. I knew that our love could not possibly die that day. I knew that our love would give Charlie the strength to survive – that fate would not be so cruel as to deny us our happiness.

I made myself believe that I would see Charlie again.

Jane and I watched Charlie disappear into the operating theatre, and then we sat down on the bench at the entrance to the ward and wept. We wept for Charlie and for ourselves. We wept at the unjustness of it all, at the senselessness and the pain. We wept; and with each falling tear the time passed, marked only by small salty pools on the shiny red vinyl.

Jane's arm was around my shoulders and she was trying to comfort me. She had so much strength in her tiny frame, she had given it to Charlie when he needed it and now she was giving it to me. We sat and waited, walked and talked for five long hours, and then at last, Alan Wood emerged from theatre. He took me to one side and gave me the news I had been desperate to hear – Charlie was going to be all right. He was very blunt with me but I needed to hear everything – I wanted him to tell me everything.

The first thing he told me was that Charlie was very lucky to be alive. When he had opened up Charlie's heart he found it to be florid with infection – something that he was not used to seeing in the heart of such a young man. The bacteria had taken hold of Charlie's heart and had formed gross vegetations on the inside of both the aortic and the mitral valves. In the seat of the infection lay a large abscess, which went right through both valves and on into the right atrium – one of the upper pumping chambers of the heart. Alan had removed both the valves and cut away the part of the heart that had been affected by the abscess. He then inserted two pig's valves into the heart, sewed them into place and closed the hole in the right atrium. He then closed and re-started Charlie's heart, closed the chest, and once he was happy that Charlie was 'firing on all cylinders', he sent him off to the Intensive Therapy Unit.

Alan Wood saved a life that day – he saved lives every day, but that day was special because that was the day that he gave Charlie back to me.

The walk down to ITU was made in total silence. Both Jane and I needed to gather our thoughts before we saw Charlie but I felt that at any moment, one of us might break into a run, so unbearable was the tension. We finally reached the outer doors to the ITU, but still we could not see Charlie. We had to wait until his nurse was happy that he was stable enough to see us, but eventually we were shown to his bed. It was such a relief to see him again that we hardly noticed all the tubes and wires coming out of his body. He was attached to a breathing machine and was heavily sedated. His skin was cold to the touch – he had been on a heart bypass machine throughout the operation and for any procedure requiring bypass, the patient's body needs to be cooled down to around 28 degrees centigrade. This helps to preserve the vital organs for as long as possible during surgery. Charlie was being kept sedated whilst his body gradually warmed back up to its normal temperature, for if he came round too quickly he would go straight into shock.

We sat on either side of his bed and watched as Charlie slowly began to regain consciousness. He was attached to a breathing machine so talking was impossible, but eventually his eyes flickered a look of recognition and he tried to smile. Jane sat and talked to her son for a while and then left us alone together.

It was late by this time and the ward was quiet, save for the constant beeping of the monitoring machines and the mechanical wheeze of the ventilator.

Charlie, recovering on Cotton Ward

I talked to the nurse whist I waited for Charlie to come round again and she explained everything that she was doing. During that long night I learned a very valuable lesson – namely that the secret of coping with the strain of having a loved one in hospital, is knowing everything there is to know about his treatment.

Knowledge is power when you are dealing with the medical profession – they have it and you need to have it. Your job is to be able to convince them to share just enough with you in order for you to understand what has happened, or what is about to happen. Some doctors are very good at explaining everything to you and some seem to consider it an affront if you dare to ask them even the most basic of questions. But it is only by questioning that you will gain peace of mind. It is in your interest to speak up if you do not understand what the doctor has said – and if professional, he or she will be happy to repeat the explanation. If they fob you off by saying it is too complicated to explain, then they are failing in their responsibilities to the patient and to you. What I believe many doctors fail to realise, is that it is the relatives who will give the patient the mental strength to continue through even the most difficult of treatments. Emotional support can only be given if the relative is fully confident about those treatments, and sometimes, emotional support is the most powerful treatment of all.

Doctors may have the power over life or death, but they are not gods, they are human beings. They are there to be questioned – so question them.

I watched the nurse throughout the night. She was gentle and kind and she let me stay with Charlie when a lot of people would have told me that it would be in my best interest to leave. I watched as she pulled out the large drain tubes that had been inserted into Charlie's chest and I watched as she sewed up the holes that were left behind. I bathed Charlie's parched lips with ice and I talked to him and reassured him every time he drifted back into consciousness. During that long night I gained an understanding about the job of an ITU nurse and I gained precious hours, which helped me to come to terms with what had happened to Charlie.

As dawn broke, he was taken off the breathing machine and soon after that he was deemed well enough to return to Cotton Ward and the safe hands of Sister Marie.

Chapter Twelve

Charlie was a boy in a man's ward. The other patients were, by and large, many years his senior, but they all shared the same slow, shuffling, post-operative gait. Charlie stood out like a sore thumb, not only because he was so young but also because he wore a nightshirt. Marie and the other nurses had never seen a man in a nightshirt on Cotton Ward, but Charlie's choice of nightwear did add a certain air of authenticity to the already Dickensian feel of the place.

It took him a while to gain the confidence to get out of bed, and his recovery was not helped by an allergic reaction which resulted in a livid rash covering his entire body, but he was soon making slow, halting steps, up and down the ward. He walked with one arm across himself, to protect the ten-inch wound, which ran down the length of his chest. His other hand gripped the drip stand, which carried the bag of antibiotic solution – something that had now become as essential to his survival as the air that he breathed.

I had the luxury of being able to stay in an accommodation block within the hospital grounds, which gave me the freedom to spend as much time with Charlie as I liked. I needed to be around, not least to police the hordes of visitors who turned up to see him. Most people were sensitive to the fact that he was in a severely weakened state, and only stayed for a few minutes. But some people just sat and let Charlie do all the talking, which weakened him so much that I often had to ask them to leave. I don't think some people grasped just how ill he was. They treated their visits like some sort of social outing and Charlie was too polite to tell them when he was tired, or when he needed to be alone. I was not nearly so polite – in fact I became a bit of a rottweiler, but I knew that the only way he was going to recover was if he was allowed to rest.

Food was the other problem. When I saw what the hospital had to offer in the way of nourishment, I wondered how any of the patients ever got better. One day Charlie ordered fish, which turned out to be full of bones and I had visions of him getting one stuck in his throat, and coughing so hard that his chest opened up. Jane and I decided that he needed at least one good meal a day if he was going to stand any chance of getting better, so we hatched a plan to bring a home-cooked meal in to him every day.

My time was running out and after staying for a week I knew that I had to get back to work. Charlie seemed to be making steady progress, although he was pretty fed-up. I wanted to stay with him but I had now become the main bread-winner and it was essential that I kept my job in order to pay the bills. Charles and Chris were committed to keeping Charlie on, but couldn't pay him a full salary – in fact, in those early days they could barely afford to pay themselves, so they kept him on a retainer until he was well enough to work again.

Once I was back at home, I found it incredibly hard to concentrate on anything. I felt that I was not in control of what was happening, that the whole force of my emotions was being directed down a flimsy phone line and it simply wasn't enough to contain what I felt. You can't make someone better unless you can touch him, unless you can hold him, unless he can feel your presence. I needed to give Charlie my strength, but I needed to do it through my eyes, through my mouth, through my fingertips – not through a bundle of twisted wires.

At five o'clock on the 15th of August 1989, I got a phone call from Charlie. It was exactly two weeks since his operation and he sounded different – not his usual upbeat self, but monotonal and sad. He said, 'I'm not feeling too good, I think I've got a bit of a cold and they're keeping an eye on me because I'm spiking a temperature'. I felt a chill go through me when he said that because I knew that if he had a temperature, then there was a very good chance that the infection had returned. And then he broke down and cried. He was sobbing and I was trying to reassure him but I was so far away and I felt utterly powerless to help him. I was frightened to hear how upset he was. Charlie was such a strong man – this was the first time I had ever heard him complain of feeling unwell and I knew that if he was as low as he sounded, then something must have gone badly wrong.

I needed to hug him, to hold him; I needed to talk to a doctor and find out what had happened, but all I could do was tell him how much I loved him and that I would soon be with him again. Jane came on the line because by this stage Charlie was sobbing too much to speak. She told me that the doctors were very worried about him and were just about to take him down to get a moving image of his heart. She told me that she would call me as soon as she found out the results of the tests, and I then put the phone down. I stood in the kitchen in a daze, chopping up vegetables for a stir-fry that I knew I couldn't eat, trying not to think the worst but thinking it all the same.

The procedure that the doctors were about to undertake was a dangerous one considering Charlie's condition at that time. He was, I learned, in severe congestive heart failure, but it was imperative that the medical team found out why. They took him down to theatre and injected dye directly into his heart; they then used a special camera to record the function of his valves. What they found was gross mitral regurgitation – meaning that the new valve that controlled the flow of blood into the main pumping chamber of the heart was not functioning at all – it had literally fallen to pieces.

Charlie's heart was failing.

The phone rang shortly after seven o'clock. It was Jane, she said, 'You have to come straight away, they're going to operate on Charlie's heart again'.

Charlie's sister was on holiday in Italy, having looked after Charlie for a week after I had returned to Devon. That same night she was awoken by a vivid dream. In her dream an old friend of the family had come to her and told her that Charlie was in trouble. The next morning she was on the first flight back to Heathrow.

I called my own parents to tell them what had happened and asked my father if he would drive me to London. When he arrived in Ugborough he found me sitting on the doorstep of Wood Cottage with my bag packed. I got into the car and we drove in total silence towards London. I just couldn't speak and he didn't know what to say to me. There were no words of comfort that he could offer me at that time; silence was the best he could do and silence was all that I wanted. I looked out of the window, wondering if I would ever see my darling boy again. In those days very few people had mobile phones, so I had no way of finding out what was happening until I reached the hospital. I was trying to pre-pare myself for the shock of hearing that Charlie had died, but at the same time something told me that he wouldn't give up without seeing me again. I held onto that as we raced up the M5, and managed not to let any more morbid thoughts enter my head.

When we reached Heston services, we realised that we did not have a clue how to get to Whitechapel. Dad filled the car up with petrol and when he went to pay he decided to ask for directions. But the problem was that we were not going to a friend's house in some suburban street. We had to get through cen-tral London and The City before we could get to Charlie and it was a rather a tall order to expect somebody to guide us, street by street to our destination. The bizarre thing was that Daddy actually found a man who knew exactly how to get there, and who was only too glad to tell us. After a few minutes I realised that neither of us would ever remember such lengthy and detailed directions and so I thanked the man for his kindness and bought an A to Z.

Navigating for another person is never easy but navigating your over-wrought father through central London and then The City, takes nerves of steel. But he didn't get cross with me and somehow I got us to the hospital entrance by eleven p.m. I left Daddy to find a parking space, and then I raced up the steps into the hospital.

In the last few moments before the anaesthetic took effect, Charlie must have been utterly terrified. Knowing that Alan Wood was about to open up his chest for a second time, about to snip through the metal ties which held his sternum together, about to pull his ribs wide apart. Knowing that he would be reaching inside and grasping his heart – holding it until it ceased to beat, but not knowing whether he would be able to re-start it after the surgery was com-plete.

Jane held onto Charlie's hand so tightly, trying vainly to take his mind off what was about to happen. She told him that he should try to think about his childhood, and of all the wonderful times that they had shared together. Charlie looked up at her, his eyes alight with fire and indignation and said, 'I don't want to think about the past, I want to think about the future. I don't want to think about my childhood, I'm going to get through this and have children of my own some day. '

When I reached Jane, she was sitting alone on the red bench at the end of a quiet, darkened ward full of snoring men in pyjamas. The man in the nightshirt was lying on an operating table, whilst the surgical team tried to once again to save his heart. The theatre staff worked to the steady hum of the bypass machine and the beep of the heart monitor, but if they had strained their ears, they would have heard a faint sound deep within the recesses of Charlie's chest. It was the sound of the fat lady limbering up to sing.

Chapter Thirteen

There was a tradition in the Boydell family that if any of the children went away on holiday, they always left their signet ring with their mother for safekeeping. Charlie had been told to remove his ring before surgery and had given it to Jane as she walked beside his trolley on the way to the operating theatre. It was the same ring that I had placed on his finger in the vestry after we were married, only six weeks before.

As I sat beside her in the oppressive gloom, she silently took off the ring and placed it on my finger. It was a simple act; a simple act that showed that she was passing on the responsibility of her oldest son to me. Charlie was still her son, but I was his wife and he was mine to care for now – in sickness and in health. Jane seemed to know what a heavy burden she was placing on my shoulders by placing that ring on my finger, but I know she wouldn't have done it if she had any doubts that I would be strong enough to bear it.

We left the ward to get some fresh air. Each of us had our own thoughts as we walked slowly up and down the road outside the hospital. I thought about Charlie, about his wonderful mind, and about all that would be lost to us if he died. I thought of his favourite poem, one that he had tried to get his sister Victoria to learn by heart, because he wanted her to love it as much as he did. It was called 'The Love Song of J. Alfred Prufrock', by T. S. Eliot. I thought of parts of it going through his head as he drifted into unconsciousness.

> Let us go then, you and I,
> When the evening is spread out against the sky
> Like a patient etherised upon a table....
>
> I am no prophet – and here's no great matter;
> I have seen the moment of my greatness flicker,
> And I have seen the eternal Footman hold my coat, and snicker,
> And in short, I was afraid.

After seven hours of surgery, Charlie was taken back to intensive care. My father could not bear to see Charlie stuffed full of tubes, so once he knew that his son-in-law was alive, he got in his car and drove back to Devon, leaving Jane and I to make our way once more down the gloomy corridors that led to ITU.

Alan Wood met us at the entrance to the ITU. He looked totally knackered, so I assumed that Charlie was not going to look too hot either. He told me that when they had opened Charlie up again, they had discovered that the replacement mitral valve had been sewn into the site of an abscess and that as the abscess had grown, the valve had pulled its stitches, leaving a gaping hole inside Charlie's heart. The valve was full of pus and there was more diseased tissue around it that had to be cut away.

Dr. Wood had removed both valves and replaced them with two new pig's valves. He then repaired damage to the aorta and left atrium. He also drained over two litres of fluid from Charlie's chest cavity, which had collected as a result of him being in heart failure for so long.

No wonder he looked so tired.

He told me that they had done their best to repair the damage, but that Charlie's heart was so badly infected that there was a very strong possibility that the valves would come loose again, and that he might need a third or even a fourth replacement operation. He said it was just a case of watching and waiting, but that in the final event it was all 'down to Charlie'.

When I walked up to his bed I thought that it was all over. Charlie looked like an emaciated corpse. His skin was totally devoid of colour and he seemed to have grown much thinner since I last saw him. He had lost over four stone in weight over the course of the illness and was now barely eight stone. The skin had shrunk from around his head, hollowing out his cheekbones and accentuating all the features of his skull. His hair and nails had stopped growing – in short, his body was shutting down all non-essential services in order to maintain life.

As I sat down beside Charlie I noticed a new piece of equipment had been attached to his body. It was a small metal box with a meter and a needle and it ticked like an electric fence box. It was an external pacemaker. The second bout of surgery had disturbed the area of the heart which is responsible for creating and regulating rhythm, and now a simple blue box had taken the place of one of the most intricate wiring looms that God had ever created.

I watched the needle tick from right to left for over an hour, wondering if Charlie would ever regain consciousness and imagining what life would be like for a 28 year old man with a two pigs valves and a pacemaker. My attention was drawn back to the needle, which had suddenly started going in the opposite direction. I called the nurse over and asked her what had happened and she began to smile. She told me that it was good news, for it showed that Charlie's heart had taken over from the box and was now beating by itself.

Charlie wasn't going to give up that easily.

I held on to his hand and promised him that I would spend the rest of my life trying to make him happy. I told him that I would never get cross with him again and that I loved him more than life itself. As I sat and waited I thought about fate and of how it had taken a number of totally unrelated circumstances to bring us together. I decided that God had put me on this earth for one reason, namely to take care of Charlie and to make his life a joyous one. And if I had been made for that reason, then Charlie would have to live for long enough to let me to do the job I had been created for.

I dozed in the chair beside his bed and the nurse brought me a blanket to keep me warm. She was bending the rules by letting me stay but she knew that we were newly-weds and that I wouldn't leave Charlie's side until I was sure that he was all right.

After what seemed like an eternity, Charlie began to stir. He opened his eyes and tried to smile when he saw me. He seemed to want to speak but the breathing tube made it impossible, so he gestured to the nurse to come over to the bed. He pointed to her clipboard and then to her pen, and she placed the pen in his hand and the clipboard on his lap. He had a needle in the back of his hand, which made it difficult for him to hold the pen, and he was still woozy from the anaesthetic, but there was obviously something that he was determined to tell me. I watched him as he struggled to write but I couldn't read what he had written because all the letters were on top of each other. He tried again – and this time he was satisfied that I would be able to understand his post-operative scrawl.

I took the clipboard and looked at what he had written – and what I saw left me emotionally eviscerated. In a jumble of mis-formed letters were the words, 'You are very brave.'

If anything summed up Charlie, then it was those four words. He was a man totally lacking in self-pity – his first thoughts were for me and me alone. I felt totally unworthy of such a love, but at the same time I knew that it was precisely that love which was keeping him alive. I started to dread what he would write next, but I needn't have worried – it was 'Blackcurrant sorbet'.

One of the side effects of being on a breathing machine is parched lips and a very dry throat and as soon as the tube is removed the patient craves iced water. Charlie decided that he needed sorbet, which presented me with a bit of a problem. It was six o'clock in the morning and all the shops were shut – but if Charlie wanted sorbet, then I would get him sorbet. Luckily for me there was a Seven-Eleven just down the road, and I was its first customer of the day.

Chapter Fourteen

Not everybody had been aware of the traumatic events of the past few weeks. Charlie's brother Eddie was travelling around South America for a couple of months whilst he waited to start his life as a pupil barrister. After a couple of weeks touring Ecuador he was joined by a friend called Simon Grange, who brought with him a letter from Jane. The letter explained that Charlie had been taken ill, but added that he was in Derriford hospital and was starting to make a full recovery. Jane told Ed not to worry, and so he took her advice and carried on with his trip.

As a consequence, he was totally unaware of the unfolding drama that was taking place at home. He was out of contact in the wilds of the Andes and it was only when he reached Bogotá and called Jane, that he found out that Charlie had undergone heart surgery. Jane told him that his brother was stable and that there was nothing that he could do, but added that he should start making arrangements to fly home.

After spending several days trying to rearrange his flights, Eddie decided to call Jane again. It was Jane's husband John who answered the phone; he told Eddie that Charlie was gravely ill, that Jane was with him and that they were just about to operate again. Eddie was totally 'pole axed' by the news. The last he had heard was that Charlie was making a good recovery in Devon, and now John was telling him that Charlie was at the London Hospital and about to go under the knife for the second time in a fortnight.

Eddie thought that Charlie was going to die and that there was no way that he would get to see him before that happened. There was no time to lose – he had to leave straight away. Simon Grange rushed down to the British Embassy to ask the Ambassador for help, but it was past six o'clock and the Ambassador said he could do nothing until the following morning. Ed raced over to the airport and found the KLM desk. He explained what had happened and begged the girl on the desk to get him on the next available flight home. As it turned out the only seat was in Club Class and he didn't think he had the funds to cover the cost of the ticket. Amazingly, the girl on the desk offered to lend him the money to cover any shortfall, but thankfully he had just enough credit left on his Visa card to pay for his flight home.

Eddie had always seemed to me to be supremely levelheaded, and later he would tell me that throughout the long flight back to England he went through all the possible scenarios, which might take place as he walked through the arrivals gate. What he said he dreaded most of all was seeing Jane and me standing there to meet him. Eddie knew that if we were not at the hospital, then it could only mean that Charlie had died.

His last memory of his father was watching him get onto an aeroplane bound for a business trip in South America. His father had never returned from that trip and now by some perverse twist of fate, Eddie was returning from South America with the full realisation that he might never see his brother again.

The tension must have been unbearable, but as he rounded the corner of the arrivals lounge, the first person he saw was his sister Pixie – and she was alone. Jane was at home in bed. She was emotionally wrung-out and needed to rest. Pixie took Ed back to Godalming and when he saw that Jane was still in her nightie at eleven o'clock in the morning, he knew that he could relax. Back at hospital, Charlie had gobbled up almost a whole tub of blackcurrant sorbet and was sitting up in bed looking a little less cadaverous than he'd done when I first saw him. He was enormously buoyed-up by the news that Eddie was on his way, and I felt as if all my troubles had just been halved.

Eddie was a rock. Charlie and I both needed him and when I saw him stroll into the entrance lobby of the hospital with Pixie, I felt waves of joy and relief washing over me. He looked fit and tanned and so healthy; in fact at that moment I was reminded that he was everything that Charlie was not. I ran up to him and threw my arms around his neck.

There are times when words are redundant; times when everything that you want to say can be channelled down your arms and through your chest and squeezed into the person you are holding. At that moment all I needed was to be held tightly. It had been so long since Charlie had been able to hug me that I had almost forgotten what it felt like to be in the arms of a man.
It felt good.

I took Ed and Pixie to see their brother and although Eddie disguised it well, it was clear that he was visibly shaken by his first glimpse of Charlie. He looked more like an aged uncle than an older brother, but Eddie said that when he spoke to him and saw the fire in his eyes, he was left in no doubt that he was going to get better. There was something fantastic about Charlie's will to survive. It was a powerful, tangible thing which burned inside him. We knew he would live because he knew he would live. Here was a man who had no strength left; yet he was stronger than he had ever been before. It was remarkable to see such courage and it made me humble.

Seeing Eddie again was the best thing that could have happened to Charlie. It gave him tremendous peace of mind knowing that I was going to be looked after. Of course I had Jane and Pixie with me, but Charlie knew that I needed Eddie. He and Charlie were very similar in the calm, rational way that they dealt with problems, and Charlie knew that his brother would take care of everything for me whilst he was in hospital.

Charlie was soon sent back to Cotton Ward but he was not out of the woods yet. His heartbeat was very erratic and he had to have a further litre of fluid drained from his chest.

He had a few days of bed rest but then he got bored and asked if he could have a bath. I helped him out of bed and held his arm as he shuffled gingerly across the ward to the bathroom. Charlie had not looked in a mirror for nearly a fortnight and so he had no idea of just how bad he was looking. He reminded me of those terrible images of British soldiers walking away from the newly liberated Japanese labour camps at the end of the Second World War. Charlie stood with his knees slightly bent, his back was hunched and I could see the outline of every bone sticking out beneath his pale flesh. His buttocks hung down like two empty skin bags – all the fat and muscle had gone from him. He looked utterly pitiful.

He stood at the mirror, gripping onto the edge of the basin for support and slowly looked up at his reflection. It was clear to me that he was barely able to recognise the awful image that presented itself to him. I didn't know what to do, but I could see what was going through his mind, so I smiled at him and told him that he was doing really well and that he looked fine. But all the while I was thinking, 'How can you do it? How can you bear to look out of the eyes of a twenty-eight- year- old and see the gaunt, sallow face of a seventy-year-old staring back.'

But he did it.

He stood and he looked, and then he slowly turned away.

Charlie had his bath, sitting on an inflatable cushion to keep his bones off the enamel; and afterwards, as I helped him dress, I wondered how either of us was going to get through the next few weeks.

Chapter Fifteen

Charlie's body may have been frail but his mind was still as sharp as a razor. He was very switched-on and no matter how ill he was feeling he made it his business to know exactly what was going on regarding his treatment – but without appearing to be a busy body or a know it all. He knew the names of every other patient on the ward, he knew what drugs he was being given and he knew each of their doses. He had been on intravenous drugs for so long that all of the veins in his arms had collapsed; in desperation they began to put needles into his neck and ankles, but eventually it was decided that he should have a central line fitted.

A central line is a tube that is inserted into a major blood vessel leading directly into the heart – usually in the neck or chest. When the line is in place, the drugs can be fed through it via a drip, rather than being fed through a needle each time. This was a risky policy in Charlie's case because there was always a chance that the site of the line would become infected, but the doctors had no choice.

The man chosen to fit the line was a young Honorary Senior Registrar called Chris Burrell. Chris was tall, fair and softly spoken; he was a charming, gentle man and an extremely gifted physician and he and Charlie liked each other immediately. He fitted the line without any problems and kept appearing on the ward to check on how Charlie was doing. The two men got to know each other quite well over the following weeks, but at that time neither of them knew just how important their friendship would become.

Days and weeks dragged by, but we kept going with the help of friends and family. Both Two Four and Uncle Peter sent hampers from Fortnum and Mason, which Charlie sat and opened – looking like some naughty school boy with his first tuck box. The hampers were soon emptied but came in very useful for storing the heaps of cards and letters that arrived daily. We did have visitors every day as well; most of them were Charlie's old friends from Wimbledon and they provided a great deal of much-needed support to us both.

One couple invited me to stay with them for a few days. I was given their spare bedroom and told to come and go as I pleased. They had both known Charlie for many years, Jo had grown up with him in Wimbledon and Alex had met him during his time in Chagford. It was Charlie who had arranged their first meeting and they were married three years later.

Alex came to the hospital and took me out to lunch and Jo was at home when I got back after being with Charlie all day. I was able to talk frankly to them about his condition, which was something that I hadn't been able to do with a lot of people. They loved Charlie and they wanted to know everything, however distressing and being able to talk freely to them was a tremendous release to me.

Lots of people asked me how Charlie was doing, but in some cases if I told the truth, their eyes would glaze over and they would start to look fidgety and uncomfortable. I came to learn that however well meaning people might be, in reality they do not actually want to know the whole story – all they want to hear is good news. If I gave them news of a raging fever or a major set back then I might as well have been talking about genital warts – it was clearly not what they wanted to hear. I could see their point, after all it's depressing to hear somebody else's tales of woe – but when they turned away it made me feel rejected and at that time I was so vulnerable that rejection was the last thing I could cope with.

Charlie's close friends loved him very much and I think they knew that if they could keep me going, then I in turn would keep him going. Jo and Alex didn't mind that I cried myself to sleep every night; they just made sure that I felt safe and secure. They were looking after me because I was looking after Charlie and even though I had only known them for a few months, they made me feel loved.

I had to return to Devon after a few weeks, but it was a tremendous struggle for me to be on my own. My work suffered, I couldn't concentrate and I felt as if I was letting my colleagues down. When I got home each night I felt terribly low, and I was totally reliant on people 'phoning me up so that I could unload some of my angst.

I vividly remember one call from Jenny Dally. She was a very close friend of ours and had been Charlie's first love – until the day she dumped him, rather unceremoniously for a friend of his called David (a man whom she subsequently married). Charlie was heartbroken, and vowed never to be faithful to any girl from that moment onwards – and he was true to his word until the day he met me.

Jenny called me one night, and I picked up the 'phone in tears. She didn't say that she would call back; she just listened quietly whilst I sobbed and told her what had happened that day. She absorbed my grief without making me feel self-conscious. She didn't patronise me – she just listened and understood. I had her support that night and I knew I would always have it.

Eddie and Pixie came to stay with me from time to time, to make sure that I was managing all right and to relieve the boredom of spending so much time on my own. On one occasion I went to bed and found a small package under my pillow. I opened it and found a box containing a pair of pearl earrings, along with a note from Charlie, which read:

My darling darling Katie,

These are for you to wear every day – to thank you for your strength and fortitude through all this palaver, and to remind you of my great love for you until I am able to hold you close again and tell you myself.

I love you,

C xxx

Charlie had instructed Eddie to hide the earrings for me to find that night, to show me that although I was out of his sight, I was never out of his thoughts. I didn't need earrings to remind me of how much Charlie loved me – the mere fact that he was sill breathing was testament enough for me.

I carried on working for as long as I could, but one morning when I called the hospital to see how Charlie was, I lost it totally. The staff nurse who answered the 'phone told me that Charlie was really low and that his hair had begun to fall out in great handfuls. This was the straw that broke the camel's back; I had to get back to him and so I told my boss that I would take unpaid leave until Charlie was better. I think he was mightily relieved because, quite frankly, my work had been dreadful for the past few weeks.

I packed my bags and went to stay with Jane. Eddie put himself totally at my disposal, and either he or Pixie would drive me home from the hospital each night. In the morning I would prepare a meal for Charlie and put it in a wicker basket covered with a red checked cloth. I felt a bit like Little Red Riding Hood – with attitude, of course. I took the train to Waterloo and then the tube to Whitechapel and it was there that I faced my biggest daily challenge.

There was a small kitchen attached to the ward and it should have been relatively easy for me to heat up the food for Charlie. However, it was patrolled by two large Nigerian ladies called Aerial and Mercy, and they took great pleasure in preventing me from entering what they considered to be their personal domain. I had to wait for them to leave before I dared set foot inside the kitchen. But I was on a mission; I had to get to the microwave – my husband's well being depended on it.

I had terrible daydreams on the way over about coming face to face with the two of them, and getting into some awful fight. I had visions of Aerial adjusting her vertical hold on me whilst Mercy looked on dispassionately, but luckily for me the sneaky approach paid off and the phantasmagorical food fight never happened.

We all took turns doing the food run. Each day we watched and waited as Charlie ate the food and each day the amount of food that we prepared increased. We turned up with a selection of calorie-laden goodies; one day he would pull back the cloth to reveal steak and kidney pie, followed by rice pudding and on another day Jane might have brought her son cottage pie and apple crumble. Mealtimes became the highlight of his day and before long he was licking his pudding plate and asking for second helpings – and it was then that we knew he was getting better.

Charlie was beginning to recover but I was definitely not at my best. His

Charlie, during his first trip outside the hospital, with Eddie, Jane and Pix

illness was weighing on me like a rain-sodden duffel coat. My head was down and my shoulders had dropped, but when I walked into the ward to see him each morning, I tried to look as if I hadn't a care in the world. The most difficult thing for me was to keep my spirits up and to remain positive for Charlie. I couldn't afford to let him see when I was sad or anxious, because he was relying on my buoyancy to keep him afloat. I felt like an emotional battery – I went in fully charged each morning and during the course of the day, bit by bit, Charlie would gradually draw strength and love from me until it was time for me to leave, as drained as a dud Duracell. Whatever negative feelings I had were hidden from Charlie and stored somewhere at the back of my mind, but even though I cried when I was alone each night, those emotions were never properly dealt with. The only person who was qualified to talk me through the pain I was feeling was the very cause of that pain. I needed Charlie so badly – but his need was always far greater than mine. His family was my salvation, but I was always mindful of the fact that they were going through the same hell that I was. If I crumbled and fell apart, then their energies would be diverted away from Charlie and towards me; so I had to keep strong for his sake and for theirs.

I discovered what it was to be a Boydell in the months that Charlie was away from me. The long car journey back to Godalming became a time of great openness among Eddie, Pixie and me. They took turns it in turns to escort me home, and as we talked and laughed and ate our customary post-hospital kebab,

I could feel my emotional battery being topped up until it brimmed over. There was a warmth about them, which wrapped around me like a soft woollen blanket, and comforted me even in my bleakest moments of despair. If there had been any cracks in the seemingly perfect veneer of harmony that they presented to the world, then I would have noticed – but there were none. I was living within a family who made the Waltons look dysfunctional – but when I walked with them beside me, I felt like lifting up my head to the heavens and shouting, 'Come on, is that all you've got to throw at me? Give me more, I can take it.' And I could; with their help, I knew I could.

I soon became a permanent fixture on the ward. I sat with Charlie throughout the day and, when I got the chance, I lay beside him on his bed. The ward staff knew how difficult it was for us being newly married and yet being unable to be together, so one day they got together and devised a fiendish plan. They thought that we needed to spend a night together – in private, and so they gave me some linen and the key to the visitors' rest room and told me to make up a bed on the floor. When the ward was quiet, I helped Charlie out of bed and we locked ourselves in to the room. Charlie lay down on the mattress and I carefully lay beside him. I couldn't hold him too tightly because of his wound and because of the central line, but I was close to him and that was enough. He smelt of hospital and of the antibiotics that were being pumped into him, day and night – but it was bliss, pure bliss just to be close to him again. He fell almost immediately into a deep sleep, but I could not. I lay awake, watching his chest rise and fall, listening to the sound of his breathing, waiting for him to stop. And when he stopped I waited for him to start again. I thought each deep exhalation would be his last. I waited and I watched until dawn.

In the morning Charlie awoke looking so happy and refreshed that I totally forgot about my ghastly vigil. It was the best nights' sleep he'd had since he'd arrived – it was the perfect tonic. It wasn't exactly romantic, but it worked for Charlie and that was all I cared about.

Charlie had been on the ward for much longer than any of the other patients and the junior doctors had all taken rather a shine to him. He helped them remember what doses of drugs he was supposed to have when they were at the end of a shift and too tired to think. He also kept quiet if one of them dropped a syringe, or dozed off on his bed for a few moments. Charlie had become a mascot for the ward staff; and one night the doctors got together and decided to kidnap him. They dressed him in a white coat, put him in a wheelchair and took him to doctors' party in the hospital grounds. He had a wild night but ended up having a lot of difficulty explaining the presence of alcohol in his blood test results the following day. But Charlie was not the only one to be spoilt that week.

Uncle Peter had asked me to join him for lunch at the Berkley Hotel in Belgravia. It was just around the corner from his house and he liked to refer to it as his local 'café'. My usual lunch consisted of a jacket potato and a pint of Guinness in the pub next door to the hospital, so the thought of gourmet cooking and fine wine had me salivating all the way to Victoria station.

Peter was a gentleman of the old school. He had started his career as a humble solicitor, but had gone on to train as a barrister and gradually rose to his then position as a very senior silk and one of the country's foremost authorities on planning and diocesan law. Not only that, he was also leader of the Parliamentary Bar and Treasurer of Middle Temple. During the war he was the youngest Brigade Major in the Royal Artillery and whilst fighting in Italy he commandeered a white open-topped Bentley, from which he directed his troops. He and the Bentley both managed to survive the war unscathed and he drove it home as a battle trophy. With that kind of background, Peter could have been very intimidating, but in reality he was far from it. I always found him very approachable and utterly charming and he had a great line in anecdotes about various members of The Establishment. He often took tea with the Queen Mother and so I felt especially honoured to be lunching with him that day.

I had to be on my mettle because as you would imagine, Peter was nobody's fool – but I needn't have worried because we had a blast. We talked about architecture and art; Peter was a joy to be with but he did grill me on every aspect of Charlie's treatment to date. I managed to reassure him that Charlie was getting medical attention of the highest quality and once we got the serious bit out of the way, we had a thoroughly enjoyable meal.

It was mid-afternoon by the time I left the hotel and I made rather unsteady progress back to the station. When I eventually reached Charlie's bedside I felt like curling up and going straight to sleep. It was a hot afternoon and the journey back through the thronging crowds of the Underground had worn me out. I weighed up my options; I had a choice of sitting in an uncomfortable vinyl chair for the afternoon, or lying on Charlie's cosy bed and drifting off in a happy haze of Puilly Fume to the land of calves liver and calamari. No contest – two minutes later I was sound asleep, whilst my seriously ill husband sat bolt upright in the naughty chair, wishing I'm sure, that he'd married a tee-totaller.

Life on the ward became a continual round of poking, and prodding, followed by pricking. The only thing that broke the monotony was the prospect of visitors bringing news from the outside world. My eldest sister Jane called in to see Charlie for the first time. She was feeling a little shaken after getting off the tube because a man had stood over her for most of the journey, rubbing his groin and leering at her. When she got to Charlie's bed, she took one look at his wound and promptly fainted, gashing her head on the corner of a table on the way down. I'm not sure what the nurses made of my sister, lying, as she did, in a crumpled heap of Chanel and Escada – but it certainly gave the other patients something to talk about for the rest of the day. I didn't have any smelling salts to bring her round, but I think the thought of being kept in hospital wearing a borrowed polyester nightie soon snapped her back into the land of the living. She ended up in casualty, and didn't have the nerve to visit Charlie again.

Soon Charlie was considered fit enough to venture outside the hospital grounds without medical assistance, and his doctors decided that we should be allowed to take him out for Sunday lunch. He dressed very slowly, his clothes hanging loosely from his emaciated body, and did his best to act as if he didn't

My love and I

care. I took his arm and he gingerly made his way out of the hospital, holding onto me for support with one arm and protecting his chest with the other, terrified that we might be jostled in the busy street market outside the hospital.

Jane took us to The London Bridge Hotel for lunch, accompanied by the rest of the Boydell family. It was the first time in months that we had been able to take a walk in the fresh air together. Charlie got to feel the sun on his sallow face again, and I could have cried with the joy of being with him. Pixie took a photograph of the two of us to record the momentous occasion of Charlie's first excursion from the confines of the hospital, and the look on my face is the most complete illustration of everything I was feeling for him at that time.

The Anchor boys decided to make a surprise visit towards the end of Charlie's stay in hospital. They had been very worried about him, and had clubbed together to organise a trip to London to pay him a visit. It was a big day for them, London being a place that few of them had ever visited before – and they didn't much care for it when they got there. Charlie was sitting in the day room when Nigel, Ilkey, Chap, Anson and Jim Long came ambling round the corner, grinning like a bunch of schoolboys on a day trip. Charlie's face was a picture. I had known about the trip for some time, but he was totally taken by surprise. He was given permission to take them to the pub next door to the hospital and they all had a drink together, whilst the boys filled him in on all the village gossip. It was a mark of how highly they regarded Charlie, that they had journeyed all the way to London to see him. They had all missed a day's work to make the trip and they were not the kind of men that could easily afford to do that. They wanted Charlie to know that they cared about him and their visit did a great deal to speed his recovery.

The boredom of a long hospital stay can often play funny tricks on your mind, and one night Charlie woke up, totally convinced that he was hallucinating. There, at the end of his bed, stood a large chicken, holding what appeared to be a water pistol. He rubbed his eyes and tried to clear his head, but the chicken refused to vanish. It was only when it squirted him, that Charlie realised he wasn't having a horrible nightmare, and that there really was a large chicken at the end of his bed. It turned out that one of the male nurses had decided to break the monotony of the night shift by dressing up as a huge rooster and terrorising the other nurses. Charlie was the only witness to the fowl antics, but I think even he knew that it takes more to scare a night nurse than a six-foot cock.

Chapter Sixteen

On 29th of September 1989, ninety-nine days after he was first admitted to hospital, Charlie put on a crisp cotton shirt, a pair of button fly cords, his Mid-Devon Hunt tie and his keeper tweed jacket. He laced up his Trickers' brogues and walked out of Cotton Ward for the last time. Alan Wood had at one stage been convinced that the only thing the Charlie would be leaving in would be a black body bag, but he was very happy to have been proved wrong. Charlie had defied the expectations of all the ward staff by beating the infection that had been beating him. He was still painfully thin, and the erratic rhythm of his heart continued to give concern to his doctors, but by the time he left, his heartbeat had reverted to a normal sinus rhythm and the doctors were happy to discharge him from their care.

I was overjoyed to have Charlie back home again and I felt that we could now begin our married life in earnest. I also rather naively believed that once Charlie he was home, he would quickly get better and everything would return to normal.

How wrong I was.

It is a popular misconception that recovering heart patients are relatively easy to care for once they have returned home. What I, and I'm sure many other people failed to realise, was that the hard work begins once the cardiac care ends. When Charlie was in hospital he had round-the-clock care and a regimented routine, which provided him with everything he needed. But when he walked through the front door of Wood Cottage, he was my responsibility, and mine alone.

I did not have the reassurance of looking at a heart monitor to find out whether his rhythm was steady, nor did I have the luxury of nurses constantly checking on him whilst I was at work. I wish I had done, because one day, soon after he had returned from London, I got back early to find the house empty and a note from some friends to say that they had taken Charlie to hospital. I panicked and raced down to Derriford, to find Charlie waiting for me, looking very sheepish. He had felt peckish whilst I was out and decided that he needed a fish finger sandwich. I don't like fish fingers and hadn't bought any since he'd been away, so there weren't any to be found in the freezer. But Charlie spied a lone digit welded to the permafrost at the back of the fish drawer. He managed to chisel it free and then popped it under the grill until it was crispy, put it between two slices of bread and gobbled it up. The finger in question must have been there for at least a year, and the resulting food poisoning gave him a free

trip to hospital (as if he hadn't spent enough time there) and a major ear bending from me. I made sure after that mishap that the freezer was groaning with
the finest cod fillet that Captain Birdseye could provide, and thankfully Charlie
never felt the need to plunder the permafrost ever again.

In fact, Charlie was very irritable whilst he was at home. He desperately
wanted to get back to work so that he could feel normal again and I wanted
him to get back to work so that I could stop worrying about him and begin to
relax a little, but the reality of the situation proved to be somewhat different.
Whilst I was trying to nurse Charlie back to full health, I tripped up and fell
headfirst into the black pit of depression. I didn't know that I was depressed
at the time; all I knew was that nothing seemed to be going right. My job was-
n't going well, Charlie was taking an age to get better and we had no money. I
took it out on Charlie, who hardly deserved to be treated so badly having
already been through five months of hell – but I just couldn't help myself. I
snapped at him constantly and was forever bursting into tears, which was not
something that Charlie was accustomed to seeing. I felt so guilty about my irrational behaviour, especially as I had sworn to Charlie as he lay in ITU that I
would never get angry with him again, but in truth I was totally overwhelmed
by melancholia. I had been shovelling back all the emotion and the hurt that I
was feeling and presenting a brave face to Charlie every day. Since his return
home, cracks had begun to show in the wall of competence I had built to hide
my anxiety, and eventually the whole lot crumbled, burying me under an ava-
lanche of utter despondency.

It took several weeks to dig myself out. With Charlie's help I slowly
regained my hopeful, happy disposition, but in truth I was a changed woman.
The experiences of the past months were etched into my face; I was told that
my eyes had lost their innocent sparkle and grey hairs were sprouting all over
my head. But I didn't care about any of those things. I didn't care when people
said 'Gosh, Kate, you look so much older.' The fact was that I had aged, but in
so doing I had gained clarity of vision, which I think eluded my peers. I saw
what was important in life. When my friends had a problem, it was as though
they were looking at a forest and seeing only as far as the massed ranks of
Douglas fir. I could see straight through the trees and out onto the open fields
beyond. I had gained maturity far beyond my years, but I needed every ounce
of wisdom and insight to help me deal with the radical alteration that had taken
place in my life.

I had discovered an inner strength but I still had an innate weakness. The
fact was that I could never explain to Charlie what it felt like for me to see him
in intensive care, thinking I was going to lose him; thinking he was going to die
at any second. And for Charlie, the feeling of being so close to death was something that he couldn't even begin to describe to me. We were both haunted by
our individual experiences, bound by chains of silence – unable to exorcise our
own personal grief.

It was gut wrenching for both of us. We were living with a brooding,
potent force, which could so easily have ripped us apart – but in truth it had the

opposite effect. It was as though we had been tossed into a furnace, which burned for ninety-nine long days and nights. But instead of combusting our relationship and turning it to ashes, it melded us together, forming an impenetrable bond that could never be broken. We became two halves of a whole, I lived for Charlie and he lived for me. We were we bonded together for life.

Chapter Seventeen

It had been a very long summer for both of us, and by the end of October we were in need of a holiday. Charlie suggested that we take a trip around the country to visit friends that we hadn't seen since his operation, followed by a few days on our own, touring around Shropshire. I was really excited about having the chance to get away from it all for a few days but I couldn't understand why everyone at work kept asking me about the trip; after all we were going to Much Wenlock, not the Maldives.

We went to London to see Charlie's family before setting off for Shropshire and Charlie decided to take me to the National Portrait Gallery so that I could stand and gaze at my favourite painting, the portrait of Lord Ribblesdale by John Singer Sergeant.

When I had satisfied my need to see the dashing man in jodhpurs, we went next door to The National Gallery. We ended up in the Caneletto room and I wandered about for a while and was just about to go on to the next room when Charlie called me over to him. He was sitting on a bench opposite a view of the Grand Canal in Venice and he asked me what I thought of the painting. I said that it was a stunning view and then Charlie placed into my hands a small brown package. I couldn't imagine what it was but when I opened it I found two tickets to Venice. I was pretty emotional anyway at that time, so to be given a surprise like that totally finished me off. People must have been giving us very funny looks as we sat and embraced but we were completely unaware of anybody else being in the room with us.

Charlie was the most romantic, thoughtful man and every time I thought I couldn't love him any more than I did, he would do something which totally blew me away. He had kept the trip a secret from me for weeks but everybody else in the world seemed to know about it. Charles and Chris had even paid for the flight and as I picked Charlie up from the office and we set off for 'Shropshire', they both stood on the steps of the building, waving and grinning like a couple of loons.

We had the most magical holiday imaginable. St. Marks Square was under water when we arrived, which was a sight that I will never forget, but by the following morning the skies had cleared and we were bathed in brilliant autumn sunshine for the rest of the week.

Each day we woke to the smell of sweet rolls being baked for our breakfast, and then we set out on expeditions around the city. Charlie was still quite frail, but even so we would walk and talk until lunchtime and then picnic on one of the jetties overlooking the Grand Canal. When we returned to our room each afternoon for a nap, we found that our nightshirts had been laid out on the bed, side by side, with their sleeves touching. The maid must have thought we were on our honeymoon and in a way we were.

Apart from the waiters who took our orders for dinner each night, we spoke to nobody. We were so wrapped up in each other, rejoicing in surviving the past few months and planning out the rest of our life together. It was a new beginning for us; we hadn't really had a chance to enjoy our first year of married life – it had been a case of getting through each day and hoping the next would be a little easier. But we now felt a real sense of hope and optimism and when we flew back to England we were sure that the worst was behind us.

We chose to spend Christmas alone that year. Charlie had written to me from his hospital bed, planning the whole thing in advance in his own inimitable style. We woke on Christmas morning and he went down to light the fire and then came back up to bed carrying a tray laden with champagne and smoked salmon and scrambled eggs. We had a very lazy morning, opening presents and phoning our families to wish them a Happy Christmas.

As lunchtime approached we called in at The Anchor for mulled wine and beer. The atmosphere was as warm and welcoming as a pair of mink slippers and the festive fug enveloped us as soon as we walked through the door. It was a real social event for the village, there were vast bowls of hot punch on the bar and a huge array of delicious bar snacks kept appearing from the kitchen throughout the day. I kissed all the boys and wished them a Happy Christmas; and as I stood in the crush of the public bar, surrounded by our friends, alongside a man who made my heart swell with joy and pride, I felt I was the happiest woman alive.

Charlie cooked a brace of pheasants that evening, bought from Mr. Wilkinson in Modbury. His was a proper butcher's shop and he always managed to find the blackest beef, or the sweetest local lamb for Charlie when he called in to see him on a Saturday morning. He had put a brace of birds aside for us on Christmas Eve and by eight o'clock the next evening, we were sitting at the kitchen table, anticipating our first mouthful of roast pheasant. It was good job that Charlie went to fetch the birds and not me, otherwise we might have been eating Tawny Owl surprise.

After supper, we lit the candles on the Christmas tree, put on an Ella Fitzgerald CD and exchanged presents. We had nothing extravagant to give each other because money was so tight, but the presents were all the better because of that. I had thought of giving Charlie a new overcoat to wear for work but I just couldn't see any way of being able to afford what I wanted. I had almost given up, when I decided to take a trip to Totnes, a nearby market town, and found exactly what I had been looking for in a second hand shop. The coat fitted perfectly and Charlie was absolutely delighted. It looked brand new and as far as he was concerned, it was.

We did cut down on the luxuries of life, like expensive Christmas presents, but there were some Boydell essentials that we could never compromise on – namely wine and food. Charlie had opened an account at Berry Brothers and

Rudd when we met and we slowly began to amass a fairly respectable collection of wine. We never had enough to fill a cellar, but our small cottage had a large wine cupboard and when that was full we stored the extra cases under our bed. When Charlie came home and found yet another case under the bed, I simply looked innocent and told him that the wine fairy had paid us a visit.

We loved to entertain. I think it had a lot to do with our need to celebrate what was good about life with people who meant a lot to us. The most satisfying thing for me during a dinner party was to hear people laughing and to know that if I left the table for a moment, the laughter would still be ringing out when I returned. Charlie prided himself on the fact that none of his guests ever left our house feeling bored or thinking that they had not been given enough to eat or drink – and for that reason that people rarely refused an invitation to dine at Wood Cottage.

Charlie was as efficient in the kitchen as he was in the office and delighted in preparing wonderful dishes for our guests. He wasn't one of those men who cooks something fantastic, but uses every available pot and pan in the house and leaves the kitchen looking like a war zone. Charlie had perfected the art of washing up as he went along, so that by the time he had finished, the kitchen looked as spotless as when he had begun. If I make him out to be an anally retentive perfectionist, then I am doing him a disservice. Charlie left his socks on the bedroom floor like every other normal man; he didn't line his books up in alphabetical order, or put on a pair of white gloves and run his finger around the furniture to check I had dusted properly. His life was ordered but not regimented and that's the way I liked it.

Charlie went into 1990 with a renewed sense of purpose. He wanted to repay The British Heart Foundation for helping to save his life and had devised a ten-point plan from his hospital bed, to persuade them that he was the man who should be making their educational videos.

We were both struck by the limitations of the information that had been made available to us on leaving hospital. The small booklet on valve replacement surgery told us the basics, but there was so much more that we wanted to know. Charlie knew that if we felt that way, then many other people must have felt the same. It seemed a perfect opportunity to make a video on the problems associated with life after heart surgery and Charlie had it all planned out in his head – it was just a question of convincing The British Heart Foundation to give him a chance.

It took a while for he erratic rhythm to settle down, but eventually he was given the all clear to return to work and he immediately set about putting his plan into action. Two Four Productions was a tiny company at that time, with no track record for making videos for clients as big as the B.H.F., but after writing a treatment and making his pitch, Charlie got the commission he so desperately wanted. He not only produced, wrote and directed the video – he also made a cameo appearance with his blushing bride, talking about sex after heart surgery.

Sex is a subject that most heart patients feel loathed to discuss with their doctor, yet it is a crucial part of feeling healthy again. We were chosen to be interviewed because of our age; sex is not the first thing you think about when you are over sixty, but I was only twenty five and Charlie was twenty nine, so for us it was a major factor. We wanted to make people aware that heart surgery should not prevent you from leading a perfectly normal life, and that having sex again is a fundamental part of regaining that sense of normality.

Charlie was fine about it. He knew when he was ready to make love to me again and was totally relaxed when he did. I was a bag of nerves. I was absolutely petrified that he would over-exert himself and collapse on a heap on top of me at a crucial moment. I couldn't really tap him on the shoulder every five minutes and say 'Darling, do you feel alright, or are you going to conk out on me?' So I just kept quiet and tried to appear like I hadn't a care in the world.

However hard I tried, I just could not relax into it and so the first time we made love, the only sigh that I uttered was one of relief when it was all over. But I soon came to realise that Charlie would not do anything if he didn't feel totally fit and happy – and after a tentative start we were soon enjoying the delights of being newlyweds all over again.

As Charlie's life began to return to normal, so he discovered that the road to normality was paved with uneven concrete slabs, which tripped him with monotonous regularity. The DVLC took away his full driving licence and gave him one that only lasted three years. He was refused car insurance and it took some time before his doctor was able to convince the insurance company that he was safe to drive. At every turn he was reminded that he was not the same man that he had been and that however fit he became, or however well he appeared on the outside, what was inside made people regard him as a medical liability.

Charlie was bitter about the way he was being treated but was able to turn his negative experiences into positive advice when he came to make The British Heart Foundation video. The resulting video 'Better Than Before' is now shown or offered to every patient leaving hospital after heart surgery.

Chapter Eighteen

Over time, Charlie gradually began to build up his strength and regained some of the stamina that he'd lost during his long illness. He swam three times a week and we played tennis at weekends. I became less worried about him as time went on but I was fiercely protective of him nonetheless. I didn't worry about him while he was at home with me but when he went to work his well-being was taken out of my hands entirely.

Charlie's work ethic was beyond compare – he never gave less than 110 per cent, but it proved to be a double edged sword as people soon forgot that his stamina was not that of a fit and healthy 29 year old. As the company grew, so Charlie's workload increased, but he stubbornly refused to let anybody make allowances for him. It was easy to forget what he'd just been through as he made a point of never talking about it; in fact, most of his clients were totally oblivious of his condition and that's they way he liked it. Charlie never wanted to be singled out for special treatment, but above all, he hated the thought of anybody feeling sorry for him. He worked himself too hard – it was in his nature to do so but it was a high-risk policy for a man in his condition – and we both knew what was at stake.

Charles Wace was the driving force behind the company He was an extremely astute businessman and I always regarded him as the man who would ultimately make Two Four Productions a success. He had great vision and keen eye for exploiting new markets; I respected him immensely but at the same time I held him responsible for the wellbeing of my husband whilst he was at work.

If I told Charlie to try and slow down, he would always say that he had a lot of work on, but that he would ease up once the job was completed. It was just that he never seemed to ease up. Once one job had been completed, Charlie would be writing a treatment for the next prospective client and so it went on. He came home with black rings under his eyes, looking pale and tired and then went to work the next morning looking exactly the same. He stubbornly refused to lower his work rate, maintaining that he was just doing what he was paid to do. He was trying to provide us with a future but I could see that if he didn't slow down, he would end up in hospital again and we wouldn't have any future.

Charles Wace gradually became the focus of my displeasure. I felt he was putting Charlie under too much pressure and one day when I was visiting Charlie in his office, Charles happened to ring up. He was away on a shoot and he had called in to find out what was happening back at the office. I don't know what came over me, but when Charlie had finished being grilled by Charles,

I took the receiver off him and said, 'If you kill Charlie, you're a dead man.' Charles was stunned at first – as anybody would be in his position, but he soon came back with a few choice invectives of his own and brought the matter swiftly to a close.

I had been clumsy and blunt, to say the least, but I didn't know any other way of making him see what was happening. It took three months of silence before Charles could bring himself to be civil to me again. I didn't blame him for feeling that way – I would have felt exactly the same in his position, but my only concern was for Charlie and ultimately my shock tactics had the desired effect. Charles began to keep more of an eye on Charlie – but sensibly always tried to remain at a safe distance from me.

On October 26th 1990, Charlie celebrated his 30th birthday. He was still playing tennis, riding and walking – thus confounding the medical experts who had told him the he would be opening his presents from the confines of a wheelchair. We had chosen to celebrate the occasion with Fat Alex and his girlfriend Zanny, who had come down to stay for the weekend. Alex had known Charlie since their University days, but they had taken different paths after getting their respective degrees. Charlie went down to live in Devon and Alex decided to stay on at university and take a masters degree in English. One day Charlie called out of the blue and asked Alex if he fancied coming down to Devon to re-plaster the cottage that he was renting at the time. Alex didn't need a second invitation, came straight down and began pulling the old plaster off the walls like a man possessed.

He spent several weeks with Charlie; they went out hunting together, drank at the Sandy Park and enjoyed all the many and various delights that Chagford had to offer. It didn't take Alex long to decide that university life was not for him. He abandoned his degree soon after returning home and set his own company; and he chose to spend most of his spare time in the pursuit of game and women – but not necessarily in that order.

When Alex came to visit, we knew we were in for a riotous weekend and we were not disappointed. On the evening of Charlie's birthday we took Alex and Zanny to an excellent local hotel and had a blowout, wallet-emptying meal to remember. The food was exceptional and we drank our way through a bottle of champagne, three full and four half bottles of wine. At that point Zanny and I decided to call it a day, but Charlie and Alex managed to polish off an entire bottle of Taylor's 1960 port between them before they felt ready to leave.

Zanny and I spent the next morning in quiet contemplation, whilst the boys walked to the top of Ugborough Beacon. It was a long climb but it was a measure of Charlie's fitness at that time that he matched Alex stride for stride on the way up. And if I were asked to give a reason for my husband's miraculous constitution I would have to say that the joy being in the company of a man like Alex gave Charlie the will to do almost anything he wanted. Charlie drew strength and inspiration from his friends without ever appearing to do so. He had a whole raft of people around him who loved him and looked out for him. You could take away his house, his job and his money and he would survive – but if you took away his friends, Charlie would have been finished.

Alex Ashworth

After the climb to the top of Ugborough Beacon, Charlie began to go down hill rapidly. Looking back, it was staggering how quickly he descended into frailty, having been so fit for the best part of a year. His heart had begun to race and stutter like some supercharged sports car with a sticky accelerator cable. It made him feel wretched and I found it very disconcerting to have to sit help- lessly by and watch the fear flash across his face as his heart lurched from one odd rhythm to another.

During one particularly bad episode, I decided to call our G.P. at home, because I felt the situation was becoming dangerous. James Hill was the man I chose to call that night. He was a good friend to us both and it would be hard to imagine a more personable and considerate doctor. He was slight and rangy with a mop of strawberry blond hair; and he wore little round spectacles and a mischievous grin. Charlie visited James with monotonous regularity but they were social visits, rather than medical appointments. Once Charlie had seated himself next to James, the conversation rarely touched upon Charlie's condition. Both men knew the state of play and Charlie was much keener to know how James's family were, than he was to find out about his haemoglobin level.

James was well aware of the precarious nature of Charlie's health and had told us to call him if we ever felt that we needed his advice. We had never felt the need to do so up to that point; and even though I was loathed to disturb his evening, Charlie was in such a bad way that I felt I had no other choice. James wasn't on call that night and said in rather embarrassed tones that he couldn't drive over, as he'd just finished his third glass of wine. He told me instead to bring Charlie straight round to see him. We arrived at his house a few minutes later and after listening to Charlie's staccato rhythm, he sent us straight to hospital.

Charlie's evening took a decided turn for the better when he arrived on the ward, for who should stroll round the corner to greet him but Christopher J. Burrell, MB, BS FRCP, the new Consultant Cardiac Physician at Derriford Hospital. Charlie had kept in contact with Chris after he left The London Hospital and was delighted when Chris told him that he'd changed jobs and would be moving down to the West Country. We bumped into him by chance during the following summer; he was spending the day relaxing on the beach with his wife Beth and daughter Olivia.

The Burrells had just moved into their new home at that stage and it was so typical of his friendliness that the first person to call round to welcome them was Charlie, bearing a bottle of wine and grinning from ear to ear. Charlie never forgot a kindness and wanted to make sure that Chris knew that there was somebody on whom he could call if he ever needed anything. Unfortunately, it was Charlie who needed Chris's help first but he could not have found a better doctor or a better friend in his hour of need.

Chris gave Charlie a thorough going-over and decided that the only effective form of treatment for his dysrhythmia was a very nasty but effective drug called Amiodarone. It had all kinds of side effects – so much so that it was banned in the United States, but it would totally control his fluctuating rhythm in a way that no other drug could do. Chris was slightly reluctant to give Charlie the high initial dosage that he needed, but the supra-ventricular tachycardia that he was experiencing at that time was doing so much damage to his already-enlarged heart, that Chris had no hesitation in prescribing it.

The bugs in Charlie's heart had shown no sign of reappearing, but we were about to experience an infestation on a much grander scale. During that winter, I had begun to notice rather a lot of dust around the sitting room – despite the fact that it was cleaned every week. At about the same time I happened to mention to Charlie that the beams in the ceiling appeared to have rather more holes in them than they had in the past. One night I took a screwdriver and stuck it into the nearest joist. It went right through without resistance and when I pulled it out, more dust poured out of the hole and onto the carpet. I tried another beam and then another and each time exactly the same thing happened. We appeared to have a major problem, so we decided to call in an expert.

My parents were converting their barn at the time and had taken on a chap called Dickie Bird, to oversee the building work. He was an ex-Marine and could turn his hand to anything. He came round, gave the beams a poke, shook his head gravely and told us that the whole ceiling had to come down. Every beam was infested with deathwatch beetle and they had over many years, tunnelled through each joist – leaving the outsides relatively intact but turning the insides to fine powder. There was it seemed no earthly reason why our bed hadn't come crashing down into the sitting room years before and Dickie told us that we had no time to lose.

If things weren't bad enough, we were trying to sell the house at that time. We were finding Wood Cottage a little cramped for all our wine and weekend guests, and had decided to try and find somewhere a little bigger, but the discovery of our little visitors prompted a hasty call to the estate agent and they immediately took the house off the market.

We had no money to spare, so we asked Charlie's mother if she would lend us the cash to pay for the building work. She agreed and my parents released Dickie and another builder, so they could start pulling our house apart. They took out the entire floor, so that we were able to walk in through our front door and look straight up at our bedroom ceiling. The more timber they exposed, the more problems they uncovered, and so the job just kept on getting bigger and bigger. Eventually, after a considerable amount of effort, Dickie and his mate finished the job. We were left with a new floor, a large loan to repay and a considerable amount of decorating work to do.

I set about working on the beams during the day, sanding and waxing them until the new pine began to look in more keeping with the interior of a 17th century cottage. Charlie came home to help me in the evenings, painting the plasterboard and generally making good. We were up a ladder one night, finishing of and anticipating our first pint in the Anchor, when the phone rang. It was Charlie's friend Tom Harris, calling from Canada. He and his wife Ali had moved out to Toronto shortly after our wedding, after Tom had been made financial controller of HMV Canada. He wanted to know how we were doing but after hearing the saga of the deathwatch beetles, I think he must have wished he'd never asked. Our beetlemania soon evaporated when Tom told us that he would be sending us a pair of tickets to Toronto, so that we could fly out and join them for a fortnight's holiday in the summer.

He might as well have told us that we'd won a million pounds on the lottery. Despite being a considerable improvement on 1989, 1990 had been problematic for us to say the least. All our friends seemed to be sailing along without a care in the world, whilst we were struggling to stay afloat in a leaky tub with a spluttering outboard. Now, just when we thought things couldn't get any worse; they suddenly got a whole lot better. We had something to look forward to in the coming year – something to aim for which we hoped might go a long way to dispel the general feeling that our luck would never improve.

July was soon upon us, but the gentle warmth of an English midsummer afternoon did nothing to prepare us for the full force of a Toronto summer. Walking outside the airport was like being hit by a blast from a giant hairdryer. The air was hot and dry and there was a delicious contrast between the heat of the day and the icy chill of our first cold beer.

Tom and Ali had bought a small house near the edge of Lake Ontario. It had been rather a ramshackle affair when they moved in, but when we arrived

Summer on Lake Huron, Canada, 1993

they had transformed it into a stunning home.

We sat by their pool, chugged another cold one and set about the difficult business of seeing just how much fun we could have in a fortnight. We did all the touristy things whilst we were in Toronto; visiting Niagara Falls, going to a baseball game and eating foot-long hot dogs, inch by delicious inch. For the most part though, we just 'chilled'. Floating about in the pool gave us time to appreciate just how lucky we were. Charlie was alive, I was lying in his arms on a Lilo made for one and there was steak on the barbecue and beer in the fridge – what more could anybody ask for?

Tom decided to broaden Charlie's horizons a little by taking him to a table-dancing club for the evening. I pressed five dollars into Charlie's hand as he was leaving, so he could have a dance on me, but when the girl came over to perform for him he suddenly took a great interest in the label of his beer bottle. I think he felt a little uncomfortable being in such close proximity to a gyrating naked girl, but he did come home grinning like a Cheshire cat. He'd had a nice chat with her after she'd finished dancing for him, which I think he found a good deal more enjoyable than watching her sleazy striptease.

Being in Canada was the best possible tonic for both of us. I couldn't believe that the tanned, muscular hunk, walking beside me into the arrivals lounge of Heathrow airport, was the same man who only two years before had clung onto my arm looking for all the world as if he'd just staggered out of Bergen-Belsen.

Chapter Nineteen

As autumn arrived and the leaves began falling from the trees, I noticed again that Charlie was beginning to shed an alarming amount of weight. It had taken him most of the year to regain the muscle tone that he'd lost during his time in hospital, but suddenly in only a few weeks he seemed to be regressing – he was literally shrinking before my eyes. I tried not to make a big thing out of it, but I had to ask him if he felt all right. When I did he just shrugged his shoulders and said he felt fine. That was the problem with Charlie, he never, ever complained – not to me or to anyone else. It was constant guessing game trying to figure out how he was feeling. I had to monitor him continually, whilst appearing to be as unconcerned about his health as he seemed to be.

But his seeming indifference hid a very real worry – one that he could never voice. Charlie knew that if he told me every time his heart lurched or raced or fluttered I would have been a nervous wreck, so he kept it from me. He would often lie awake at night worrying, but if I asked him the following morning why he looked so tired, he would just shrug his shoulders and say that his head was buzzing and he couldn't sleep.

As time went on he lost more and more weight and began to develop what appeared to be a large goitre on his neck. He became very tired and irritable and started having extended bouts of tachycardia (racing heart beat) which made him feel dreadfully ill. Being mindful of the consequences of waiting too long to see a doctor, I took him straight to see Chris Burrell.

Chris hadn't seen Charlie for a while and I could see that even for a seasoned professional, Chris was startled by his appearance. The same thought was going through all our minds as Chris examined Charlie – had the infective endocarditis re-occurred? Chris took some blood and to our relief the cultures all came back negative – but it was clear that Charlie's thyroid function was extremely abnormal. His Thyroxin level in September had been well within its normal range, but in only two months it had risen to a level which was so high that it went totally beyond the testing capabilities of the labs. Charlie had managed to produce a test result that had given him the highest thyroxin level ever recorded by Plymouth Health Authority. He was certainly not a man who did things by halves, but the staggering thing was that he was still working hard and behaving as if he was in rude good health.

Charlie was admitted to hospital suffering from acute hyperthyroidism brought about by prolonged exposure to Amiodarone. It turned out that the very drug that had kept him healthy for the past year had poisoned him. Chris had no choice but to stop him taking the Amiodarone immediately and start him on a course of medication to bring the thyroid under control. It took many weeks for the drug to work its way out of his system, but as his thyroid function eventually returned to normal, so his heart began to race uncontrollably.

Charlie started to look cadaverous. His eyes had sunk back into their sockets and the black rings which sometimes appeared, were now a permanent feature. His heart kept lurching into supra ventricular tachycardia – a very fast rhythm of between 150 and 180 beats per minute, and the strain of maintaining such rate was taking its toll on his already battered pump. His heart was, by this stage grossly enlarged, and his cardiac function was severely restricted as a result. Every time the heart went into tachycardia it placed further strain on his weakened left ventricle. Any normal man would have been laid up in bed, suffering from total exhaustion, but somehow Charlie just carried on. He was admitted to hospital on several occasions as Chris tried in vain to find a solution to the problem, but as soon as he was released he went straight back to work. The irony of it was that Charlie was working for British Heart Foundation at the time. They had become Two Four's main corporate client and Charlie was adamant that he would not let them down. He kept the severity of his condition to himself and tried to carry on as normal

We had been asked to go away for Christmas but I had to put my foot down and keep Charlie at home. It was Charlie's Uncle Stephen who had invited us to stay and he pleaded with me to relent, but I could not. I knew that if Charlie were away from home, he would be buzzing around, cooking, clearing up and generally being sociable. It was what he loved to do, but it wore him out and I had to make him see that he needed to rest.

It wasn't the first time that I'd made myself unpopular and it wouldn't be the last, but my only priority was Charlie. His well-being was paramount to me and if I appeared like some over protective mother hen, I really didn't give a damn. Anyway, I wasn't a mother hen where Charlie was concerned, I was a snarling tigress, and the older I got, the sharper my teeth became.

Charlie's heart became cause of many sleepless nights for Chris Burrell. He was trying desperately to find the right combination of drugs to replicate the effectiveness of the Amiodarone, but he was fighting a losing battle. His professional concerns for Charlie's well being were now compounded by a high personal regard for his rather demanding patient. Chris had seen Charlie often over the past months and they had become very good friends during that time. It pained him to see Charlie struggling to deal with the uncertainty of his fluctuating rhythm, but he was very well aware that he was dealing with a problem to which there was no easy solution.

Things suddenly began to go wrong in a big way for Charlie and Chris knew he had to act fast. Charlie had developed incessant tachycardia with bouts of atrial flutter – in other words his heart was playing Stockhausen at 45rpm when it should have been ticking away like a metronome. Chris needed to know the exact cause of the electrical problems in Charlie's heart. He needed a wiring diagram and the best man to supply such a diagram was Professor Ronnie Campbell of the Freeman Hospital in Newcastle. Ironically Charlie had interviewed Professor Campbell for one of his B.H.F. videos, so he was well aware that he was being sent for treatment by the country's foremost authority in the field of cardiac electrophysiology. It wasn't going to be a pleasant social visit by any means; time was of the essence and a solution had to be found quickly.

I had every confidence in Chris Burrell and the skill of the doctors in Newcastle but it was clear to me that Charlie's options were narrowing by the day. I didn't want to consider the 'worst cast scenario' but at around that time I did start thinking about Charlie's funeral – not his death; I never thought about that, but I did think of his funeral and I thought about it every day from then onwards. It wasn't as morbid as it sounds; I would be driving along in the car listening to the radio, a certain record would come on and I would think to myself, 'that would be a lovely song to have a Charlie's funeral'. Now, I don't know why I had those thoughts, but maybe it was a way of preparing myself for the worst. Over time it became a mundane thought; I became so used to it that I failed to be shocked by the very act of allowing myself to think it. But always at the back of my mind I held on to the belief that Charlie wasn't going to die; he was tough and strong – stronger than anyone I had ever met and I was sure he would never leave me.

In March 1992 the situation became serious. Charlie's arrhythmia was totally out of control; he had struggled on, but after only a few days his condition deteriorated so much that Chris made the decision to fly him to Newcastle in a private aircraft. Charlie was in need of immediate attention and had to be accompanied on flight by a doctor equipped with a defibrillator, in case he arrested en-route. I was allowed to fly with him and I can't say that I spent my time idly sitting by the window admiring the view. Charlie was in extreme discomfort, but managed to remain as polite and convivial as always to the doctor who flew with us. She spent the journey monitoring his chaotic rhythm with a distinctly worried expression on her face, and seemed greatly relieved when the plane eventually touched down at Newcastle airport.

When we got to the hospital, a doctor came to see us and explained what would be involved in the electrical mapping procedure. When he was sure we were fully cognisant with what he'd told us, Charlie signed yet another consent form and waited for yet another nurse to appear, bearing a faint smile and a large syringe.

He was taken to theatre, where the surgical team inserted a wire into his femoral artery, which was then fed directly into his heart, where they mapped out each electrical signal that the heart was creating. When Charlie came back from theatre I was pretty optimistic that we had seen the end of his rhythm problems. We were in a centre of excellence and we both knew that if anybody could fix the problem, Professor Campbell could.

Our doctor came to see us later in the day and explained what they had found during the exploration. We were heartened by the news that Charlie's problem could almost certainly be brought under control by drugs and that more surgery was unlikely to be necessary. As a precaution the doctor explained what would happen if all drug therapy did fail, but it seemed like such a drastic solution that I chose not to consider it an option.

What he proposed as final resort was something called a-v node ablation. It entailed burning out the part of Charlie's heart that was creating the rogue rhythm, and fitting a pacemaker. It would be a drastic step to take, as the surgeon would effectively be burning the conductive bridge between his upper and lower pumping chambers, and it would mean that Charlie's heart would never be able to beat normally again.

The drug therapy continued, but after a week in hospital Charlie was still in acute discomfort. His heart was locked into a constant rate of between 150 and 180 beats per minute and he was totally exhausted. Our kindly doctor came in to give us the bad news. None of the drugs they'd tried had succeeded in bringing Charlie's chaotic rhythm under control and they were faced with no other choice than to burn out his atrioventricular node and fit a pacemaker.

It was a shocker to say the least. Charlie hated taking so many drugs but the thought of being totally reliant of a pacemaker for the rest of his life was an even more depressing one. And there was more bad news to follow. The operation could not be performed for a further three weeks and so we were given the option of staying in hospital, or going back home. We decided to go home.

We were booked onto an evening flight back to Plymouth and by the time we got to the airport, Charlie appeared to be on the verge of collapsing. In fact I'm sure he would have done if he hadn't already been sitting in a wheelchair. He couldn't walk because he'd sustained a massive haematoma (blood clot) on his thigh as a result of the surgery. His right leg was now a livid patchwork of black and purple, which stretched from his groin to his toes and made movement of any kind extremely painful.

The flight itself was uneventful, but when we landed I had to half-carry Charlie down the aisle of the aircraft. When the pilot saw how much I was struggling he was kind enough to help Charlie down the aeroplane steps and into the terminal. It was such a relief to be so close to home, but when we got to the entrance we discovered that some scuzzball on our flight had taken the taxi that we'd ordered – leaving us stranded in the cold drizzle of a February evening. Luckily, the airhostess from our flight saw us standing by the entrance and offered to give us a lift to the hospital to pick up our car.

I drove Charlie back home and we called in to see our next-door neighbours, Walker and Deb Lapthorne. They had lit our fire and were waiting up to see that we returned safely – but I don't think they were prepared for the shock of seeing how Charlie had deteriorated over the period of a week. Deb was an ex-nurse and very down-to earth, but even she went pale when Charlie's ghostly visage appeared at the door. She thought he should have been hospitalised immediately, but the thing that struck her more than anything that night about the wizened little man who stooped in her sitting room, was how ebullient he still was. He was struggling to stand upright and yet his eyes were still sparkling. And though most of his strength had ebbed away, his wit and charm were as potent as ever. He never lost that spark; and even though at times the sight of him was enough to make you break down and weep, the pleasure of being with him was always a totally uplifting experience.

We thanked Walker and Deb for their kindness and then I helped Charlie upstairs and put him to bed. As he lay back on the pillow, I could see his lips beginning to take on a bluish tinge and I thought for a split second that he had finally lost the will to go on. I got the 'phone and was poised to call an ambulance, but as I sat and watched him, a faint blush of pink began to replace the blue. His body seemed to relax a little and as he soon drifted into a deep sleep. I climbed into bed beside him and prayed silently that he would still be alive when I awoke.

It is difficult to describe the experience of lying beside a man whose heart is beating so hard that that it makes the mattress beneath you shudder. The massive pump within his chest was being tested to the point of destruction – the braking mechanism had failed and the throttle was stuck on wide open. I had no way of alleviating his discomfort – all I could offer was words of encouragement, but that hardly seemed enough.

We had to move into my parent's house the following day. They had gone on holiday and we had offered to house sit for them. They had sold their original house and converted the old barn by the river into a spectacular home and once we'd settled in, I began the task of getting Charlie fit for his next operation.

Charlie had begun to find it a struggle to complete even the simplest of tasks. He woke up every morning in a state of near exhaustion and his leg was still impossibly tender -which only added to his general discomfort. He would try to dress himself, but usually got only as far as pulling on a single sock, before lying back on the bed and calling out for me. I would finish dressing him and help him up the oak staircase to the kitchen above. Once he was seated, all I could do was tune the wireless to Radio Four, give him The Daily Telegraph and keep him supplied with enough food and drink to fuel the monstrous engine which pounded away beneath his ribcage. I had to find something to keep me occupied whilst he rested because I had a very strong urge to run around the house, pulling at my hair and screaming 'Why him? Why does it always have to be him?'

The answer to my predicament lay in the barn. My father had very generously given me his trusty old Toyota, after I was forced to sell my own car to pay off some of our debts. The car had done a considerable mileage – neither of us was sure of the exact figure – as I used to disconnect the speedometer cable after every service, but it was mechanically perfect. The only fault was in the bodywork; the front wings had rusted away to nothing, and needed replacing. I managed to track down an old Toyota Celica in a local scrap yard and after I'd bought the wings the next bit was easy. Fitting the new wings was just like playing with a grown-up Meccano set, and it certainly took my mind off the old gentleman whom I'd left sitting in the kitchen.

Charlie was an old gentleman at that time to all intents and purposes. Every task he managed to perform was done in a kind geriatric slow motion, but the torpor of his movements belied the frantic motion within him. It was painful to watch a man imbued with such a lust for life being reduced to hobbling around like an octogenarian, but I was sure that with his incredible strength of will and my cooking, he would get fit again.

For a while I thought we'd made the wrong decision in coming home, but after only a few days Charlie was eating well and had begun to look a good deal better. He had been given a massive incentive to get fit again by Walker, who had offered us a pair of tickets to watch England beat Wales at Twickenham. It was the best kind of bribe imaginable and it certainly spurred Charlie on to make a recovery that startled even his jaded wife.

But we had a great deal more than rugby tickets to thank Walker and Deb for. They had moved next door to us shortly before we got married but it was only after Charlie got back from London that we had become good friends. We had many things in common – they shared our love of good food and wine and we all enjoyed entertaining, but whilst we embraced life, they took it by the throat and shook it. At Christmas, whilst we sat at the table struggling to finish off a brace of pheasant, Walker and Deb were seated next door, enjoying a candlelit dinner a deux. They were a couple who gave the expression 'living large' a whole new meaning, for between them on silver salver, sat the tattered remains of a whole goose!

Walker was a giant of a man, but it would be hard to imagine a more gentle and loyal friend. He and Deb had the same kind of relationship as Charlie and me. We never saw them bickering and we never felt any tension between them. They were also generous to a fault – so much so that when they heard us bemoaning the fact that we didn't have enough space to grow vegetables, they offered us part of their own garden, in return for a bottle of gin and a lettuce every now and then. Part of me thinks it was chance that they chose to come and live next door to us, but part of me knows they were put there for a reason.

Soon after we'd moved in to the barn the Boydell family came down to stay, to see how Charlie was getting on, and also to give me a bit of moral support. Jane and I took a trip to the fish market in Plymouth and bought scallops and salmon to feed to Charlie, and I knew that with each mouthful, his chances of getting through the next operation were increasing. He got fitter every day, and by the time it came to travel down to Twickenham, Charlie looked like a different man. He was still very weak and emaciated, but under the circumstances his recovery was startling to say the least. Our happiness was complete when England hammered Wales, and with high hopes we took the next flight to Newcastle.

Chapter Twenty

There were many things that preyed on my mind at that time, but one issue remained at the forefront of my consciousness. All of our friends had started to produce children; and whilst initially I was unconcerned, as time passed my body clock kicked in and I started to yearn for a baby. Everywhere I went there seemed to be beaming mothers with angelic children in tow, and the more fertile females I saw, the more I wished to be counted in their number. I wanted to be in the club, but Charlie had to put me up for membership and so far nothing seemed to be happening.

Charlie wanted children more than anything in the world but the cocktail of drugs that he'd been taking would have made it extremely difficult. We couldn't bear to think that there might be a problem, so we just kept on trying and watched as more and more of our friends bathed in the reflective glory of their fecundity.

Luckily, we didn't have to go straight to the hospital once we'd landed in Newcastle. Jane had decided that we needed a treat before the next big hurdle and had paid for us to stay in a swanky hotel for the night. We booked in, got changed and then took a taxi to Stowell Street, which is the centre of Geordie Chinatown; and on the recommendation of one of the nurses, paid a visit to The King Neptune restaurant. We had been told to order King Neptune's feast, which was a sumptuous seafood banquet for two, featuring a mind-blowing dish of Szechwan lobster as its star attraction. The nurse had been spot-on with her top tip, as it turned out to be the most fantastic Chinese meal either of us had ever eaten.

Charlie was on spanking good form. It didn't seem to matter to him that he felt wretched, or that he was about to have yet another bout of surgery, all he cared about was making me happy. He was such a delight to be with, it made me feel sorry for all the other diners, knowing that they were missing out on a wit that was dryer than the Sauvignon Blanc that sat chilling beside our table. The evening passed all too quickly. We didn't talk about the impending operation at all; we just laughed out loud at each other's jokes and savoured the seafood and the moment.

When we got back to our room we were both very tired but we wanted to make love before we fell asleep. It was very risky for Charlie to attempt any bedroom athletics but he did it just the same. There was a kind of sad desperation about our lovemaking that night which would be hard to explain to anyone who hasn't been close to death. I needed to get pregnant. I wanted so badly to have something of Charlie, in the event that he didn't make it through the next operation and that night he gave his last ounce of energy to try and make it happen. We never discussed what might happen in the future but we both understood that if he died, a part of him would remain growing inside me – a living, breathing testament to Charlie and to the strength of our love. The next morning dawned in a shroud of grey drizzle. At breakfast, Charlie's eggs were scrambled – and as I would later discover, mine were unfertilised.

I had arranged to stay in the hospital accommodation block for the duration of Charlie's stay. I had a new job at the BBC at that stage, it was only part time but I needed to hang on to it, as it was our main source of income. My boss was extremely understanding and gave me compassionate leave so that I could be with Charlie for as long as I needed, which was a huge relief to us both. And so began another period of bed sitting.

The life of a hospital visitor is one long bore, interspersed with moments of intense joy and anguish in equal measure. To give us both a break, I would take the bus into the city centre every day and spend my time trudging round jewellery shops. I had made up my mind to give Charlie a gift. Soldiers get a medal for acts of courage and Charlie already had a Purple Heart of sorts, so I wanted him to have something a little more useful to serve as a reminder of his bravery. I decided that a pocket watch would be the ideal thing – one that he could wear on a short chain attached to the lapel of his jacket on special occasions. He didn't like jewellery and only ever wore a signet ring, but I knew he would love a gold watch because it was old fashioned and proper. And so I set about finding one.

I had very little money to play with and all the watches I saw were fearsomely expensive, but after days of searching, and miles of walking, I finally found a tiny shop, which had exactly what I wanted. I paid a deposit to the jeweller to secure the watch and chain that had taken my fancy, and promised to pay off a little more each week until the watch was mine. In the meantime, Charlie was about to be fitted with a different kind of timepiece, in a procedure, which he would later compare to 'being skinned like a chicken'.

The pacemaker was about the size of his pocket watch and had to be squeezed into a pouch of skin just beneath his collarbone. Charlie was under local anaesthetic at the time and could feel the surgeon pulling the skin away from his muscle and stuffing the pacemaker into the hole – in much the same way as he would have stuffed a clove of garlic beneath the skin of a leg of lamb on a Sunday evening.

The pacemaker was attached to two wires, which had been fed directly into the heart. One was screwed into the wall of the atrium, or upper pumping chamber, and the other lay within the right ventricle. The idea was that the atrial lead would sense the electrical signal from the atrium and then pass it back into the pacemaker. The pacemaker would then react to the signal, sending a charge down the other lead and into the ventricle. The electrical charge had the effect of making the ventricle contract, and thus the heart would beat in exactly the same way as a normal heart.

That was the idea – but in practice Charlie had to be different.

He was in atrial flutter, which made it impossible for the atrial lead to be used. The atrial lead can only be switched on if the heart is in a steady sinus rhythm – otherwise all hell would break loose. The surgical team decided that the safest option would be to use only the pacing wire in his left ventricle and ignore what was happening in the fluttering atrium. To use a seafaring analogy; the chief stoker was dancing around the boiler, throwing in a sackful of coal one minute and a single lump the next, but the massive turbine was being told to keep pumping the pistons in and out – regardless of how much steam there was to drive them. I think Charlie would have happily swapped the experience of being fitted with his new device, for a little root canal work sans anaesthetic, but he was in no position to complain – his heart was still going and that's all that mattered.

Charlie and I flew back from Newcastle feeling a mixture of relief and despair. We were both strung out but had each met people who were in a far worse state than ourselves. I had shared a room with a woman who was sad, confused and utterly alone. Her eighteen-year-old son was about to have a heart transplant and she had nobody to support her. I spent my evening trying to reassure her and convince her of her need for real emotional support.

On that same evening Charlie had met a young Geordie called Iain, who was totally distraught about the prospect of having his own heart replaced at the age of twenty-one. Iain and his parents were in the day room when Charlie walked in with a takeaway curry. Charlie later told me that he felt that he couldn't just sit there and watch such a young lad sobbing his heart out, and so he started up a conversation. When I asked him about it the next day he said that he had just tried to reassure Iain and his parents about the surgery, but as Iain would tell me years later, what Charlie said to him that night stayed with him – and would continue to do so for as long as he lived.

Charlie was totally frank about his own situation, expressing himself to Iain and his parents in a way that he never could to me. He simply said, 'Listen, Iain, every morning that I wake up and realise that I'm still alive is a bonus to me. I don't expect any more than that, I just live each day to the full and consider myself very fortunate when the next day comes along.' I'm glad he never said those words to me – I don't think I could have carried on knowing what was going through his mind as he opened his eyes each morning. I was oblivious – all I ever saw was the face of a happy man.

We flew to the Isles of Scilly a few weeks after returning from Newcastle for a well-earned holiday. It was a magical time for us both, full of hope and laughter. Charlie was feeling a good deal better since his heart rhythm had settled down and we were able to walk for miles across the islands. One day on a deserted beach, we came across a small ruined fort. I told Charlie that there was an old legend, which spoke of pirate treasure hidden somewhere within the ruins. I urged him to go and search for it and he came out after a few minutes bearing a small blue box (Little did he know that I had hidden his pocket watch in a crack beneath one of the windows a few minutes earlier.) He was delighted with his booty and spent the rest of the holiday opening up the box and admiring the glistening gold watch, which lay within the soft folds of satin. I was as proud of him as I had ever been and if I could have bought him a whole chest full of gold watches, it still wouldn't have been enough to show him how much he meant to me.

Charlie now had two visible reminders of his heart condition – the operation scar and the bulge of the pacemaker. The pacemaker didn't seem to trouble him that much but his fitness and stamina had lessened quite dramatically since the thyroid trouble. When we returned from our Easter holiday he tried to keep up the same punishing schedule as he had previously. The company had expanded despite the recession and Charlie now had far more responsibility than before. He was eager to play a full part in the running of the company, which ultimately meant working harder and travelling further in order to find new clients. I could see that he wasn't up to it, but I was powerless to stop him. Charlie hated anyone reminding that he wasn't as fit and strong as the next man. If I had voiced my concerns every time I felt he looked tired, it would have been like nudging him in the ribs and saying, 'Hey, weedy bloke, are you up to it, or what?' Charlie was a proud man and I refused to dampen the spirit, which burned so brightly within him.

When he came to bed at night he would often fall asleep as soon as his head touched the pillow. I would lie awake beside him, wishing that I could give full vent to my passionate nature, but knowing also that he would have loved me long into the night if only he had the heart to do so. When he felt fit enough to make love to me, if I was tired or not really in the mood, I would never refuse him. In the back of my mind was always the thought that it might be the last time he ever had the chance to make love to me. How could I deny him that chance? I could deny him nothing.

 I would have given him my life if he'd asked for it.

Chapter Twenty-One

Life went on but it seemed I couldn't get pregnant and we couldn't sell our house. Charlie was struggling to stay out of hospital and our debts were piling up. A friend of mine at work happened to mention to me that she had been to see a famous fortune-teller on the Barbican in Plymouth, so I made up my mind to pay her a visit. I needed to know whether Charlie was going to live or die. I needed to know if we would ever have children and I needed to know if we were ever going to sell our house. I think if the poor clairvoyant had known what a burden of responsibility I was placing on her, she might not have been quite so keen to see me.

I walked up and down outside for some time before I could summon up enough courage to enter the shop. But eventually I went inside, pulled aside a faded velvet curtain and took my seat in the dingy cubicle. A young woman entered, I crossed her palm with a tenner and then she laid my cards on the table.

The first thing she said to me was, 'You've had three terrible years – but from this moment onwards your life is going to get better.' She continued by telling me that we would have two children of the same sex, to which I replied, 'Hurrah.' She also said that we would move within six months and would be very happy in our new house. She said my husband would be very successful in business and that she could see a lot of money around us. She told me I would be changing jobs shortly, but was unaware of the fact that I had just had an interview. She said we would soon have a new car, which would be red. I told her that was nonsense because we had no money, but she was quite adamant. She mentioned that fact that Charlie had trouble with his leg, but didn't mention his heart at all, and when the reading was over I felt totally elated.

Charlie was horrified that I had been to see a fortune teller and refused to hear what she'd said. But I was so happy I told him anyway.
And this is what happened shortly afterwards...

I went to the village shop one day and a lady came up to me and introduced herself. She said, 'Hello, I'm Gwen Pearce and I live by the school. I know you want to sell your cottage and I wondered if you would be interested in coming to see my house, with a view to doing a swap.' We moved in six months later. Charlie was given his first company car – a red Peugeot estate. I got a job at Westcountry Television – a company that had just won the franchise from T.S.W. But as for the children – my womb remained resolutely empty.

We had been to see Dr. Halliday, but he just looked at Charlie over his glasses and said, 'Listen, old chap, don't you think you have spent enough time in hospital, without having to go in for more tests? Once you embark on the road to finding out where the problem of fertility lies, life can get very depressing indeed. I want you both to go away and forget about it, but if after two years you have failed to conceive, then we might think about doing some tests.' It was very good advice from a fine doctor, and we went home thinking that we weren't quite so abnormal after all.

Over the past months I had become good friends with Beth Burrell and saw her almost as often as Charlie saw her husband. She and I were very similar and I knew that I could say anything to her in complete confidence. She was very funny and she always got my jokes – no matter how obscure they were. I would call round to see her whenever I felt low and she would give me coffee and make me laugh. She had been a midwife before she came down to Devon and so she knew all there was to know about getting pregnant. She told me to stop worrying, and advised me to elevate my pelvis after sex. I took her advice, but I did feel rather foolish standing on my head – and God only knows what Charlie thought.

Chris Burrell was still very concerned about Charlie. He had been trying to come up with a remedy for his continuing fatigue, but true to form Charlie decided to come up with his own solution. One day his heart stopped fluttering and went back into sinus rhythm quite of its own accord. Chris was quite unable to offer any explanation as to why this should have happened but he was obviously delighted when Charlie's E.C.G. results rolled of the machine, showing a continuous line of regular little spikes. He was more accustomed to looking at a trace, which resemble a straight line drawn on a cold Arctic morning by a naked Eskimo with St. Vitas Dance.

Chris was always looking for ways to improve Charlie's quality of life and the new steady rhythm gave him the chance to fit Charlie with a spanking new state-of the-art pacemaker. It would give Charlie a new lease of life and what's more, it could be tuned and tweaked with a cunning electronic gizmo that could perform a full diagnostic check on the pacemaker, simply by being rested on top of it.

Just over a year after Charlie had his original pacemaker fitted, he went into hospital and got fitted with a new model by the best doctor in the Western Hemisphere. Charlie was cooking on gas at last and boy did I know it!

The time limit for getting me pregnant was fast approaching; we had been trying for nearly two years and although I was only twenty-nine, we both knew that we couldn't live with the uncertainty of not knowing any longer. June was our deadline, so in the middle of May when I was sure that I was at my most fertile, we 'gave it large' in the bedroom. We christened the new pacemaker with a road test that would have left Jeremy Clarkeson stuttering for adjectives – and on 'Three-times Thursday' our first child was conceived.

It is impossible to underestimate the importance that Charlie placed on the news that I had at last got pregnant. He was away filming when I did my pregnancy test and he could hardly contain his joy when I phoned him to tell him that he was going to be a father at last. He was having dinner with the film crew and tried to sound nonchalant but he kept cupping his hand over the receiver and saying. 'I can't believe it, Katie, are you sure? Am I really going to be a daddy? You're so clever, Katie. We're going to have a baby!'

We wanted to tell the world about the pregnancy but we kept quiet until we were sure that the baby was anchored properly and from then on it was just a case of waiting and watching as the buttons pinged off my trousers. I went to my first antenatal class with Charlie and during the evening, the midwife asked all the fathers what they thought their role was during the labour. Charlie put his hand up and said 'The father's role is to provide fresh straw.' And that was the last time we ever showed our faces at the clinic.

We were in the midst of renovating the house when we found out about the baby, so I donned my dust mask and sanded the beams in the kitchen with a new sense of purpose. The house was quite something. It had been built in 1697 as the malt house for the Anchor Inn and had undergone a number of alterations since that date. The structure was sound but the house needed new central heating, a new roof and a lot of tarting up before we could live there in comfort. We couldn't afford to do everything right away, so we decided to get the basics sorted out first. The roof was sagging and creaking but we had to ignore it, along with the hideous purple and brown bathroom, until we felt brave enough to tack another few thousand pounds onto our huge mortgage.

I had done a lot of work to the house before I found out I was pregnant, which was very lucky as I wouldn't have attempted it otherwise. I went up into the roof space with Dickie Bird and strengthened the joists and purlins. We put in a new king post and generally beefed up the rickety timbers that held up the undulating roof.

Gwen had told us that there was an old fireplace behind the ancient Rayburn in the kitchen and one night as we were sitting eating our supper, I told Charlie that I was going to chip away a tiny part of the plaster to see if the fireplace really existed. When the dust began billowing into the sitting room, Charlie came into the kitchen to investigate and found me sitting in a pile of rubble, looking very meek and clutching a bent screwdriver and a lump hammer. He went to get a cold chisel; carried on with the excavation and by the end of the night we had exposed a large fireplace, which had been bricked up many years before. It was just the right size for an Aga, so we enlisted the help of Jeff the builder and Pete the slave to clear out the cavity.

On the day that they were supposed to arrive, we put polythene up over all the doorways and waited for the work to commence. The boys were late and I decided that I couldn't sit and look at the sledgehammer any longer – so I picked it up and began to pound away at the brickwork. It was very awkward because the Rayburn was in the way, and during one swing, the sledgehammer glanced off a lump of stone and I crushed the tip of my finger between its handle and the corner of the brickwork.

It was quite a novelty being rushed to hospital by Charlie, but the pain was so excruciating that I failed to see the irony of it all. The doctor took off the

Eddie, Pix and Charlie – summer 1994

remains of my mangled nail and stitched up the bloody mess beneath it. Deb Lapthorne came over and cleared up the blood that I had sprayed over the walls, floor and ceiling and when we returned, Walker took Charlie off for a pint. The professionals finished the job that I had started, and a few weeks later we had a stunning fireplace, resplendent with a racing green Aga, which Charlie lovingly polished every morning before he went off to work.

My pregnancy was a complete joy. I had no morning sickness, in fact I felt no ill effects whatsoever – and to cap it all, my bust size increased from 34B to 'magnificent'. I felt so sexy and so pneumatic. My hair shone with a deep lustre, my skin glowed and my husband had a job to get to work in the mornings! Life was very good for us then; we had a wonderful home, I had a job that I loved, a husband whom I adored and I knew a beautiful baby was growing inside me.

We went back to Canada to see Tom and Ali that summer and they took us up to a cottage on the edge of Lake Huron. To give you some idea of the scale of the lake, the bay where we were staying was bigger than the English Channel. The waters of the lake were warm and clear and we would take a swim off the end of the jetty in the evenings, knowing that in the depths below there lurked huge green turtles and fish with great big teeth and absolutely no sense of humour.

The islands dotted around the bay were mostly deserted, and had white sandy beaches that shelved out gently into the lake. We spent our days swimming and lazing in the sun. Charlie looked absolutely edible. He was bronzed and fit and for the first time in years I was able to relax and enjoy what most women of my age take entirely for granted – being married to a healthy man.

Chapter Twenty-Two

On January 29th 1994, Charlie squeezed me into the car and drove me to the maternity unit of Derriford hospital. My 9-hour labour was punctuated by a visit from Dr. Burrell, who had called in on his way home to see how I was getting on. As he and Charlie gossiped, Beth rang him on his mobile and so I was able to chat to her between contractions. It turned into quite a social occasion, although I'm not sure quite what the midwife made of it all. She was called Sarah and with her help, and a little gas and air, I found the whole experience very easy. When I went for the big push, Sarah was putting on her gown and gloves – so Charlie ended up catching the baby, which came flying out just like a newborn lamb. When I saw her, I cried out, 'It's a baby!' As if it were a miracle that I hadn't just given birth to an armadillo or a small fridge freezer.

Charlie held his daughter and the pride and joy that radiated from him seemed to fill up the whole room. He was totally speechless with the wonder of it all and I could see that the tiny bundle that lay in the crook of his arm had filled his heart with love until it was overflowing. For my own part, I knew I had given Charlie the gift of immortality. Rosanna Jane Stirrup Boydell would carry his genes far into the future. She was his future, she was his baby girl – she was his whole world.

We called our parents to tell them the news and then Charlie called Eddie, who was also in hospital at that time. He had been involved in a serious road accident – the girl sitting next to him on the back seat had been killed and he had broken his neck. Eddie was lying in head traction when the phone was brought to his bedside; and when Charlie told him that he had a new niece called Rosie, he broke down and cried.

I went up to bed and lay awake, unable to take my eyes off the tiny miracle that lay asleep in a cot by my bedside. She had a squashed nose and a dent on the side of her head, but to me she was the most beautiful thing I had ever seen. Charlie drove wearily back to the Burrell's house, where Chris opened a bottle of Cloudy Bay Sauvignon Blanc and Beth cooked him supper. When he eventually got home, he opened a bottle of scotch and called everyone he knew. He called most of them more than once and he called all of them between 11.00am and 3.00am. He was very drunk and very happy.
The following day he sat down and wrote this letter.

My Darling Rosie,
I'm sitting in the kitchen and thought I'd write so that one day way

off in the future you would know what it was like for Mummy, and for me, when you were born.

We went to the hospital at about lunchtime – it was pouring with rain, and we kept getting delayed on the way – telephone line repairs, horses, etc. The midwife, Sarah, helped throughout, and at about 7.15pm wanted to give Mummy something to help ease your birth. Chris Burrell appeared and put a drip line in Mummy's arm – and about an hour after, around 8.30, she really wanted to push you out. With much encouragement, shouting a bit, and a mixture of kneeling and squatting, at about 9.05 she sat back on her 'haunches' to rest – then she said she felt like pushing again, gave two almighty heaves, and out you came. You looked wonderful, cried noisily, and then we laughed because your nose was a bit squashed! You were put straight on to Mummy's tummy and chest – and then she cried a little bit too!

After making lots of phone calls, I made sure you were both OK, and came home. Your first day – a Sunday, as you were born on Saturday night, was gloriously sunny, clear and cold. You were a treasure – the most precious thing I've ever seen or held – and I've never experienced the rush of emotions like I did that first day. But now I'm sure I'll feel it every day.

I love you,

Daddy xxx

Rosie was a model child. She hardly cried, she slept well and when she was only eight weeks old we took her on holiday to Ireland. We stayed with the Levignes, in their converted granary, and introduced Rosie to the delights of Guinness. She went for walks with her daddy whilst I fished the river Slaney, and then I sat down in my waders and fed her on the riverbank as if it were the most natural thing in the world.

Nineteen ninety four proved to be a landmark year in more ways than one, for not only was it the year of Rosie's birth, it was also the year that Two Four Productions turned over a million pounds for the first time. More importantly, it was the first year that Charlie had remained fit enough to stay out of hospital. He had worked very hard that year and was rewarded by being made a company director, which was such a proud moment for him. He loved his job and got a big kick out of telling me that he was going to his first board meeting.

Charlie indeed played a very important role in the running of the company. He had become Charles's right hand man and ran the office when he was away. He was seen as being totally loyal and trustworthy, which inspired a lot of confidence around the office but which I found rather irritating, as he never came

Charlie and Rosie at a wedding, May 1994

home with any juicy gossip. He also acted as unofficial personnel manager and became very adept at handling emotional crises when they inevitably arose.

The most surprising thing to me about Charlie's work persona was how ruthless he could be. I never saw that side of him at home. He was always so gentle and kind – he never raised his voice and I can honestly say that I never once heard him bad-mouth any of his friends or colleagues. I used to bitch away like an old fishwife about all sorts of people, but Charlie always remained resolutely silent. He was totally without malice – except when it came to donkeys, and the business of handling car dealers.

Charlie was given the job of negotiating the price of all the company cars and he was utterly ruthless when it came to making a deal. He relished the challenge of getting one over on some hapless dealer and in car showrooms all around Plymouth, salesmen soon came to realise that Mr. Boydell was not a man to be taken lightly. He applied the same ruthless attitude to getting deals on crewing and editing. He was christened 'The Bald Rottweiler' by one facilities house, but he was so charming on the phone that he invariably got what he wanted without too much of a fight. I once asked Joe, the man who gave him the nickname, what Charlie was like to deal with. He said, 'I get people on the phone to me all the time, trying to screw me down to the last penny and I really hate it. But when Charlie calls, he is such a pleasure to deal with that I don't mind him getting one over on me from time to time – it's just impossible not to like the man.'

Charlie had a number of admirers among his female clients and many of them continued to call him long after their video projects had been completed. Charlie was immensely flattered by their attentions, but always kept his relationship with them on a purely professional basis. I was fully aware that the qualities that I had recognised in Charlie would be equally appealing to other women, but I never worried. Charlie was as devoted to me as I was to him – and anyway, I had dealt with the subject of infidelity very early on in our relationship. I told him that if he were ever unfaithful to me, I would take off his testicles with a blunt knife and hang them from the top of Ugborough church tower. I think that clarified my position once and for all and Charlie was never left in any doubt that had he strayed, I would have carried out my threat to the letter. I was not without admirers of my own and used to delight in telling Charlie all about the men who tried to chat me up. His reaction was always the same. He would listen to me, let me finish my story, pause and then say, 'I'll kill the bastard.'

I went back to work part-time in August 1994, leaving Rosie in the capable hands of our new nanny, Anna. Rosie took to Anna immediately and became a very social baby all of a sudden, and I was able to go to work with a clear conscience because I knew how much fun she was having in my absence. Although most of my salary was used to pay Anna, I was once more able to feel like I was making a contribution to the running of the household and I was very happy being back in a job that I loved.

We spent the remainder of the year delighting in the joys of our baby girl, who accompanied us on trips all over the country. Our new home thronged with weekend guests and the sound of laughter rang out from our dining room, across the fields and mingled with the wood smoke drifting lazily up from the chimneys in the village below us. This was our time. We had waited so long for the chance to live our lives as others lived theirs – without worry, without endless trips to hospital – Charlie was fighting fit and all was well with the world.

29 i 95

My Darling Rosie,

It's a year since I sat down to write – and try and preserve the memories of the day you were born. Now, I'm going to try and tell you a bit about that first year.

Today is your birthday, it's a Sunday, and I'm writing in the study, looking out over the fields to White House Farm. It's grey, cold and gloomy outside – the rain at bay for only a short time, I suspect. In the kitchen you are in your high chair, chuntering a familiar sound – 'doc-a-doc-a-doc' which we've not yet deciphered. Your mother is getting your breakfast; we've opened your presents in bed; you slept well; all's well with the world. This first year you've learnt to move, then crawl and you're very nearly walking now. We've been to Ireland for Easter to stay in the Levigne's cottage, and had a holiday in Malvern in October after Granny's 60th birthday. You've been to lots of weddings – including Sam and Julian Culhane's, Emma and John Birkin's; and Jo and John's. We had your Christening in July – and Tom and Ali came over from Canada. You were spoilt terribly by everyone, and returned their generosity by behaving beautifully!

We've also discovered that you love water – you've never minded being bathed or having your hair washed, but with Granny's pool and the one down the road, we know that you like to swim too. When Mummy went back to work we also met Anna Nanny – who now looks after you. You're great friends – and with her you have a very sociable time going to the zoo, parties, swimming and play group. But at the moment, your greatest pleasure is pointing at pictures of animals and getting us to do the noises – although your version of a horse 'chick' and a pig 'grunt' are very funny.

You have changed my life since the moment you came into the world, I think about you at work, and when I'm away, but never more than when you are close, and I can just put down my pen, fold up the letter, pop it in an envelope and come and give you a big birthday hug – right now!

Your ever loving

    Daddy xxx

P.S. I love your Mummy more than I can say or write.

Chapter Twenty-Three

In the spring of 1995 Charlie started to get breathless again and began to feel increasingly tired. And as we lay in bed one night I heard a high-pitched 'squeak' coming from his heart. I knew that it could only mean one thing – one of his replacement valves had begun to leak. Pig valves have a limited life span; they begin to stiffen over time and eventually the seal that is formed by the cusps begins to leak. The valves generally last between seven and fifteen years before a replacement operation becomes necessary and Charlie's had been in place for six years.

He was admitted to hospital in May 1995 and Chris gave him a thorough going over. As we suspected, Charlie had developed a leak in his mitral valve – but with the added complication of atrial fibrillation. Chris had to switch his pacemaker to single chamber, rate-responsive mode, which would mean that Charlie's cardiac output would be severely restricted. It all came as a tremendous blow for Charlie. He had been so well for over a year but now, seventeen months later, he felt continually fatigued and extremely depressed.

His depression manifested itself at home as mild irritation at his lack of energy and a kind of sad resignation about the declining state of his health. He never burdened me with his fears for the future because he knew that I had exactly the same fears. We never dwelt on the negative aspects of our life together because as far as we were concerned there were none. Both of us carried a very heavy burden, but we never bowed under its weight because it was always counterbalanced by the strength of our relationship.

People often used to comment on our closeness and the fact that we always behaved like a couple of newlyweds, but they never realised the strain that we were both under. I worried about Charlie more as each year passed and although we tried to live as normal a life as possible, it was becoming increasingly evident that he was finding it more and more difficult to disguise the frailty of his health.

I vividly remember one occasion when we went to visit some friends at their cottage, near Rock, in Cornwall. They had decided to take us to the local pub for lunch and to get there we had to walk across the beach for about a mile and a half. Charlie began well but after a while it was clear to me that he was struggling to keep up. By that stage it was too late to turn back, and so he had to continue, and by the time we reached to pub he was totally exhausted.

It was at times like that I felt like ripping out my own heart and giving it to him. I couldn't stand to see him gasping for breath whilst his heart struggled to cope with the strain of what to him was a massive exertion, but to the rest of us was nothing more than a gentle stroll. I couldn't bear to see him having to suffer the indignity of asking if somebody could go back to fetch a car because he knew he wouldn't have the energy to walk back across the beach.

On the way back I watched the other men in the party, all ruddy-cheeks and rippling muscles, striding out before me without a care in the world. And I wished I could have told them what it was like for Charlie – what it was like to be so aware of his future; what it was like to know so much about the state of his own health that he could virtually plot his decline, year by year. But I couldn't say anything because I didn't want anyone to pity a man who had no pity for himself. So nobody knew. Nobody really knew.

There was no doubt that Charlie was going to have to cut his workload. He simple couldn't sustain such a punishing schedule whilst he was in such poor health. We talked about the possibility of him doing part of his work from home – but that was never really a viable option. It was what I wanted but it was not what Charlie wanted. I saw it as a way of limiting the strain that working at such a rate was having on his health – but he saw it as the first step in becoming an invalid; because the easiest way to make Charlie feel like an invalid was to stop him doing what he loved. His work was exhausting at times, but it gave him such a buzz to be in the office that he didn't seem to mind how tired he got. Giving Charlie time at home would allow him to rest, but separating him from his colleagues would just make him miserable – so what could I do?

In the end I borrowed some money from Eddie and bought Charlie a computer. This gave him the option of being able to bring work home without the stigma of people knowing that he wasn't well enough to work full-time. It would also give him the chance to start the book that he'd always talked of writing.

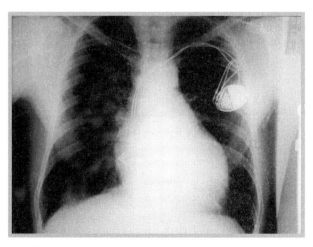

X-ray of Charlie's chest – his heart by this stage almost filling the lower left side
of his rib cage

Whilst I was worrying about how to keep Charlie happy, Chris Burrell was applying his sizeable brain to the problem of his erratic heartbeat. The solution he came up with sounded scary, but if it worked, Charlie would have a steady rhythm and thus a greatly improved quality of life. Chris had decided to try a procedure called cardioversion, which would involve passing a current through his heart, high enough to interrupt its own electrical signal and stop it beating. The intended outcome would be that Charlie's heart would re-start in a rhythm that would allow his pacemaker to work normally again. He was in for a big shock – literally.

Charlie went into hospital and was placed in the safe hands of Chris Burrell. He was given a general anaesthetic and taken into theatre. Chris placed two small pads on Charlie's chest and two on his back. He would then pass a D.C. current through the pads to stop the heart. It was then a case of waiting until the heart restarted to see if it had reverted to sinus rhythm. Chris tried the standard charge of 100 joules, but it had no effect. He then doubled the charge, but still Charlie's heart continued to flutter. As a last resort, Chris decided to use the maximum charge of 360 joules, but he had to repeat the shock three times before Charlie's heart reverted to a steady sinus rhythm.

Charlie said he came out of theatre feeling as if he'd been kicked by a horse. It was possible to see exactly where the pads had been placed, because the strength of the current had been strong enough to burn four rings into his skin. Chris had performed the procedure countless times in the past, but he'd never before had to resort to giving such a massive shock to a patient with atrial flutter. Even though he was a seasoned professional, Chris found the experience of seeing his friend contorting and grimacing during the procedure extremely upsetting and disturbing, and it would be hard to say which of the men was more relieved when it was all over.

Charlie took a while to recover from the cardioversion, but once he had rested for a few days he returned to work. I made the decision to start working full-time because we had a huge mortgage and I knew that we would struggle to keep up the repayments if Charlie became ill.

There was no 'if' about it – he was ill.

The heart of a normal, healthy male is generally about the size of an orange. Charlie's heart was by now the size of a melon. It was so distended that it virtually filled the right side of his ribcage and when he lay on his back, the movement of the pulsating pump was so pronounced that you could measure his heart rate simply by looking at rise and fall of his chest.

We knew that it would be only a short time before Charlie had to go under the knife again. Chris Burrell had spoken to Charlie about the benefits of undergoing a heart transplant and we were pretty hopeful that it would give Charlie a better quality of life. But that rosy, soft-focus picture of a new life was soon brought into sharp relief when we went to see Dr. Alan Wood a few weeks later.

It was a routine check-up for Charlie, but it also proved to be a real eye-opener for both of us. Alan listened to Charlie's squeaking heart and then pronounced the leak very small and added that the valve itself would not need replacing for at least a couple of years. He then said, 'I'll do the operation for you, but I can't say I'm looking forward to it. I know what's inside there and it's not pretty, I can tell you.'

When we asked his opinion about transplantation, we received a reply that was as blunt as a vegetarian's steak knife.

Alan Wood was a very experienced surgeon who performed transplants on a regular basis. He was under no illusion about what the future had in store for Charlie if he were to receive a donor heart. I think his exact words were, 'Don't have one.' He qualified that stark message by saying, 'When they take out your heart and give you a donor heart, you know that you only have a certain number of years left to live. You may get seven years out of the new heart but when that one gives up, you have to go in and get another one fitted. That one may only last three years and so it goes on. The psychological problems associated with having somebody else's heart beating inside you are also very hard to deal with, and you will be taking vast quantities of anti-rejection drugs for the rest of your days. Stick with the one you've got, that's my advice.'

It wasn't the kind of advice that he would have given to most of his patients I'm sure, but then Charlie wasn't 'most patients'. Charlie's heart was immensely strong – the very fact that it was beating at all was nothing short of a miracle. It was scarred and battered but it was his, and we both knew that if they took out his heart, they would take away his will to live.

We walked out of the hospital into the bright sunlight feeling a mixture of relief and dread. There was only one thing for it – lunch at Rules. If a piece of clothing could sum up Charlie's character, it would be Farmer's Friend button fly cords, a wine merchant – Berry Bros. and Rudd. But the restaurant that reflected all of Charlie's idiosyncrasies was Rules in Covent Garden. Reputedly the oldest restaurant in London, it typified all that is good about British cooking. Walking through its doors was like stepping back in time, and one glance at the menu was enough to tell you that you were in serious red meat country. The restaurant specialised in game from its own estates in Yorkshire and button-bursting dishes like steak and kidney pudding and spotted dick. We loved it and tried to eat there whenever we were in London. The house claret was £9.00 a bottle, and if you went for lunch, you could stay all afternoon – which is exactly what we did.

The prognosis was not good. We tried to remain positive about the future, but just when we thought that everything had gone wrong that could possibly go wrong with Charlie's health; it became my turn – I had a miscarriage.

It wasn't a total surprise to me; I'd had a bad feeling about the pregnancy right from the start – but that didn't mean that I wasn't affected when I lost the baby. To make matters worse, when it began, Charlie had to go away to do some filming for the B.H.F. Rosie was only just over a year old at the time and I needed Charlie to look after her whilst I rested, but I ended up putting him on a train to Newcastle, and was left standing alone on the platform at Exeter station – holding onto one child and losing another.

I went to stay with Chris and Beth and they looked after me until Charlie could get back home. I didn't blame him for leaving me, the filming was crucial and Charlie refused to let his friends at The British Heart Foundation down at such short notice. He was torn between his concern for me and his commitment to his work, but in the end we both knew that his staying to look after me wouldn't stop me losing the baby.

I got over it, and at the beginning of the summer I got the distinct impression that I was pregnant again. I went to get a testing kit and rushed home. I got a blue line, and I was so excited I went straight round to see Beth. Charlie had been for a check up with Chris and when he got back to work I phoned him to tell him about the baby. He seemed a little distracted as I burbled out the news to him and when I'd finished he tried to sound pleased, but there was obviously something wrong. I asked him what the matter was and he sighed and said, 'My heart's gone into flutter again.' Charlie was clearly devastated. I felt all the excitement and joy drain from my body as he told me the news, and I knew at that moment that I was going to miscarry for a second time.
It had not been a good year.

I buried myself in my work and all but a few of my colleagues were totally unaware of what had been happening in my personal life. I needed to retain an air of professionalism and consequently I always kept my work and my home life separate. If you come into work every day in floods of tears, people soon become tired of your histrionics and expect you to get a grip on the situation and get on with your job. Nobody knew about the fluctuating state of Charlie's health or the strain that we were both under. But you only had to look at photographs of us both at the time and you could clearly see the truth behind the smiles. It was in our eyes – the fatigue and strain were plain to see – if only people had looked a little closer.

We both carried on working hard through the autumn and at the end of the year I accompanied Charlie on a shoot at a nearby estate. I was feeling tired and full of flu and the last thing I wanted to do was to spend a day tramping around after Charlie in the cold and wet. But he pleaded with me, saying, 'Please come with me, Katie. I really want you to be with me today.' So what could I do?

It rained torrentially throughout the day but I zipped up my Barbour and resolutely trudged from one drive to the next by the side of my happy huntsman. I was happy too, for even though I was freezing cold and soaked to the skin, I knew that there was another little life growing inside me; floating lazily around in a warm amniotic bath, listening to the dull thud of Charlie's gun and the pattering of the rain on my Barbour.

28 i 96

My Darling Rosie,

It hardly seems yesterday since I sat down to write to you on your first birthday – and now, tomorrow, you are two. This time last year we couldn't discuss things – and you certainly couldn't make yourself understood, unless you were tired or hungry. Now, your vocabulary is amazing, and you have learned so much.

I don't suppose I will ever know how you feel when you read all these letters – but for us, and for me in particular, they are a way of communicating how it feels to be the parent of someone so very special – and to record the details of another year.

We've had a lovely time, Anna is still with us and now lives in the village with Adam. You had your first French holiday – staying on Clive's farm and then with the Mayhews. You loved the farm – especially the pigs, and since the autumn your Mummy has been making you your own farm in the barn, which we gave to you this morning. If you're wondering why – it's a Sunday – and Mummy and I are both working tomorrow.

By the time you read this you will, hopefully, have at least one brother or sister – expected in July this year. I hope whatever happens that you will never forget your family being the most important, irreplaceable thing in life, and I hope that Mummy and I will have filled your life with as much love as my mother did for me, Eddy and Pixie.

As our first child there will always have been things we experienced together which will never be repeated, but all the love I have, is shared today with Mummy and the baby in her tummy, and you my very very special Rosie.

I love you, always, wherever I am.

Daddy xxx

Walking in Ugborough Square, summer 1996

Chapter Twenty-Four

Nineteen-ninety-six would be a landmark year for Charlie – it was the year he fulfilled his greatest ambition and went to sea with Her Majesty's Royal Navy.

Our friends seemed to fall into three broad categories – doctors, telly types and naval officers. Charlie especially loved being in the company of naval officers, because it gave him the opportunity of talking in that peculiar abbreviated language that is specific to the services. Once Charlie got into his stride, his language was peppered with words like Soo, Peewo and Fost. I had no idea what was going on, so I just carried on talking about knitting patterns and the latest innovations in crochet hooks with the other wives and let him get on with it.

One of our closest naval friends was a charming man called Charles Style. He lived in a kind of ordered chaos with his wife Charlotte and their three daughters, in a village on the edge of the moor. We saw them often and Charlie would go out for a sail on Charles's boat whenever he got the chance.

Charles had just been stationed in Plymouth, after an extended tour at sea, and his new job involved training naval personnel from all over the world. F.O.S.T. (Flag Officer Sea Training) staged a pretend war every Thursday in the waters off Plymouth, to give sailors a chance to become battle-ready. Charlie asked the top brass to give him permission to make a film about the 'Thursday War' and when they agreed, he thought all his Christmases had come at once.

It was the start of a golden period in Charlie's career. He was helicoptered onto ships of all descriptions and spent a good deal of his time in the company of men whose jobs he envied more than they would ever know. It gave him immense satisfaction to be so closely involved with the Royal Navy – of course it was no substitute to actually being an officer himself, but it was a fair compromise.

Whilst Charlie was being a Navy tart, I was busy trying to grow us a healthy baby. It wasn't too difficult – I thrived when I was pregnant and continued to work as if nothing had happened. The only difference being that I took two punnets of plums and six custard tarts into my edit suite each morning, which I proceeded to gobble up as I edited news packages for a succession of rather startled journalists.

We made the decision to address the issue of our rickety roof that year. It was a problem that had been literally hanging over our heads since we moved in and because we were both earning we felt it was time to go for broke. The strange thing was that regardless of how much money we both earned, our bank balance always remained resolutely in the red. I'm sure it had something to do

Charlie and baby Alice – July 1996

with the number of people we entertained, but we both felt it was much better
to be overdrawn and happy than well-off and miserable. Our guests knew that
when they came to stay, they would be treated to creamy kedgeree for breakfast
and rare rib of beef for Sunday lunch. Charlie loved to do the cooking and never,
ever scrimped on his ingredients – and it was all I could do to stop him filling
our house with guests every weekend of the year.

It was a very exciting time, with the impending birth of our second child
and the expansion of our home. Our careers were blossoming: I cut my first half-
hour documentary and Charlie was busy planning another big project with the
Navy. I think the excitement must have filtered through to our unborn infant,
who decided to make an appearance eleven days early. We rushed off to
Derriford; it was a long, drawn out process, but eventually Alice Elizabeth
Stirrup Boydell agreed to grace us with her presence.

Charlie put us both to bed and then went to the Burrell's house for a celebratory glass of Cloudy Bay. When he got home, he had the presence of mind to
make a list of the people he had telephoned. He was determined not to repeat
the multiple phone call fiasco that happened after Rosie's birth, but after getting through almost an entire bottle of Johnny Walker Black Label, he could neither read nor write, so he decided to call everybody again, just to make sure.

12 vii 96

Darling Alice,

I'm pretty sure that by the time you read this, your birth day will
seem a very long way away, and we will all have forgotten what it

was like. Now, just a day after you were born, seems a good time to jot down a few things about the day you arrived – not the boring things of politics and world events (like the divorce of the Prince and Princess of Wales and the state visit of Nelson Mandela) but our life at the time.

You arrived after a long day in hospital – a gloomy misty day in Plymouth, with some blue patches – but 11 days earlier than expected! The house, which we have recently added to with a new bedroom for your sister Rosie, a new larder and downstairs loo – still has much work to do, or rather be done, to it. You were born at 10.23 at night, and I had a blissful 15 minutes with you while your Mother had a bath, before seeing you both safely to the ward. You were so calm and unbothered by the very lengthy ordeal of being born – and took to feeding very quickly. The doctor said you were 'perfect' – and no better word can I find to describe you. It seemed so funny to me that I would have the capacity for more love after meeting your Mother and the arrival of Rosie – but last night I looked at your beautiful face and found further love in store for you, and I hope I never forget that – I love you, my special Alice (or Princess Baby Alice as Rosie is calling you at the moment)

Daddy xxx

We had it all – lovely house, lovely daughter, lovely baby who never cried. Charlie, who gave everybody a nickname, called Alice 'Squeak' after the sound

Charlie, Rosie and baby Alice

she made during her first two weeks of life. However, if he'd waited just a week longer he might have opted for a 'Dances with Wolves' kind of name – something like 'Drives Parents to the Brink of Insanity.'

Alice developed chronic colic and turned from a placid little baby, into a screamer – and when I say a screamer, I really mean a SCREEEEEEEEAMER. It wasn't just the volume of her cry; it was the ear-splitting pitch of it that made it so painful. Our house was relatively large, with two-foot thick walls, but there was still no way of escaping the teeth-grating torment of our daughter's gasso profundo.

The Iraqis are rumoured to have a torture chamber filled with massive speakers, which emit a sound frequency so low and so loud that it literally shakes the human body to pieces. I think they could have saved a lot of money and put Alice in there for a few minutes. The output of her lungs would be enough to make even the toughest soldier run screaming for the door, begging for the map and the big red felt-tip.

There was nothing we could do except dance the 'jiggy dance' with our apoplectic infant and pray for a cure for her colic. I was utterly exhausted and began to get unnatural bedroom desires. When I came upstairs each evening with the screaming Alice, my eyes were immediately drawn towards one object in the room – my pillow. I desired my pillow. I wanted to bury my face in it – I needed it and I needed it badly. Once Alice was asleep, Charlie didn't get a look-in. I turned away from him, looked down and thought, 'I want you and I want you now.' The pillow was whispering to me in a deep, seductive tone, 'Give me head.' And I was powerless to refuse.

Night after night it went on, but thankfully after four hellish months Alice decided to stop torturing us and began to entertain us. We tore up the adoption papers and decided to keep her and she rewarded us by turning into an adorable little girl. Charlie suffered the trials of the tiny terror in silence but the stress of having to come home each night to a wall of sound that would have made Phil Spector weep, certainly took its toll. He was still maintaining a punishing work schedule; he began to tire more easily and felt exhausted for much of the time. But the company had just embarked on a massive broadcast project with the Navy and Charlie was their first point of contact. He couldn't let them down – he was totally dedicated to his work.

His work for BHF served as a constant reminder of the frailty of his own heart, yet he remained committed to producing the videos that he knew would help the lives of others like him. It made me proud to see him begin to enjoy the fruits of his labours. His videos won awards from the BMA almost every year, but he was typically modest about his success because to him it was just a way of saying, 'Thank you'.

Westcountry were taken over by Carlton Television that year and the few company shares that I had managed to buy, rocketed in value overnight. I dreamed of buying some nice furniture and some lovely new clothes for myself with the spectacular profits – but my prudent husband had other ideas. When I started to talk about all the goodies we were going to be able to afford he just looked at me and said, 'Wouldn't it be better to put the money into the house?' As usual I couldn't argue with his logic, but I can't say I was happy about it.

Charlie had his own reasons for wanting to get the house finished. He took Walker Lapthorne to the pub one hot Sunday afternoon, ostensibly to ask his advice about the building work, because at that time Walker was a chartered surveyor. As Walker would tell me some years later, he and Charlie walked into the pub and took their seats in the corner of the bar. The sunlight was streaming in through the window, lighting up the gloom, and as they sat and enjoyed their pints of bass, Charlie told him the truth.

He said, 'I want to get the house finished for my girls. It's really important to me that we get as much work done as possible now because I want to leave them a home that's in the best possible shape. I know that I'm not going to see old age and that I won't be around to walk my girls down the aisle and so it is vital to me that they have some sort of security when I'm gone.'

Walker said he was shocked by what Charlie had said, as any man would be in his situation; but being an intensely practical man he replied; 'Well, I do think you're wise to put the money into building a new room – it's a great investment – but you really mustn't talk about leaving your girls – you're only thirty six for God's sake, you've got years yet.' But Charlie was deadly serious. He had obviously given the matter a great deal of thought and had focussed on the house as the main security for his family once he was gone. He was preparing himself for what might happen in the future. It must have been desperately hard for Walker to hear his friend talking in such a way, but for Charlie, vocalising his deepest fears must have been heartbreaking.

Each night before he went to bed, Charlie would go and kiss baby Alice goodnight, and then he would go into Rosie's room and perch on the edge of her bed. I would often walk past the room and catch him, sitting and gazing at his sleeping daughter and I knew exactly why he was there. It was almost as if he were drawing her into himself through his eyes, storing her up in his memory for a time when he would no longer be with her. 'Come and look at this beautiful child,' he would say; and I would go and join him by her bedside. But I didn't look at her as he looked at her, because I had the certainty of knowing that I would be there to see her in the morning. Charlie didn't.

29 vii 97

My Darling Alice,

This is the first of the 'birthday' letters to either you or Rosie not actually written on a birthday. This year, though, we were in France on holiday – and spent part of the day playing in the garden of the house we rented in Normandy, followed by a birthday lunch of pizza and salad (for us) and French baby mush (for you) with James, Debbie, Emily and Grace.

It had been an extraordinary year – within two weeks of your arrival you developed appalling colic, driving you to cry in agony, and leaving us for the best part of four months to try and live with a screaming bundle of almost inconsolable baby. From August to November you emitted the kind of ear splitting, blood curdling scream that one hopes never to hear. Day (often) and night (a lot) this went on. During one period Mummy and I could not even hold a conversation, watch television, or eat a meal together. Then, suddenly, as if emerging from a dark tunnel into sunlight, you stopped. By the time we went on holiday for Guy Fawkes 1996 (also to Normandy, this time staying with James and Debbie and the girls) you had become the quiet (ish) bubbly, very funny, little baby girl that we know and love. But, what a nightmare.

We could, of course, never have not loved you with all our hearts – but maybe one day you too will find yourself pushed to the limit like we were. I hope not!

I worked through Christmas and part of Easter – and this year we have had more work done on the house, building the new porch and the Carlton Room. You have nearly learnt to walk since Easter, crawling hesitantly at first, then with increasing boldness, until now, when you are not safe to be left anywhere without supervision because you move too fast!

You are a very funny little girl, with a cheeky little smile, an eye for any man (who invariably melts at your look), and a good ability to flare up with anger for a very short period of time. The words are beginning to come – I can hear you shouting 'Mummy' from upstairs – I must get you from your cot.

I love you, as I have loved you from the moment I first saw you.

Daddy. xx

So the room got built and the money was spent and my plans for a whole new wardrobe were dashed. I did get to buy myself a new pair of shoes, which was compensation of sorts, but then I had rather got out of the habit of buying clothes for myself.

I did occasionally go out on shopping expeditions but they were usually taken up with my endless search for sodding button-fly trousers. The shop assistants became used to seeing me furtively fingering the openings of their merchanise in my eternal quest for the zipless fly, but I was always disappointed. I loved Charlie dearly but he simply didn't realise that the zipper fly was king in Plymouth – it is not a place overburdened with bespoke tailors or quality

Charlie and Alice in France, July 1997

gentleman's outfitters – so I gave up my search completely and told Charlie that he had to make do with what he had. And then one day I got lucky; the Boden catalogue turned up on our doorstep and imagine my surprise when I opened it up and discovered page upon page of trouserings, replete with buttons and not beastly zip fastenings. I was beside myself with joy. My search was over – Charlie was at last sorted for strides.

Chapter Twenty-Five

I had returned to work in March 1997 when Alice was eight months old – but without the help of Anna, who had left to have a baby of her own. The nanny who replaced her seemed proficient enough, but turned out to be so unsuitable that I decided to give up my job, rather than put my children's happiness at risk. It was a difficult decision for me; I had been in television for 14 years and I felt I that I was at the height of my creative powers – but my children had to come first. I couldn't bear the guilt of getting ready for work each morning, with Rosie tugging at my arm, saying, 'You're not going to work this morning are you Mummy? Please don't go to work this morning.'

Charlie had been admitted to hospital a fair few times over the past months and the strain of worrying about his health was taking its toll on me. I needed to rest and I wanted to be able to care for my children and my husband, so with great sadness I wrote a letter of resignation to my beloved boss, Duncan.

Charlie was unhappy when I told him I was resigning. He never gave me a definitive explanation as to why, but he didn't have to – I knew. He was worried about becoming ill again and he wanted me to remain on staff so that I could return to work quickly if I needed to. But I knew that Duncan would take me back like a shot if I asked him to, and so I didn't worry too much when the time came to say goodbye to all my colleagues and embark on a career as a full-time mother.

Charlie's heart continued to trip out of the sinus rhythm that Chris Burrell was trying so hard to maintain. He had to suffer the terrible process of cardioversion a further three times and on the second occasion, an unthinking anaesthetist just walked up to him and put him straight under without any warning whatsoever. Charlie was terribly shaken when he came round – he thought he'd died when the anaesthetic was injected – one moment he was wide awake and the next he was out of it and for all he knew he wasn't going to wake up ever again.

When I went to collect him he was still visibly shaken. He looked like he'd seen a ghost and it frightened me to see him that way because I knew that he'd just had a glimpse of his own mortality. The man who bounced back so easily after each set-back was now cowed and deflated. The anaesthetist had done more than just put him to sleep – he'd awoken him to the possibility that death might now only be a heartbeat away.

I took Charlie home and put him to bed, and it was all I could do to stop myself driving back to the hospital and giving the anaesthetist a taste of his own medicine. Charlie seemed to get over the experience, just as he had done so many times before, and I started to believe that he was invincible. He was all fired-up about work and went back to the office the following day.

I began to enjoy being at home with my girls and took real pride in preparing Charlie delicious meals for when he came home each evening, because to me, being at home was a job like any other. I made sure that the kitchen was spotless before I took the girls up for their bath, so that he didn't have to come home and start clearing up. I always felt a huge sense of relief when I heard the familiar sound of his confident footsteps echoing in the hall, because it heralded the end of my working day and the start of our evening together. It didn't matter how tired or fed up I was feeling, just knowing that he was home was enough to put me back in a good mood.

Charlie adored his little girls and would creep up the stairs and surprise them, as they played in the bath together. His face just lit up at the sight of them and I knew that he had been waiting all day just to hear them shout, 'Daddy, Daddy, Daddy, as he came into view. He often used to undress and jump into the bath with them before getting out and changing into jeans and a polo shirt and going downstairs to make himself a Bloody Mary. Rosie and Alice invariably demanded an extra story from him after I had read to them, but eventually he was able to sit down and relax with his B.M. and *The Daily Telegraph*.

Friday night was fish and chip night at the Anchor. I knew how much Charlie loved going down for a drink with Walker and Deb and the rest of the locals, so as soon as he came home I would send him off for an hour or so. He would often protest, saying, 'I don't want to go out, I want to be with you and the girls.' But I knew that the best thing for him at the end of a punishing week, was a pint of Bass and a laugh with his mates.

We both adored Friday nights. Charlie would bring a jug of beer home for me with the fish and chips and we would sit at the table, talk about our week and plan what we were going to do over the weekend. We never did anything terribly exciting, just the normal things that parents with young children do, but it was a joy just to be together.

Charlie would sometimes leave a list of things for me to do when he left in the morning to go to work, and often I would only get through half of the list before getting bored and taking the girls off somewhere. Consequently, when he rang later in the day to ask if I'd done everything, I had to say that I'd been too busy – even though I knew that he knew I hadn't. But he never got cross with me; he just took the list to work the next day and did it himself.

I liked leaving him to do all the bills and talk to the bank manager because he did it so well, and also because he was always much more diplomatic than I was. My forte was writing the stinging letters of complaint, which were sometimes needed when Charlie's diplomacy wasn't enough.

Apart from my reluctance to do certain jobs, which I considered better suited to my husband, I usually managed to keep the household running smoothly. And when Charlie came home in the evening and I had occasion to tell him of an achievement of which I was particularly proud, I would always end by saying, 'Did I do good, Charlie?' and he would look at me and reply, 'You did good, Katie.'

And that was all I needed. That was all the praise I ever needed.

One weekend we went to stay with Charlie's mother Jane in Godalming. Charlie told me to pack something smart to wear. He said we would be going away for the night – his mother was going to look after the girls and we were going to escape, but I didn't know where to.

I was very excited as I drove the car out of Godalming; Charlie was navigating but wouldn't give me any clues about our eventual destination. When I saw the signs for Winchester, I guessed where Charlie was taking me and I knew we were going to have a great night. We booked into the Hotel Du Vin, and the manager, Michael, made a point of coming over to greet us. Charlie was a regular guest at the hotel. Cinewessex, the facilities house that he used for most of his editing, was just across the road, and The HDV (as it became known), was very handy for entertaining clients.

I was always very jealous when he said he would be staying there because he always went on about what a fantastic place it was – very relaxed but with really exceptional food and a top-notch wine list. He always said he wished I could be there with him and now I was – and what's more, we were alone. But when we got to our room, things got even better.

The room had a big wrought iron bed, with crisp white sheets. The bath was large, the towels where huge and fluffy and I could have quite happily stayed there all afternoon, dozing in the soft autumn sunlight that was filtering in through the window. Charlie could see me eyeing up the plumptious pillows and being mindful of my fondness for goose down, decided to take me off to the cinema. It was just a short walk down the road – a tiny place that only seated about thirty people, but they served real cappuccino and there were no screaming children or ladies with big hats to spoil the view. We settled down in our seats and watched *The English Patient* and I don't think I have ever been more captivated by a film.

We walked back to hotel, bathed and dressed for dinner. When we got down to the bar we ordered a drink and settled into a comfy sofa to study the mouth-watering menu. I hardly knew what to do with myself – Charlie and I were alone for the first time in months and we had the whole evening ahead of us. Knowing the phone wasn't going to ring and that we weren't going to be awoken at some ungodly hour of the morning by one of our daughters was a delicious prospect indeed.

The evening was everything it should have been. The food was superb and the company was, as always, an utter delight. We had been married for over eight years, yet the thrill I felt at being alone with Charlie was just as strong as when we'd first met. Being in his company was utterly addictive. I had never taken any drugs – never even had a drag on a joint, but I knew what it was to be high. I didn't need cocaine, I had my own private stash of 'charlie' – and he gave me such a rush that I was permanently blissed-out. When we were asked out to dinner together I usually started off fairly quietly, but by the end of the evening

I was flying. It wasn't that I'd had too much to drink – I was just intoxicated by the balding bloke at the other end of the table. A naval friend of Charlie's once told him that I was the most exciting woman that he'd ever sat next to at dinner. I don't remember what I did to make such an impression, but I did know that my vivaciousness was due entirely to my being under the influence of C.J.S.B.

We left the Hotel Du Vin and drove back to Godalming feeling relaxed and refreshed and decided to take the girls out for a walk in the grounds of Charterhouse School. We set out across the playing fields with Rosie running on ahead of us, and eventually found ourselves at the newly-built running track. Charlie had a quick look, took off his jumper and said, 'Fancy a race?' I was a little startled at such a suggestion, but agreed, and we lined up at the start. Jane shouted 'Go!', and off we went.

I can run pretty fast, but Charlie powered past me and I just managed to catch up with him at the end of 50 meters, beating him by a head. It was only when I stopped to catch my breath that I thought, 'Hang on a minute, he's not supposed to be able to do that – he can't do that, it's just not possible'. Jane and I stood in stunned silence as Charlie sat down to recover, saying nothing, but both realising that we had just witnessed something truly remarkable. Charlie's fitness had declined over the years and he had reached the stage where he tired easily – in fact he couldn't walk more than a few hundred yards without pausing to rest. Yet we had just seen him sprint like an eighteen-year-old – so how did he do it?

The answer is I do not know.

He had done something for which there was, and still is, no rational explanation. His left ventricle was grossly distended and barely functioning. A healthy ventricle contracts with the same action as a hand making a fist – Charlie's ventricle had deteriorated to such an extent that it now contracted with the action of an arthritic hand squeezing a ripe peach – in other words hardly at all. Chris Burrell was constantly amazed that Charlie continued to lead a normal life with such limited cardiac output, so the fact that we had just seen him hurtling down a running track was nothing short of a miracle.

Charlie's heart went into flutter again that September and Chris refused to consider traumatising him with a further bout of the dreaded cardioversion. He had written to Professor Campbell in Newcastle with a view to him doing a bit more electrical jiggery pokery, but in his reply, Prof. Campbell was very negative about the chances of success. The horrible prospect of more open-heart surgery seemed to be looming ever closer, so we decided to go and have a chat with Chris.

He wasn't a happy bunny. It had been a constant battle for him to try and keep his friend out of hospital and he knew that Charlie would find it a struggle to maintain his present quality of life when his heart was jumping about like a flamenco dancer on speed. He went through the all-to-familiar routine of telling Charlie to take off his shirt and lie on the couch and then attached the electrodes to his chest with the weary resignation of a man who knows too much. When it was all over he sat studying the trace – but then his care-worn demeanour was suddenly replaced by a look of complete bewilderment. Charlie had done it again – his heart had decided to stop fluttering and settle into a lovely sinus rhythm just for the hell of it.

We sat in the consulting room feeling a bit dazed – after all we had been bracing ourselves for bad news. I still had to ask my question, even though I knew that Charlie really didn't want to hear the answer. I had to know when Charlie would have to undergo a valve replacement operation, but Chris was rather reluctant to give me a firm answer. If I'd been honest with myself, I would have known that Charlie's only chance lay in a heart transplant. His poor battered heart was simply not capable of undergoing any more surgery and his left ventricle was totally shot. I couldn't face it, so I didn't face it – Charlie and I both knew the score, but we never talked of it.

It was understood.

Chapter Twenty-Six

We spent Christmas 1997 at home. Jane, her husband John, Eddie and Pixie all came to stay with us and we had a ball. Charlie looked really well and he was happy doing what he loved most – entertaining. Building the new room was the best thing we could have done, even if it did mean that I had to wear the same clothes I had been wearing for years.

We spent Christmas evening sitting around the new 8ft chestnut table that we had commissioned to fit in the room and we laughed and talked long into the night. It was so good to see my mother-in-law throwing her head back and roaring with laughter; she had been through so much in her lifetime that if anybody deserved to be happy, she did.

Ed was on stonking form, which probably had something to do with the fact that he was just about to announce his engagement. He had met a fantastic girl called Christobel de Cruz. We had only seen her on a couple of occasions, but we knew right away that she was the one for Eddie. Charlie christened her Bubble and soon everybody abandoned calling her Christobel, and chose to use her new nickname – even Ed.

She was definitely not the kind of girl that any of us expected him to choose, but she was perfect for him. I had always envisaged him ending up with some Alice-banded Bennedon girl, with a mouthful of plums and a head full of frippery and bobbins – but Eddie decided to surprise us all.

Bubble was from Canvey Island, talked with a total absence of fruit and had a head full of literature. She was smart as a whip and she loved books – devouring them at an astonishing rate – but her greatest asset was her generosity of spirit. She was uncommonly kind and thoughtful and when she sent us birthday cards, she always looked up an appropriate quotation to write inside. Her love for Ed was apparent from the day I met her, but she didn't take any nonsense from him. If he ever got puffed-up and pompous, she would fire off a few well-chosen words in his direction and totally deflate him. We were very similar in that respect, because if Charlie started showing any signs of pomposity I did exactly the same thing. She was a perfect foil for Ed; they had a mutual love of football and opera and it was a foregone conclusion that they would make each other very happy.

Pixie had also fallen in love, with a girl called Alex. Her past relationships had been notable for their transient nature, but this time she seemed to be totally committed. It was wonderful for me to see how the whole family had become so happy and settled. I think it was the best Christmas we'd ever had.

In the New Year, Rosie celebrated her fourth birthday with a party at home. A woman came dressed as a mermaid and entertained twelve hyperactive children, whilst I stood in the kitchen with Beth, eating Cadbury's mini rolls and drinking tea – it was the best £50 I've ever spent! Rosie had a fine time and was very excited when her Daddy walked in through the door. He'd come home from work early to join in with the party, and stood watching proudly as his birthday girl blew out four pink candles and then decapitated a hideous fondant Barbie.

Home (well, as if from!!)
2nd Feb '98

Darling darling R,

I can't believe that the time has come again for me to write to you – and this time I'm in the office. I suppose one of the features of the year – and you've just turned four years old – is that I've been balancing work and family, and trying to make sure that I get enough of you and Alice. But there's been a big change in that this year because Mummy has stopped working.

After Alice was about seven months old Mummy went back to work at Westcountry, and you were looked after by a girl called Karen. Mummy began to be very affected by you being unhappy at her continuing to work – you used to get up in the morning and say to her 'Please don't go today, Mummy'. When it came to you telling us that 'Karen's not a nice lady' she had to go; Mummy left work, and you were much happier.

You've also been at playgroup for the first time. You took the move very well – without batting an eyelid – and are very happy at The Jays. You've also been going to Ugborough playgroup as well. And, after much pestering Mummy got you into ballet classes – from which you emerged exhausted and, after about week three, declared that you never wanted to be a swan again !!

What else, this year? As Alice has got older, started to walk, and then started to talk, she has become more interesting to you – and you have actually started playing together. This morning, charm itself, you wandered in in your pyjamas and said 'Good morning, darling' to her and gave her a big kiss. You are very polite, always (or almost always) saying 'please' and 'thankyou' – and knocking on doors. You still fight at most mealtimes, and largely seem incapable of sitting still and feeding yourself – leading to huge stand-offs with Mummy. Your mind is ever active, and you are very cute in an argument. You've also decided – largely unprompted – to teach yourself French, and have started counting to ten to anyone who will listen.

In the last year we have had a lovely holiday in France, staying in a rented house near James and Deb – giving you lots of chances to play with Emily and Grace. Tom and Ali came out for a week, and one evening she showed you how to be a ballet cat and horse in the sunshine on the lawn, while you were in your nightie – it was magical. This year Granny is taking us to Southwest France and we'll have a house with a pool. She and Grandpa came down for Christmas, with Ed and Pix. It was heavenly and you and Alice were deluged with presents.

I love you, always,

Daddy xx

Charlie and I celebrated ten years of being together that year. He rang me from work and told me to go and look in the study for a parcel. I found the package hidden in a cupboard and when I unwrapped it, I found a pair of tiny silver photograph frames, complete with pictures of Rosie and Alice.
He never stopped surprising me.

There was a card along with the present, showing a picture of a naked couple, each holding a glass of wine and pirouetting around a Hoover – entitled 'Passion'. The inscription inside read:

My darling Katie,

Was this what you imagined it would be like? !
Thank you for ten years of your love.

I will always love you.

C xx

Chapter Twenty-Seven

In February 1998 we were at home with the girls; it was a pottering Sunday and Charlie had decided to reorganise the wine room. I was in the new sitting room with the girls when he staggered in looking grey and breathless. He held onto the sofa for support and said, 'I've just found myself face-down on the floor. One moment I was lifting a box of lager and the next I was lying beside it. I think I must have fainted.' I was desperately worried and I told him to lie down on the sofa – which he stubbornly refused to do, saying, 'I'm fine now, I just need to get my breath back.'

I got the 'phone and broke a golden rule by calling Chris Burrell at home. He came straight over and brought his portable E.C.G. machine with him. After he'd examined Charlie he told him that he'd fainted because he'd been bending over and had stood up too quickly. He warned him that this might happen again and told him to go carefully. But it was what he didn't say which worried me.

Charlie had struggled for years to overcome the burden of his failing heart but it was always an unequal battle. He was working as hard as ever and had just entered his twentieth BHF video for a BMA award – but he was slowing down. Our walks became shorter and it broke his big old heart to have to pass Alice over to me because he was too tired to carry her. His weekend afternoon naps had now become a necessity rather than a luxury.

Tom and Ali invited us to stay for the weekend in the old rectory they'd just acquired near Tewkesbury in Gloucestershire. There was a huge amount of work to be done inside the house, but that weekend was spent tackling the garden. There was a lake was choked with bullrushes which needed to be cleared. but Charlie had to stay behind whilst Tom and I waded about, hacking away at the offending plants. I looked up from my labours and saw him looking plaintively out of the window. He just didn't have the energy to come down and help us and it crucified me to see him that way; but there was nothing I could do to help. There was nothing anyone could do – and Charlie knew it.

A few weeks later we bought a climbing frame for the girls, and had to dig a section of our raised lawn away to accommodate it. Charlie just stood and watched me dig away at the turf and barrow away the topsoil, because that was all he could do. He tried to help me a couple of times but after lifting a few shovelfuls of soil he was panting for breath and I had to take over again. It was obvious to me that he was changing. The signs were very subtle but I could see that he became weaker with each passing day. When I say weaker, I don't necessarily mean physically weaker – although that was apparent. No, what I noticed was much more significant.

Charlie had spent many years building up a kind of armour plating around him, which protected him against each new set back and against each new disappointment. It also served to make his worries invisible to the outside world and kept all the frustration and rage deep within him, bubbling and spitting beneath the shiny surface like a hot pot inside a pressure cooker. The years had weakened his armour. The salt of our tears had fallen on the rivets that held the polished steel plates together and they had started to rust away.

Charlie used to walk into the bathroom each morning with a weary resignation, knowing that he was once again going to have to take a potent cocktail of drugs -but he always did it without complaint. But when he began to grumble about the pills, I started to worry. He had bounced back so many times that I had grown complacent about his ability to cope with the strain of it all – he even began to proudly pat his tummy at one stage, saying, 'I'm building up my fat reserves so I can be ready for the next operation.' But he'd stopped saying that to me and he'd grown much thinner of late.

Nevertheless, all that was unimportant because he wasn't simply losing weight – he was losing will.

The armour was falling away from him piece by piece, leaving him vulnerable and unprotected and I was helpless to prevent it. It didn't matter that I took Alice from his shoulders when he tired, or that I left him to sleep longer on Sunday afternoons – he was tired, but it was a fatigue that no amount of rest could abate. Charlie was tired of the worry, of the endless injections, of the horrible electric shocks that left him physically battered and mentally scarred. I think by that point he was just tired of it all.

A few weeks later he sent this e-mail to Alex Ashworth. They had dispensed with the formality of addressing each other by their Christian names some years before, and now Alex and Charlie had simply become 'Fat' and 'Bald':

Subject:	The loveliness of you
Sent:	20/3/99
From:	Charles Boydell
To:	Alex Ashworth

Dearest waistline-challenged friend,

I'm sitting here killing time until the management relief column arrives and I can disappear and get a sandwich or pasty for my lunch. So far just a Cup a Soup and a bag of Doritos, not nearly nourishing enough for a growing boy. All is well at home; we had a very good weekend when we went to Tom and Ali's. Their house is quite extraordinary – circa 1720 Georgian red brick rectory in a Queen Anne style (according to Pevsner) with big rooms, tall ceilings, and overgrown grounds including a small temple, reflecting pool, and pond/lake. They have taken on a job similar to painting the Tamar bridge with a nailbrush, though.

We're looking forward to booking you in for a weekend when you feel that you have exhausted all the hospitality on offer from your real friends in the county. I'm sure Kim can be persuaded to bring you with her, if we pay her the same rate as last time to ease the discomfort.

I'm so pleased that it is Friday – it has been a nightmare week trying to prepare a £500,000 plus tender for some Channel Four work. So early starts, late finishes – not as late as yours though. I hope that you don't overdo it – not with your advancing years. That milestone birthday draws ever closer – and I shall be E-mailing everyone to let them know.

Love squeezes through the 'phone line to you from us.

As ever, yours until it ends.

The hairy man of Ugborough.

'As ever, yours until it ends.' – those are not the words of an optimistic man. Charlie knew he was slowly declining and all I could do was watch it happen and scan the papers each day for a medical breakthrough that might buy him a little more time.

His clients were still totally unaware of his failing health because he never discussed it and he gave no physical indications that he was anything other than totally fit. He flew to Norway for a couple of days to do some filming, but the job was delayed slightly and he arrived late at the airport for his flight home. When he went to check in, the girl at the desk told him that he was too late to board his flight, and that it was just about to take off. Charlie looked at her and said, 'But you've got to get me on that flight.' The girl gave him a hard Scandastare and told him that he had to have a pretty good reason, so he looked imploringly at her and said, 'I've got the best reason there is, I want to get back in time to bath my daughters.'

The ice melted away and she told him to run to the departure gate as fast as he could, and then called ahead to stop the plane leaving – and yes, he did make it home in time to bath his girls.

Chapter Twenty-Eight

Two Four were about to pitch for the biggest broadcast contract in the company's history. Channel Four had recently won the rights to broadcast the Chelsea Flower Show and Charlie had been given the task of writing the proposal document to tender for the job of producing programmes which had the potential of making his company a household name. He was very pumped-up about it. He worked long, long days and I barely saw him, but he was terribly excited about the whole thing and I loved seeing him that way. There are many men who find their work dull and tedious, but Charlie really loved his job and he gave it his all.

He was working with a chap called Anthony, who was the company's financial controller; writing detailed estimates about the cost of everything to do with producing each live programme from Chelsea. He came home one night with a page full of calculations to show me. I was very impressed and I told him how proud I was of him, but typically for Charlie, he refused to take any credit for the work. 'It's all Anthony,' he said, but I knew differently.

When the pitch was finished Charlie's working week returned to normal. He had to go away to the H.D.V. for a couple of nights whilst he edited a video for Audi, and he rang me from his room the next morning. He told me that Michael had put him in the best suite in the hotel and that the bathroom had a magnificent slate-lined shower, which was big enough for several people and a really big loofa. He said he was lonely and that it was of little consequence where he was, because I wasn't there to share it with him. He also said that he hadn't slept very well and that he thought he was coming down with flu. I berated him for squandering a lovely quiet night alone, when he knew that he wouldn't be disturbed at 6.00am by his noisy daughters.

I had prepared a Delia Smith special for his return and waited with the fidgety anticipation of a newly wed for the sound of his Tricker's on the quarry tiled floor of the hall. He looked all-in when he came into the kitchen to greet me and said he felt a bit rough and that his throat was sore. He didn't eat very much and went up to bed early.

The next morning he couldn't speak. He had totally lost his voice, but managed to whisper that his chest felt very heavy. Charles Wace rang up during the morning because he was off on a family holiday to the Caribbean and needed to make sure that Charlie was up to speed on everything whilst he was away. He knew that I hated Charlie being called about work at the weekend, but even he was a little startled when he asked to speak to him and I said, 'No.' I allowed a delicious pause before explaining that Charlie couldn't speak to him because he couldn't speak. I even passed the phone to Charlie so that he could demonstrate that I wasn't telling a big fib, and eventually Charles said goodbye and told Charlie that he would call again when he felt better.

I left Charlie to rest, checking on him every hour or so, but he didn't seem to want to eat anything or do anything except lie still and listen to his beloved Radio Four. That night I was aware that he wasn't sleeping. He was very restless and couldn't seem to get comfortable. On Sunday morning he looked truly shocking. He obviously hadn't slept a wink, and when he got up to go to take his pills, he turned to me and said, ' Katie, I feel really bad today – I think you'd better call the doctor.'

Alarm bells went off in my head. Big bad alarm bells. Charlie had been ill for so much of our married life that I had almost become complacent about it. But in the ten years that I'd known him, he'd only once said that he felt ill – and that was in the London hospital and then he wasn't ill – he was dying.

I could have called James Hill at home, I could have called Chris Burrell, but knowing them as friends was different from asking them to come out and work. I decided to do it by the book and was eventually put through to a doctor in a clinic in Plymouth. She was obviously in charge of deciding whether to send the doctor on call out to me, so I carefully explained what was wrong with Charlie and told her about his medical history, and then waited for a reply. Admittedly a very sore throat and tight chest does not sound life threatening, but I did stress that Charlie's condition appeared to be acute. She paused, and then in a chirrupy, doctorly, condescending voice, said, 'Right, what I want you to do is pop him in the car and bring him down to the clinic and we'll take a little look at him.'
'But I can't pop him in the car, he's too ill to go anywhere. I've got two small children who've been throwing up all night to cope with, and I can't just leave them.'
'Well then, just pop them in the car too and bring them along with you.'
'But you don't seem to understand, my husband is ill, he has a history of S.B.E and he's worried that it might have re-occurred.'
'So, what your saying is he needs I.V antibiotics? Well just pop him in the car, bring him down to us and we'll give him some.'

I couldn't argue any more, I put the receiver down, went over to Charlie, buried my face in his chest and wept. I just couldn't seem to make her see that Charlie was really ill. I felt so helpless and frightened, but Charlie just put his arm around me and silently held me with all the ebbing strength that was left in his tired body.
When I'd pulled myself together I decided to kick ass.
Nobody was going to put me down like that. I would not be dismissed out of hand by a woman who had no regard for my very real concerns and who had no right to call herself a doctor. I called her once more and said, 'Hello, I'm Mrs. Boydell, we've just spoken and you refused to send out a doctor to see my husband. I can't do anything today, but tomorrow I will pop my husband in the car and drive him to see his G.P. If anything should happen to him between now and then however, I will hold you personally responsible.'
Two minutes later she called me to say that a doctor was on his way.

I had given her conscience a big, painful, prick, but what I really felt like doing was pinching her ear lobe very tightly between my thumb and forefinger, popping her in my car and driving her over to see what 'acute' looks like, so that she wouldn't be tempted to put anybody else through what I'd just been through.

I know that many people call out doctors with spurious complaints – they get a slight headache or they stub their toe and then they rush to the phone and drag some poor G.P. out of his bed in the middle of the night. I understand all that, but I really feel that they should be able to recognise when a person is in real trouble

John Halliday was on call that day and when he saw Charlie's name on the list he came straight over. I was still seething about what had happened and my jaw was clamped down so hard that I was barely able to say hello. I took him upstairs and left him alone with Charlie.

When he came downstairs I could tell that he had not liked what he'd seen. Charlie was very ill. He did indeed have flu, which had settled on his chest and his weakened heart was not able to clear the fluid that was steadily accumulating in his lungs. John told me that Charlie really ought to have been in hospital, but because he knew how much Charlie loathed being admitted, he decided to let him stay at home. I was to keep an eye on him and not let him lie flat when he slept. He needed to be sitting upright, so that his heart didn't have to work so hard at clearing his chest. John told me that he would call the next day to see how Charlie was getting on, and then left me with my charge.

Charlie spent a week at home in bed. He hardly slept during that time and my nights were fractured by the sound of his coughing and the knowledge that he was just not getting any rest. I told him to try sleeping in the spare room, so that Rosie and Alice wouldn't disturb him in the mornings, and one day he came in to see me with a huge grin on his face. It wasn't anything extraordinary; it was just that he'd managed to find a position within his eight pillows, which allowed him the benefit of an undisturbed night's sleep. He even took me into the spare room to show me how he'd arranged the pillows – which sounds strange until you consider just how much that one night of complete rest meant to him.

His days were spent resting, and once or twice I left Alice with him whilst I went on errands. The weather was fine for most of the week and he would watch from our bedroom as the girls and I played in the garden in the warm spring sunshine. On one occasion I glanced up at the window and thought I saw a skull looking back at me. It gave me a real fright but it was only when I screwed my eyes up that I realised that it was not a skull at all, but Charlie.

Even though he'd been told to rest, Charlie was still worried about how the office would function without him. Charles had placed him in charge and he wanted to make sure that everything that Charles had briefed him about, was sorted. I could see the way his mind was working – he was fidgety and grumpy and so I rang the office and asked Charles's P.A., Amanda, to come round and take instructions from Mr. Conscientious. She arrived early one morning when I was in the middle of getting the girls dressed. She came up to our bedroom to say hello to Charlie and found Rosie tormenting her Daddy. 'You should look after your Daddy, Rosie', she said, ' You've only got one Daddy'.

Chapter Twenty-Nine

After seven days of complete rest, supplemented by numerous steak sandwiches for breakfast, and whatever else he wanted for lunch and supper, Charlie was given the all clear to go back to work. He had been hell to live with for the whole week because he was so desperate to get back into the office, and part of me was glad that he had been given a clean bill of health. He called the office straight away and spoke to Jill Lourie, another company director who was in charge of broadcast productions.

'Hello. Old girl', he said, 'I'm coming back to work tomorrow'.

I still had a nagging doubt that he wasn't sufficiently recovered to be allowed to return to work, so I rang Beth and told her about my worries. She knew me well enough to know that I was asking for her help, and she gave it. She mentioned to Chris that I was still concerned about Charlie and he duly came over on the Sunday to take a look at his troublesome patient.

He gave Charlie a thorough check-up and then in his soft, halting voice, told him that he would not be going back to work full-time for the foreseeable future. Charlie's face hit the floor. He had been on such a high about the prospect of getting back into the office, that he didn't even realise he'd been in heart failure for the whole of the previous week. I knew how disappointed he was and I knew he was cross with me for calling in the big guns, but I also knew I was right. Chris told Charlie that he could work for a maximum of two hours per day for the next week and then he would review the situation

Charlie didn't sleep well that night. I lay awake listening to his laboured breathing and feeling the each massive beat of his heart. I moved across the bed and placed my hand in his. We didn't speak. Sometimes words are needed, but that night touch alone had the power to transfer my thoughts and feelings with far greater effect.

The next morning Charlie was up and dressed and raring to go. Rosie called him over as he was putting on his tie. She nuzzled up against him – she always loved the feel of his face after he'd had a shave because he still used the same Trumper's Rose shaving soap that he'd used when we first met, and it always left his skin with a wonderfully soft glow.

He had acquired a thick growth of stubble during that past week and I realised to my shame that I had hardly kissed him in all that time. I found him incredibly sexy when he had stubble and I loved to take a part of his chin between my teeth and nibble it. I had let the opportunity pass – Charlie had shaved off the growth of hair which made usually made him irresistible to me, so why had I found it so easy to resist him?

I was scared.

Passion is quenched by fear, like a glowing steel blade in the inky water of a blacksmith's bucket.

I was scared.

He skipped off to work without a care in the world. His two-hour working day was supplemented by a two hour lunch break, and he came home as chipper as very chipper thing on its way to the chip shop. I had bought skate wings for our supper, as I wanted to give Charlie a treat. He poured over Rick Stein's 'Taste of the Sea' and came up with a recipe for a black butter and caper sauce. I offered to make it, but he said, 'I'll give it a go', and started rustling up our fish supper. It was delicious. His cooking was always delicious – he was happy in his work and I really began to think that he was going to be all right. The next day he went into work a little earlier and came home a little later, but I let it pass. I had never been a nagging wife and I knew enough to recognise that he loved being in the office and that it was giving him the impetuous to get better.

That night I sat reading *Private Eye* and found myself scanning the lonely-hearts column. It was something that I often did, because although I never allowed myself to imagine what it would be like to lose Charlie, something inside me knew that one day I would. It was like standing on the edge of a crumbling cliff – part of me hoped that the cliff would suddenly stop crumbling, and part of me understood that the fall was inevitable. But you never think what it will be like to lose your footing and fall, head first into oblivion. You don't let yourself imagine it until it actually happens, and then there is no time to imagine because you are already experiencing the fall. I didn't want to fall; but I could already feel the ground giving way beneath my feet.

When Charlie came in and saw me reading Private Eye, I looked up and said, 'I'll never love any man the way I love you.' And then I quickly corrected myself by saying, 'I could never love any man the way I love you.'

But we both knew what I meant.

We both knew.

On Wednesday the 8th of April 1998, Charlie was up and on the phone before nine and in work by ten. He was incredibly buoyant and his colleagues were startled to see him coming out of his office and bounding up the stairs, two at a time. He called Chris Burrell at lunchtime and said, 'Hello, it's me. Don't worry, I feel absolutely fine.' He stayed at work until 4.00pm and was home shortly afterwards. When he walked in the door I was busy battling with the girls. I came into the sitting room to see him and leant wearily against him and said, 'I'm tired.'

'Give me a hug, poppity', he said, and then he lifted up my arms and placed them around his waist.

I wish to God that I'd run up to him and flung my arms around his neck as soon as he'd walked through the door, but I didn't know. I didn't know that it would be the last time I ever got the chance to hold him.

He had asked a young researcher from the office to come over and discuss a forthcoming project, and Kent arrived at around 4.45pm. They came into the kitchen to make a cup of tea and then went into the small sitting room to talk about the script. I had a hard time trying to keep Rosie and Alice away from Kent, as they were determined to run up to him and tease him about his rather unusual name. His was not the only unusual name in the office at that time; the company also boasted a Saffron and an Apricot – she bore the name of the fruit tree beneath which she was conceived. I always thought it was rather lucky that her parents hadn't chosen to conjoin beneath a Kumquat tree or an Uglifruit for that matter.

Charlie and Kent were sitting on the sofa, talking over the script. There was a pause in the conversation and Kent started looking at the stereo, wondering if it sounded as good as it looked. Charlie began to talk – but he wasn't talking, he was just stuttering the same sound over and over – trying to say something but only getting as far as the first syllable. I was faffing about in the kitchen when Kent came in looking ashen and said, 'I think you'd better come and have a look at Charlie'.

I rushed into the sitting room to find him sitting back on the sofa with his arms outstretched and a look of complete bewilderment on his face. He looked like he was having 50,000 volts passed through his body. He couldn't understand what was happening to him and neither could I.

I think I shouted 'Oh my God, Charlie, No!' and then I rushed over and grabbed the phone to call for and ambulance. Charlie suddenly slumped forward and so I pulled his legs up and laid him back on the sofa. I knew what I had to do. But all the time I was thinking, 'It's not supposed to happen this way'.

I had prepared myself for Charlie's death – but I had prepared myself to walk with him down a long corridor, holding on to his hand as he lay on the trolley. I had prepared myself to lean over him and whisper that I loved him. I had prepared myself to see him disappear through the doors of the operating theatre. I had prepared myself to see the surgeon coming out through those doors and to walk towards me looking sad. He would tell me that Charlie hadn't made it. I was prepared for that. But I had not prepared myself for sudden death. Sudden death was just not an option.

I loosened his tie and checked for a pulse, but I couldn't find one and so I started cardio pulmonary resuscitation. I had never had any instruction, but I didn't need any, Charlie had made so many films for the British Heart Foundation that I could almost read the script as I went through the motions, 'A,B,C, airway, breathing, chest....'

I started to do chest compressions and then breathed air into his lungs, but between breaths I was trying to tell him – I wanted to tell him, 'Stay Charlie – don't go my darling, you can't leave your girls now, you just can't leave us now, please Charlie, don't go.'
I had to make him hear me, I had to stop him leaving me – but I knew that he was leaving me.
He was leaving me.
My love was leaving me.

I kept breathing and pushing down on his chest and the man on the phone was telling me to calm down, but I was calm. I told Kent to talk to him and carried on breathing into my dying husband's lungs. After the first few breaths the air was coming straight back out at me and I couldn't understand why. I could see his chest rise with each breath and I wanted my air to stay in him just long enough to give him the oxygen he needed to stay alive. I didn't know that his lungs were already flooded with blood and there was nowhere for my air to go except back the way it had come.

I pulled him off the sofa and onto the floor so that I could work on him better, and then Rosie and Alice came into the room and saw me pummelling their Daddy. Rosie was laughing – she didn't know what was going on, and Alice was crying because she was only little and she didn't understand why Mummy wouldn't talk to her. I yelled at Kent to get them out of the room but he was trying to give instructions for the ambulance crew. He asked me if I knew someone in the village who could come and take the girls away but my mind was blank. I just couldn't remember any telephone numbers. I couldn't think.
I couldn't think about anything except Charlie.

In desperation Kent took the girls out of the house, away from the ghastly scene, away from the pitiful sight of their mother trying to keep their father alive. He took them down to the end of the lane – they had no shoes on but he had to get them out of the house. A car drove past and the driver waved. Kent flagged the car down and asked the driver if she knew who lived in the house at the end of the lane. She said, 'That's Charlie and Kate's house.' And then Kent told her what had happened and she bundled Rosie and Alice into her car with her own children and drove home.

Anybody could have driven past at that moment, but by some miracle it happened to be the most capable person in the village. Peggy, the most level headed, down-to-earth woman in Ugborough scooped up my children and took them away, without fuss and without panicking. She never expected my gratitude, but she had it.

The 'phone rang – it was John Halliday calling to see how Charlie was feeling. I told him what had happened and he said he would come straight round. The 'phone rang again – it was Anthony at Two Four. Kent had called the office to tell them that Charlie had arrested and Anthony became terribly worried and called to find out if he was all right. I listened to him, but all I could say was, 'I'm sorry Anthony, I can't talk at the moment, can you call me back later?' It was a bizarre thing to say under the circumstances but it demonstrated how I was feeling. I wasn't panicking; I was on top of it. My mind was fixed and focussed on one thing and one thing only – keeping Charlie alive.

I kept pumping his chest and breathing into his mouth, but by that stage it wasn't just air that was coming back at me, it was blood and bile and all kinds of horrible internal fluids. It sprayed into my mouth, it was in my hair and it was all over my face – but I couldn't stop.
I couldn't stop.
Charlie was beginning to turn blue, but I couldn't stop. I heard ambulance com-

ing up the lane and then the two paramedics flew through the door. They told me to leave them and I let go of my love.

I let him go.

I went to the 'phone and rang Jane and she said she would get Eddie and Pixie and leave right away. I rang Beth and she said that everything would be all right and that Chris would be waiting for Charlie when he got to Derriford. John Halliday arrived and I asked him if Charlie was going to be all right. He looked up at me with his kindly eyes and said, 'It doesn't look too good I'm afraid, my love.'

I had to stay away from Charlie but I wanted be with him. I went to the kitchen door and looked out across the field that Charlie had coveted since the day we moved in. That was all he ever wanted – a field that he could stroll through on a crisp autumn morning and maybe a few sheep to keep the grass down. But when we had talked about his field latterly, he just sighed and said, 'What's the point of having a field when I don't have the energy to walk around it?'

Kent was in the kitchen with me. He was agitated and looked utterly shell-shocked but still he tried to comfort me.

I could not be comforted.

John came out of the sitting room, walking slowly and deliberately and I knew what he was going to say to me.

I knew.

'I'm afraid he's gone, my love. I'm so sorry.' My mind registered those words but I couldn't quite comprehend the enormity of what he'd just said. The absent minded librarian in my brain was busily trying to hide the words beneath a pile of pink mohair, but they kept bursting back out of the wool shop, back into my head, going round and round in my head.

'He's gone.' 'He's gone.' 'He's gone.'

Chapter Thirty

The End

John couldn't look at me, the paramedics couldn't look at me, Kent couldn't look at me. I went into the sitting room.

Charlie lay on the floor and I knelt down beside him and held him in my arms. And then I felt it welling up inside me. It was welling up inside me and I could feel it forcing its way out of me and I sat up, threw back my head and let out the wail.

The widow's wail.

It came from the very centre of my being and it came with a sound, an inhuman sound – the sound of a soul in torment. I opened my mouth and the sound came out and came out and came out. I felt my lungs emptying and still it came out. And when the sound had left my body, I leant forward and kissed the lips of my love. They were warm and soft, but his laughing eyes were closed. And with that kiss, a small trickle of blood emerged from his mouth and slowly made its way down his cheek. I watched it fall; and as I watched, I felt it extinguish the bright, bright flame of joy that had burned within my since the day I met my Charlie.

I felt the flame gutter and die.

When Charlie died, my joy died with him; but my love for him remained – as strong and passionate as it ever was. But there was nobody to receive that love. I had nobody to kiss, nobody to hold; nobody to laugh with, to lie with – nobody to love.

All I had was a body.

A dead body.

The house was suddenly full of people. Anthony had sent half the staff of Two Four over because he didn't know what else to do. There were people in my house. I didn't want people in my house. I didn't want people hearing the words I was saying to Charlie. I wanted to be alone with my Charlie, but there were people in the house.

I called Jane to tell her that her beloved son had died and I knew that she had been waiting for that phone call for the last nine years. I called my parents and then I rang Beth. I wanted Beth. She was the only person that totally understood me and I needed her now. I went into the kitchen and a woman that I barely knew came up to me and flung her arms around my neck and sobbed 'Let it out. Go on, just let it all out.'

I didn't want her arms around me. I didn't want her to touch me. I couldn't bear being touched.

And I had nothing to let out.

I had no tears to cry.

I felt nothing.

Nothing.

I wanted to tell them all to go away. Why couldn't they go away? They were just standing in my kitchen, listening to my last words to my husband and they had no right to hear those words. Those words were for Charlie.

Beth arrived and I told her to tell everyone to leave. Dickie Bird was sitting in the kitchen looking totally stunned. He wouldn't leave me. We had been through so much together. We'd serviced my Landrover together and we'd built stud walls and put up roof timbers together. He'd watched with pride as I married Charlie. He'd watched us build a life together and now he sat mutely and watched as my whole world fell apart. He left eventually and I took Beth in to see Charlie.

Chris Burrell arrived and we all stood and looked at Charlie's beautiful body. It was beautiful to me. It bore the scars of so many operations but to me it was perfect, unblemished – mine. There was something fantastic – something miraculous about the way Charlie looked as he lay on the floor of the sitting room. He had just been through a terribly traumatic ordeal. He had been pummelled and pulled about and yet he looked wonderful. His face was radiant, his cheeks were pink and his lips were red. But it was the look on his face that was strangest of all. He looked so happy, so peaceful – so content. The black rings under his eyes had gone, the strained expression had gone and all that remained was the face of a man at peace.

Beth had seen many dead bodies in her time. She had been a Casualty Sister and was familiar with death, but even she had to kneel down and place her hand on Charlie's chest. She had to reassure herself that he wasn't still breathing. He looked so alive. He looked so healthy – so happy.

Chris was in shock. He held on to my hand and said, 'I loved him, you know.'

I knew.

Chris had struggled so hard to keep Charlie alive and I owed him a debt that I could never repay. Charlie would not have lived as long as he did had it not been for the dedication of Chris Burrell, and Chris knew that he would never have another patient quite like Charlie.

Chris and Beth left the room and I knelt down once more and placed Charlie's arm around my shoulder – and I cried. He was warm and soft and I kept expecting his strong arm to tighten about me and for everything to be all right again – for it all to be some horrible dream.

But it wasn't a dream and it wasn't all right.

I reached inside the pocket of Charlie's button fly jeans and pulled out his pocket knife. It was a sailing knife with a blade and a marling spike, which had been given to him by his Uncle Stephen when he was a boy. He had spliced a short piece of rope to it and at one time there was a Turk's Head knot at the end. I held that knife in my hand and I cried again. Charlie had carried that knife with him every day since the day we first met. He carried it in his shorts during the summer and he carried it in the trousers of his dinner suit when we went somewhere smart for the evening. It never left him.

But now it was all that was left of him.

My parents and my sister arrived and I brought them in to see him; and none of them could quite believe what had happened. There was a body on the floor but Charlie was still in the room. My sister felt him there – we all felt him there. John Halliday was trying to get me to call an undertaker amid all the commotion, but I didn't know who to call.

He said, 'You can call the Co-op, or Perring's.' Well, there was no competition really. Charlie would have been so horrified at the thought of being carted away by the Co-Op, that he would probably have started unzipping the body-bag as they tried to get him out of the door. It suddenly dawned on me that I knew the owner of Perring's, he was a lovely man called Tim, and we'd had dinner with him and his wife on a number of occasions at James Hill's house. I tried the number over and over again but there was no reply. The only thing I could think of was to ring Annie Hill and get Tim's home number.

I called Annie, and when she answered I said, 'Hello, Annie, it's Kate Boydell. I'm sorry to trouble you but Charlie's just died and I need to get hold of Tim Perring, but I can't seem to get through.' There was a pause and I realised that I had just given Annie the kind of news that requires a very long pause before one is able to give an answer. I had blurted it out, but I was just not thinking straight. Annie told me that she was so dreadfully sorry and assured me that she would get hold of Tim. And when James Hill came home from the surgery, Annie told him the news, and he went outside and took a long, slow walk around the garden.

Deb Lapthorne came in through the door. My father had gone down to the square to tell her the news, and when he told her she started running up and down the stairs – she didn't know what else to do. She came over to me and gave me a big hug. Being hugged by Deb was like being embraced by a lovely, comfy sofa. Hers was a hug to beat all hugs.

Rosie and Alice came back home just as the men from Perring's were putting Charlie into a body bag. I hurriedly shut the door to the sitting room and as the girls stood in the hallway, nobody would look at them. Nobody wanted to catch their eye; nobody wanted to give away the fact that they would never see their Daddy again. I took them upstairs and got them into bed. I tried to read Alice a story but I couldn't stop myself crying. She didn't seem to notice and soon went off to sleep. I then went into Rosie's room and sat down on her bed. She turned to me and said, 'Mummy, you smell funny.'

I did smell funny. I was still covered in Charlie's blood and bile, my hair was matted with the stuff, but I was so out of it that I failed to notice. I read her a story and it took everything I had to get through that story without breaking down. I knew I had to tell her about her Daddy, but it had to be done in the morning. I would do it in the morning.

My parents were totally poleaxed. They wanted to stay with me but decided to go, so that I would be alone to greet Charlie's family. Beth and Deb took up their positions on the stools in the kitchen and kept a silent sentinel as I picked up the phone, opened our address book and began the terrible, terrible task of telling all the people that Charlie loved, that he had just died. It was like being in the school playground, playing 'Stuck in the Mud' – and I was it. All our friends were running around, getting on with their lives without a care in the world. But when I called them and told them about Charlie, it was as if I had just tagged them. They stopped running and stood still for a moment. They stopped laughing. They stopped playing. They just stopped.

I started with names beginning with 'A' and slowly went through each page of the book, dialling the number and hearing first a breezy 'Hello' and then a long silence as the impact of my words hit home. When I rang Chris Sutton, his wife Rebecca answered the phone and after I'd told her what had happened, she asked if there was anything she could do. But there was nothing anyone could do. Nothing.

Jo and Alex Mackie were visiting from Hong Kong. We were supposed to be seeing them over Easter, before they flew back home. I rang the number of Alex's father and asked to speak to Jo. The man who answered the phone started shouting at me. He told me that he was fed up with people calling his number when they were trying to speak to the Mackies. I didn't want him to shout at me. Why was he shouting at me? Didn't he realise that my husband had just dropped dead? He was a horrid man.

It took a very long time to ring everybody and still there were people to call. I hadn't spoken to Charlie's Uncle Peter, or his Cousin Nick, but I couldn't do it any more. Beth told me to go up and have a bath and so I went upstairs, undressed and tried to wash away the evidence of my husband's demise. As I lay amid the bubbles, I realised that it was the first time I had been on my own all day. But I didn't want to be alone. I washed Charlie out of my hair and off my skin, and then Beth came into the bathroom and told me that there was somebody downstairs who wanted to see me. I hurriedly dressed and went to see who it was, walked into the kitchen and found Chris and Rebecca Sutton standing there.

Chris mumbled something about wanting to see if I was all right and then took me in his great big arms and hugged me. He had driven 25 miles just to hug me. He was trying to be brave but I could see that he was fighting a losing battle. He just kept mumbling 'No worries.' whenever I asked him a question but he couldn't look me in the eye. If he'd looked me in the eye he would have lost it. I thanked them for driving out to see me, and then they left. They had been very brave, but Rebecca told me later that when they'd walked down the lane, they let go.

I got a fax from Charles Wace that same evening. He had had a strange feeling that something was wrong, and had called the office just after Anthony got the news about Charlie.

The fax read:

Dear Kate,

Sally and I are utterly devastated at today's news. You and the children are in out thoughts and we send you and the children all the love in the world. Words and letters are totally useless at a time like this, but know that if there is anything at all that we can do, please do not hesitate to let us know.

I hope in this horrendous time that you can take comfort that Charlie was probable the most loved person I know. He was so incredibly brave and so desperately loved you all.

As you know I am abroad – I am making arrangements to come back as soon as possible and hope to be back in England on Monday. Please excuse the brief note, but Sally and I were so anxious that you should know how much we are thinking of you. I hope that we will be able to meet up as soon as you feel able to see us.

In the meantime, all out love and thoughts,

Charles.

I couldn't imagine what Charles must have been feeling that night. He had been so close to Charlie and now he was so far away.

I opened a tin of draught Guinness – something that had always given me solace during times of stress – and sat down with Deb and Beth. My legs had gone into an involuntary spasm and I couldn't stop them. I was shaking all over. I was in shock.

We sat and talked until we heard the front door open and then Deb and Beth silently got up and left. Jane, Eddie and Pixie walked through the door. They came to me and I held them in my arms and they all three broke down at once. Jane had always been so strong for me and now it was my turn to be strong for her. I was giving back what she had given me, because I knew what she had been through all those years ago. I knew, because now I too was a widow at the tender age of 33, just a year younger than she had been when Charlie's father had died.

After I had told them how Charlie died, and that he hadn't suffered at all, I went upstairs to bed. I was exhausted but wired at the same time and I knew I wouldn't sleep. I closed the bedroom door and broke down.

The indentation of Charlie's head was still on his pillow. He had been lying there only a few hours before and when I had awoken that morning, I was greeted with the familiar sight of his beaming face. He would lie awake just waiting for me to open my eyes, and the first thing I saw each and every morning was my happy husband, smiling back at me. But I would never again wake to see his face. I would only see his face in my dreams, and in the faces of my children.

I lay in bed with an empty space beside me and I was trying to talk to Charlie in my head. I just wanted to know if he was happy – that was all I really cared about. Some women get angry when their husband dies, but I wasn't angry with Charlie. How could I be?

He had kept himself alive for me for nine long years and now he was free. Free of the pain and free of the worry. He had been living each day with a time bomb ticking away in his chest. He was constantly aware of every odd beat and fluctuation within the massive organ that hammered away beneath his ribcage. Day and night it went on, for nine long years. And one day the bomb stopped ticking and Charlie didn't have to worry any more. And I was glad of that – but when the ticking stopped, my world imploded.

I lay awake, asking for him to make a noise – not just a creak and groan but a big noise to tell me that he was happy. I heard the house creak and groan and all the while I was saying, 'No, Charlie, make a really big noise.' And then there was a really loud bang, over by his chest of drawers and I had my answer.

I stayed awake all night, and when dawn broke I waited for the sound of Rosie getting up and brought her into my room. I had to tell her something that no little girl should ever have to hear. I sat her next to me on the bed and I told her that her Daddy had died. I told her that what she had seen the previous day was her Mummy trying to save his life. She was only four years old and although she was bright, she had no way of understanding the full implication of what I had just said. She got up and ran to each bedroom, shouting 'My Daddy's dead, Granny. My Daddy's dead, Eddie. My Daddy's dead, Pixie.' She was very excited and I was worried that I had not explained myself properly. But when she went downstairs, she picked up a piece of paper and drew a picture of her Daddy, with a large, black heart in the middle of his chest and an angel above him.
She had just drawn her understanding.

Chapter Thirty-One

In the next few days, my house was besieged by a constant stream of people, who all wanted to come and talk about Charlie. One person would turn up; I would show them into the sitting room, they would cry, I would comfort them and tell them it would be all right. Then the 'phone would ring, and it would be somebody else calling to tell me how sorry they were to hear about Charlie. Then the door would open and it would be somebody else who wanted to share their grief, and so it went on. And all the while I was trying to sort out the funeral and deal with all the tedious time-consuming practicalities that needed to be addressed.

Charles Wace came over to see me as soon as he got back from the Caribbean. We had always maintained a cordial, if somewhat distant relationship; but after Charlie's death the focus of his affections was directed towards me and he became my friend and mentor. He pledged himself to protect and guide me, and in so doing provided me with a solid base from which to start rebuilding my life. Without his help I would have been lost.

After he left, I had to go down to the burial ground and choose a plot for Charlie to be buried in. The lady who came with me had a plan, which reminded me of the plan that you get to look at when you book a seat at the theatre. I had to be careful – after all I didn't want Charlie ending up with a restricted view and spending the rest of eternity stuck behind a celestial pillar.

When I got back home the man from Perring's came to collect the clothes that I had chosen to bury Charlie in. I had forgotten all about it and was suddenly thrown into turmoil because I wanted him to be comfortable in heaven. It sounds stupid, but it was important to me that he was wearing something that he could feel relaxed in. I raced around and collected his navy blue button fly Levi's, a country shirt, his Mid Devon hunt tie, a holey jumper of which he was particularly fond, suede brogues and socks. I brought them downstairs and then I broke down.

I'm sure that the man from Perring's had seen it all before, but he didn't know what it felt like for me to be holding the last clothes that Charlie would ever wear. He didn't know what it felt like to walk into the bathroom and see a small wooden shaving bowl, with a soft, creamy swirl which had been made by the shaving brush, the badger bristle shaving brush – Charlie's shaving brush, held by Charlie's hand only hours before.

He didn't know.

Nobody knew.

Eddie showed the man to the door and then took me in his arms and held me. He was a rock during that time. He shouldered the burden of my grief as he was struggling to deal with his own – he was brilliant. We worked on the order of service for the funeral together every day. We worked hard, because we knew it had to be right for Charlie's sake. And it was right.

Charles had put his office totally at my disposal. They arranged the flowers for the church, and organised the caterers. Being an ex-sound recordist, the most important thing for me was the sound system. I asked for the service to be recorded on mini disc. I wanted my girls to have a lasting record of their Daddy's funeral and I wanted to be able to give a C.D. to all the people who couldn't attend in person. There had to be fuck-off speakers in the church, because I wanted Elgar's 'Nimrod' to stir every single member of the congregation. It is a tune that sums up everything that is good about England and it summed up Charlie to a tee. When the music swelled, I wanted the hairs on the back of every neck to rise and quiver in unison. I wanted everyone to have a picture in their minds of button fly cords and Tricker's shoes; of rare roast beef and rich brown gravy and of the joy and the struggle which marked and marred that quintessential Englishman's brave and brief life. And at the end I wanted even Charlie to hear the fabulous Ella Fitzgerald singing 'With a Song in My Heart' – and I know he did.

The day before the funeral was dreadful – it poured with rain. The day after the funeral was dreadful – it poured with rain. But the day of the funeral dawned clear and bright, as we all knew it would. Something took me over that day – something very powerful. I felt benevolent, I felt happy. I felt that I wanted to hug every single person as they stood and waited to go into the church. I wanted to tell them that it was going to be all right; they didn't know what to say to me but on that day and that day only, I knew exactly what to say to them.

I wasn't doped up with tranquillisers because I don't believe in taking them. I wasn't upset – I didn't even take a handkerchief into the church with me. I was just proud. I was so proud to see over 400 people turn up from all over the world, to say farewell to Charlie. I was so proud of the service, which was simply perfect. I was proud of Eddie, who wrote his eulogy to Charlie on the morning of the funeral, just as he had done with his Best Man's speech on the day we married. I was proud of Pixie, for reading so beautifully the poem she had chosen by Christina Rosetti. I was proud of Alex Mackie for telling everyone about Charlie's colourful past and making them all laugh. And I was proud of Charles Wace for writing such a fitting tribute to his friend and colleague.

Six strapping men – six of Charlie's closest friends, lifted his coffin onto their broad shoulders. And six pairs of broad shoulders shook and trembled with the strain of holding back the tears of those six strapping men.

They carried the coffin slowly down the aisle of the church and I followed on behind. I held my head high and I kept my eyes fixed on the coffin, the simple pine coffin that had no adornment of any kind. It even had wooden handles because I knew that the bloke inside would have thought it much too ponsey to have twiddly bits of shiny brass all over the place.

I had walked down the aisle of that church with Charlie on our wedding day and now I was walking back down the aisle on my own. I was on my own, and the organist, who had known Charlie since he was a boy, chose quite by chance to play the same tune that he'd chosen to play when we'd signed the register.

We slowly made our way through the village and down to the burial ground. If you had to choose a place to be buried, then you couldn't do much better than Ugborough. The view is stunning and you can look right down the Ludd Valley and out to the coast beyond. Apparently, when Judgement Day comes, all the dead will rise up and be addressed by the vicar, who should be buried opposite them. But when Judgement Day comes to Ugborough, all the dead will rise up and say, 'Oi, vicar, why did you bury us facing the wrong way? We can't see the view.'

Peter Leverton, the vicar who had married us, had retired years before, but I asked him to perform the burial service, because I knew that he was the only vicar who was qualified to say goodbye to Charlie. He was saying goodbye to an old friend, not a faceless member of a dwindling congregation. He came because he loved us both.

The box with the case was lowered into the ground. The box with the case was sprinkled with soil – until Rosie decided that sprinkling was too slow and simply tipped a whole shovel full of earth into the grave. The box with the case was left in the hole and we all turned and walked away. The case was Charlie's body; but to me it was no longer Charlie's body, it was just an empty container. I had been to see the body in the funeral parlour and I wish to God that I hadn't. It bore no resemblance to my Charlie. It was grotesque – it was a thing, not a person. It looked as if it was just about to go for an audition for The Rocky Horror Picture Show and as I stared down at it, I half expected it to sit up and start belting out, 'Let's do the Timewarp Again...'
It was a cold, white, lifeless thing and there was nothing cold about Charlie. I would remember Charlie lying on our sitting room floor, looking pink and peaceful and I would forget the case in the box.

The air that day was heavy with the weight of sorrow from 400 grieving people. Some bit their lips and dug their nails into the palms of their hands. Some sobbed, some wept, and some were simply inconsolable; and I watched it all with the calm detachment of a woman who knows that the time for weeping is yet to begin.

People came up to me all day long, saying, 'If there's anything we can do, please let us know'. And to each person my answer was the same. 'It's not now that I need you, it's in six months time.' And they smiled weakly and walked away.

The funeral cars drove slowly out of Ugborough and I made my way to the village hall for tea and sympathy. The faces that bobbed up and down in the sea of black were all known to me, but the downturned mouths and welling eyes that had replaced their once-happy countenances made them appear strangely unfamiliar. I went to each group in turn; sometimes people talked freely, but the confines of the room and the crush of other mourners made some conversations awkward and stilted. I can't say that I felt particularly relaxed myself. I was no longer a wife, but a widow, and I had a duty to listen to what every person in the room had come to say to me. People were there to give me words of comfort, offers of somewhere to stay when it all became too much, and sympathy – most of all, sympathy

I had a duty to remain dignified, to receive the words and to offer comforting words of my own; but it's not as easy as it sounds. If you talk too openly you can make people cry, if you hang around for too long after people have offered their condolences, they run out of conversation and become uncomfortable. I listened patiently, and when I felt that the words were drying up I went on to the next group; and as I left I knew that averted eyes were looking up and shuffling feet were standing firm once more.

The room was stifling and the atmosphere was highly charged, but Rosie lightened the proceedings a little by prancing around the back of the hall, waving two chocolate éclairs skewered onto a long twig. As the mourners watched the carefree little girl they momentarily forgot why they were all gathered in a dismal village hall on that bleak April day. But when they turned back to their volavants and Battenburg cake they remembered; and their fleeting gaiety was replaced with the grim realisation that they had just been watching a little girl dancing at her Daddy's funeral.

As the mourners gradually dispersed I took Rosie and Alice back home for their tea. I left my family to put them to bed and walked down the hill to the Anchor. It was standing room only in the bar that night, we all needed a drink and it seemed fitting that the place where Charlie had first been welcomed into the village was the place where people came to say goodbye. The pub had changed hands over the years and not many of the old Anchor boys were still regulars. Trevor, the man with the big, white beard was already upstairs with Charlie; and Anson, the laughing Brummie who had trimmed his straggly beard especially for the funeral, would join them soon afterwards.

But that night the Anchor boys old and new, were united, upstairs and down.

As the barrels of beer were emptied, people felt able to talk more freely. There was no shame in getting emotional, no awkward pauses or mumbled condolences – people just let go. There was not a dry eye in the free house that night and when we had exhausted the supplies of beer, we drank what was left behind the bar.

I will remember that night for as long as I live. I will remember the people who were there with me and I will remember their warm and wonderful words.

I felt that Charlie was with me that night – but for the first time in ten years I walked home alone.

PART THREE

The reality of being a widow hit me shortly after the funeral, when the last of my guests had left for home. In the days that followed Charlie's death I was carried along by a kind of negative euphoria, that nullified the shock of what had just happened to me. I was totally preoccupied with the all events that led up to the funeral, and the duties that I was charged to undertake for the sake of my husband and my children. I had a house full of people to look after me; I felt comforted and supported. I felt loved. But people had families of their own, and their own grief to deal with; I knew they couldn't stay indefinitely and within a few days of the funeral they had all said goodbye and returned home.

You can read books on the subject of dealing with grief, and books about widowhood, but nothing can truly prepare you for your first night alone. Nothing can prepare you – nothing can protect you from the overwhelming feeling of loneliness, of helplessness and of hopelessness. You suddenly realise – 'This is it. This is how it's going to be for the rest of my life.'

And you don't want to go to bed, because bed is a place for being together. Bed is where you laughed and loved; bed is where you made your children and dreamed of growing old together. Bed is a desolate place for a widow – the one place that you cannot bear to be, but the one place that you need to be because of all the memories that lie under the covers and rest on the empty pillow beside you. You reach out in the dark but there is nobody there; and then you pray that he is happy – wherever he is; and you let your hand rest on the empty space and you try to recall what is was like to touch the naked skin of another person. But you cannot remember – and then you wish you could remember what it was like to be touched, but that memory has also faded into nothingness. And so you lie awake and wish that you were anywhere else than in bed, and in the early hours of the morning, when sleep eventually comes, your mind takes you back to when you were happy. And on waking you reach out again, and the sweet dreams suddenly evaporate into bitter reality – and you begin to wish that one day you will fall asleep and never wake up.

Chapter Thirty-Two

I received over three hundred letters and cards after Charlie died; I was inundated with flowers and every time I came home there would be a small pile of gifts and cakes waiting on the doorstep from concerned villagers. The drama of Charlie's death was played out in houses all over Ugborough; the story of how he died altered slightly each time it was retold but one thing stayed constant – the impact it had on everyone who heard it. The village was united in grief, but many of the people who grieved never really knew Charlie – they were grieving for me.

When a man dies so young and leaves behind a wife and two small children, the tragedy of it all cannot help but touch other families. People were affected by Charlie's death because it made them re-evaluate their own situation. There was a sense of 'My God, what would we do if that happened to us?' They took a fresh look at their marriages and the way they behaved with their children. It made them stand back for a moment and appreciate just how lucky they were.

Each evening I sat alone and looked at the hamper full of letters, not knowing what I would say to all the people who had written to me after Charlie's death. I couldn't possibly reply to each letter individually, much as I wanted to, and so I decided to write one letter. I knew it would be the most important letter that I ever wrote and therefore one that could not be hurried.

And then one day I felt that it was time. I sat at my computer and began to type the letter and when I read it back I realised that I had just written a love letter to Charlie; and I knew I would never write a better letter as long as I lived.

> Thank you so much for taking the trouble to write to me, it has helped me greatly to know just how many people share in my grief. The response has been so overwhelming that I have had to resort to typing my reply, but the sentiment that I am striving to express is no less deeply felt because of that.
>
> This is the hardest letter I have ever written. I have known all along that I would one day have to sit down and write to all the people whose lives have been touched by my beloved Charlie, I only wish that it had not been so soon.
>
> We shared the best of times and the worst of times; in fact, there was only one year out of the ten that I spent with Charlie when he was not admitted to hospital. But you would never have guessed that, because Charlie was always so ebullient and simply hated talking about his health.
>
> You are all very dear to me, and the sentiment that has been expressed in your letters has only reinforced the knowledge that I have had all along; that Charlie was an exceptional person in every way and that he enriched the lives of all those who knew him. He lived every day to the full, he gave me joy and

181

laughter and made me the happiest woman alive; and my girls will grow up with the knowledge that they never once heard their parents arguing – we simply had nothing to argue about.

The pain and suffering that Charlie endured would have made most men bitter and resentful, but it only made him more resolved to bring love into people's lives and to make them see that life is too short to worry about trivialities. Charlie never did; he saw 'the big picture'. He never dwelt on his own problems; instead he concentrated his efforts on helping other people, both personally and professionally. I can honestly say that Charlie only said that he felt ill twice, in all the time that I knew him – and on both occasions he was dying.

Mere words cannot adequately express the grief that I feel at this time. My heart is broken, totally and utterly and it will take all the strength I have to get through this terrible ordeal – but get through it I will. My darling Charlie would have expected nothing less from me; I have never let him down and I do not intend to start now. I have my two lovely girls to think of and I have an endless supply of strength and love from all sides to help me.

When I feel the weight of grief and sorrow has been lifted from my shoulders, I will carry on, walking straight and tall. So do not pity me that I have lost a man without equal, only envy me that I, above all others was chosen to be his wife.

Yours,

Kate.

Hundreds of people had written to me after Charlie's death to express their sympathy, but the letter that I have chosen to include here was written by Alex Ashworth. The eloquence and understatement of his words belie the depth of grief that he was feeling at the time, and still feels to this day.

10th April 1998

My Dearest Kate,

What you must be going through is beyond the comforting power of words, save that my thoughts are with you and the girls every minute of the day since I heard the awful news of Charlie's death.

You must know that your unending strength supported his own great courage to make his life with you entirely and completely happy. Together you built a wonderful home and gave life to your two beautiful girls, and you know that it all combined to make Charlie the happiest man on earth.

You both had to contend daily with the time bomb of Charlie's health, and rather than give in to the strain you came even closer in a uniquely visible, tangible and impervious love.

Even more extraordinary is that you shared this bond from the start. I know you immediately recognised Charlie as the man for you, which in itself is significant of something powerful. No less wondrous was the instantaneous effect you had on Charlie. As someone who knew his roving heart of old, it stunned me to see all his feelings and affections so suddenly fixed. In your ten years together your love for each other only intensified and he was the luckiest, happiest man I knew.

How many men are granted such a close union with another human being? A love like yours for him is granted to so few people in their entire lives. For

Charlie to have had your love for a decade is what makes sense of his short life. You were meant to be together and that cannot be denied.

Throughout the last day my mind had been filled with so many wonderful memories of Charlie. From our college capers to a day riding up onto Dartmoor, and more recent visits to your home. His presence is with me and warms me now. Of all the things I've been looking through, a recent E-mail from Charlie really captures the great battle of insults which characterised the relationship of two Englishmen who found an English way of expressing huge affection. I enclose a copy because perhaps it will bring a small smile to you, as it does to me. He was my friend and I loved him.

God bless you, Rosie and Alice,

All my love,

Alex.

I seemed to be consumed with administrative details, I had dozens of letters to write to credit card companies and to the bank and to all the people who had been used to dealing with my husband. Most of the letters were short and perfunctory, but one was not. It was very important that I wrote it because of the significance to Charlie. It was a letter to Simon Berry, of Berry Bros. and Rudd.

Dear Mr. Berry,

I am writing to you regarding the account of my late husband Mr. Charles Boydell. I know that he would have wanted me to convey to you personally just how much your wonderful company meant to him.

As I sit and type this letter to you I can see a neat pile of bills from Berry Brothers and Rudd Ltd, secured with a bulldog clip, stretching back to September 1988, which is especially poignant as that was the year that we met. Charlie kept them as a record of what we had ordered and he used to love looking back through them, musing to himself that he should have ordered more of your excellent wine to lay down when it seemed such a bargain. He would have – had it not been for his cautious wife! We did lay down a case of Chateau Batailly, which we bought to celebrate the year of our wedding in 1989, and Charlie always said that we should have bought another case at the time. How right he was, but we simply did not have the money. Now I sit and look at the case and wonder if I will ever have the heart to open it.

Charlie loved Berry's because it exemplified the values that he held so dear. He should have been born in 1900 not 1960, because although he worked in the high tech world of television, he embraced the dress and values of a bygone age. He would only wear button fly trousers, he hated shirts with pockets, he shaved using Trumper's Rose shaving soap, and he carried a pocket knife and a shilling at all times because he said a man should never be without either. He was a man of the utmost honour and integrity, a true gentleman, and the four hundred people who attended his funeral are testament to the love he engendered in all who knew him.

He did so love having an account with you, and we would always call in to No. 3 St. James's Street whenever we were in London. We never bought anything special, but your staff always treated us as if we were buying a case of Chateau d'Yquem. Berry Brothers were synonymous with Charlie and that is why I would like, if possible, to keep the account open under his name; I may not order anything for a while but I'm sure that I will in the future.

Thank you for giving my beloved Charlie so much pleasure during his short life.

I will drink a toast to you and all your staff tonight.

Yours,
Kate Boydell

Thursday, May 14th 1998

Dear Mrs. Boydell,

I returned to my desk this morning after an extended bank Holiday weekend to find your extraordinary letter waiting for me. In a modern world which seems to demand hard   headed decisions, based on maximising profit, increasing margin, decreasing costs, it is humbling to be reminded that there are intangible benefits of running a business that lie a million miles from a balance sheet. I cannot thank you enough for taking the trouble to write.

I do not think that I ever met you or Charlie when you came to St. James's street, but I have had the chance to show your letter to the team in the shop and many remember you well. What is clear from your letter is that he must have been a wonderful man. I am so pleased that a few companies remain which can maintain the old values, and that by simply doing our job as well as we know how, we can give pleasure beyond the contents of the bottles we sell.

It is also encouraging that the standards which Charlie lived by and evidently appreciated, although apparently under threat, are actually being recognised as more than an out of date way of life with no relevance to modern times. The more our wine business develops throughout the world, the more I realise that other countries appreciate the 'English' way of trading more than twentieth century England seems to do – hence the scramble by other companies to recapture a heritage which they had abandoned as unprofitable many years ago.

I took the liberty of showing your letter to my father. He started his career at BB&R in 1939 – in the days when the majority of our customers carried a pocket knife and a shilling. He was very touched that the values of his era should have been maintained by a younger generation – he retired three years before you began to buy from us, and finds great comfort in the fact that his ideals are still valid to customers and staff alike.

With your permission I will circulate your letter to the whole company. I know that everyone will be inspired by it.

Of course we will keep your account open in Charlie's name. This will mean that you will continue to receive invoices and mailings in his name as well, but if that does not worry you we would be delighted to do as you ask.

It would also be a pleasure for us to offer you lunch here at St. James's Street. I don't know how often you will be coming up to London in the next few months, but please consider the invitation an open one, and let me know a few weeks before so that we can arrange a suitable date.
Once again, thank you.

Yours sincerely,

Simon Berry

Wine Division Marketing Director

Chapter Thirty-Three

I was 33 years and I was a widow. I had a diary on my kitchen wall; the months stretched out ahead of me but there was nothing to fill them. My life was empty; the passage of time meaningless, save for the important events marked down in my husband's handwriting. Every day that passed brought new ways to remind me that he wasn't there – letters, bills, phone calls – each demanding the attention of a man who no longer cared.

I was now supposed to care – but I didn't.

I had to tell them all that he was dead. He couldn't come to the phone to discuss double-glazing, he didn't feel the draught – he was dead. He didn't care if the Visa company took away his card, he didn't need credit – he was dead. He didn't want any more shirts or shoes or time-saving gadgets – his time was up. Death certificates flew out of the house as fast as I could duplicate them.

He was dead.

My grief was visible – palpable. I wore it as an old soldier wears his battle honours – but there was no honour in what I felt and I was just beginning to fight the battle. I tried to fill the days with outings and my friends all rallied around and extended invitations to tea and Sunday lunch. Rosie and Alice took it all in their stride; they loved the extra attention and got used to spending the day with another family and falling asleep in the car on the way home. Those were the best kind of days, days when I could relax, days when I could laugh.

But there were some days when I couldn't go out. There were days when I couldn't lift my eyes from the ground. If I took the girls for a walk I would stare at the road; I didn't want to catch anyone's eye in case they tried to talk to me. I knew they would see it in my face, they would hear the catch in my throat as I mumbled a 'Hello' and they would note the down-turned mouth that failed to return their cheery smile. And then they would ask how I was doing, and I would try to make light of my situation when all about me was darkness.

The grey blanket of solitude wrapped around me; it smothered me. I could feel the weight of it pressing down on me and yet I was unable to throw it off. My girls skipped along by my side, tugging at the blanket, but to no avail. They smiled and I snapped; they laughed and I growled. I felt I was descending into madness, but hidden beneath the blanket was a straightjacket – hidden beneath my misery, a sense of responsibility. I tried to appear normal for the sake of my children – the straightjacket was holding me fast, but occasionally their innocent questions acted like tiny fingers, loosening the buckles.

Soon after the funeral, Rosie and I were in the playground and she turned

to me and said, 'Mummy, can you take me to the top of the church tower?' I said that one day I would and asked her why she wanted to go all the way up there. She looked at me and replied, 'I want to get as high as I can, so that I can reach up into the sky and hold hands with my Daddy.'
And as I put Alice to bed that night she looked up at me and said,
'Daddy gone to London.'
Heaven, London – what's the difference when you are not even two years old? They are both a long way away, they are both places that mummy says daddy has gone to when he doesn't come upstairs to put you to bed at night. I held her in my arms and told her that her daddy wasn't in London, that he was in heaven; and she said,
'Home soon.'

Death was an alien concept to Alice, but Rosie was old enough to know better. I expected her to understand why I got so angry. I expected her to forgive me when I told her that I felt like walking out of the house and never coming back. I expected her to comfort me when I broke down with the guilt and remorse of a day's unabated verbal battering. I expected too much of her. And then one day, after a major outburst, Rosie looked at me with her big, blue eyes and said, 'I know it's hard for you, Mummy, but it's hard for us too, you know.' I was brought to my knees with one sentence.

Rosie was only four when Charlie died and even in my distracted state I could see that she was beginning to suffer badly. I wasn't sure what to do at first, so I made her a book in order that she could draw all the things that she felt about her Daddy. She drew what she couldn't vocalise. She drew her Daddy lying in a coffin, with herself and Alice standing above, looking happy, holding balloons. She drew her Daddy lying on a cloud, wearing pink glasses and looking alarmingly like Christopher Biggins. She drew what she felt. She had come to the funeral and that was the best thing I could have done for her. Charlie didn't go to his father's funeral and it haunted him for the rest of his life.

I could see that Rosie needed help and so I asked a kindly lady to come and talk to me about how I should deal with her. She said I was doing all the right things for Rosie, and that she didn't feel that she needed to see a specialist counsellor, but then she asked if she could see me, and so I agreed to see the kindly lady a couple of times. She came over in the evenings after I had put the girls to bed; I talked and cried and she kept saying what a wonderful man Charlie sounded. She was patient and sympathetic, but eventually she asked me if I would like to go to a drinks party with twelve other widows and a solitary widower.
Mmm, sounds fun doesn't it?
She was a lovely lady and she meant well, but I began to have bad dreams about what I would say to the other people, when there was only one thing that we all had in common...

Widow 1.   'So, what did your husband die of then?
Widow 2.   'He was decapitated in a freak window cleaning accident.'

Widow 1.   'Gosh, that does sound interesting! My husband died of
           boring old ventricular fibrillation. Can I get you a refill
           – give me your glass, oh, sorry, didn't mean to mention
           the 'glass' word. Hemlock, wasn't it?'

I didn't see the kindly lady after that evening, but I understand why other people seek the help of a bereavement counsellor. She was fantastically sympathetic and on the few occasions that I saw her I felt like a huge burden had been lifted from me. But talking about Charlie didn't stop the anger or ease the pain of losing him.

I went to see a friend who told me that a woman from the village who had just split up from her husband had been discussing my situation. After saying how tragic it all was she had ended the conversation tactfully with the words, 'Separation is far worse than bereavement.' To that woman I would say only this, 'Try bereavement'.

Separation is painful but it only occurs when a marriage has broken down. One person usually makes the decision to leave the other, but however acrimonious the split there is always a chance of reconciliation. We had no such chance. Our relationship wasn't neatly severed – death had ripped us apart. There were no sharp words to cut the emotional ties, no heated arguments to cauterise the feelings that remained. I was raw; part of me had been torn away and what was left behind was a bloody mess.

It seemed unreal at first, rather like losing a limb. I still felt Charlie was there; I expected him to call me from work each day, to walk into the kitchen

Holding on

with a bag of goodies from Sainsbury's and start cooking supper. I saw his coat on the hallstand and his shoes by the bed – but he was dead, they didn't belong to him anymore and neither did I.

But what did I have to complain about? I was still young; I had a lovely home and two beautiful children. Charlie's pension had paid off half of the mortgage; he couldn't get life insurance, but Charles Wace had provided for me in such a way that I didn't have to worry about money for the next few years. I was laughing, wasn't I? Well no, I wasn't laughing because without Charlie nothing had any meaning – nothing gave me pleasure. I would have given anything, everything, just to have had a few more moments with him; just to tell him how much I loved him, just to hold him one last time. I looked at everything I had and felt empty; the pleasure receptors in my brain were now totally unresponsive to of any kind stimulus. I had been connected to Charlie on so many different levels. My enjoyment depended on his; my happiness was generated by seeing him happy. But the connection had been severed; all positive feelings had drained away and only negative feelings remained. I felt bitter, angry, sad – the bitterness tainted everything I did, the anger made me tense and unreasonable and the sadness nullified every single happy thought that came into my brain.

I needed time alone to come to terms with my loss but there was little time for peaceful reflection. Rosie and Alice woke up very early each morning and the noise would begin. It was there when I got up and it would continue until I put them to bed at night. It was just the sound of two active little girls trying twice as hard to attract the attention of a single parent, but for me it was torture. It might have been easier if Charlie had taken a less active role in their upbringing, but he was as important to them as I was.

When he was alive I dreaded him being away at the weekend because I found it so tiring trying to keep both of them entertained on my own. Now I had to be with them all day, every day, and they had to be with me. They bore the brunt of my turbulent emotions and try as I might I couldn't make then even begin to understand why I had turned from a calm, rational human being into a brooding, bad tempered ogre. I tried to love them and care for them just as I had done in the past, but their demands were now drawing from the reserves of a mother who was running on empty.

I was lucky enough to have the benefit of a fantastic support network of friends and family who rang me during the day and throughout the evening. But trying to explain why I felt so wretched was almost impossible. The people around me had lost a friend, a colleague, a brother, a son; but none of them had lost a husband – my husband. They just didn't know him like I did.

You take so much for granted when you're married, but when you lose everything, you start to realise that being with the same person for most of your adult life isn't boring or predictable; it's comforting and stabilising and fulfilling in a way that nothing else can be. When Charlie and I were alone he adopted a totally different persona to the one he presented to the outside world. The man in the sober business suit who boarded the train at Paddington station, was the same man who used to sneak away from me in Tesco's, hide at the end of the aisle and jump out at me when I passed. If I went to the hairdresser, Charlie would always call me from work and say, 'Your hair looks lovely', just in case he forgot when he came home. When we went out to dinner he would be the first one to pick up a comic aside that I had floated out over the conversation – my humour was idiosyncratic at times, but I knew that Charlie would always get the joke. And I could guarantee that at some stage during to evening, however deep in conversation, he would catch my eye and mouth, 'Are you alright?'

Those were things that only I saw – things that were meant only for me. They were part of the tapestry of our marriage – golden threads woven between the muted shades of everyday life. Individually unremarkable to the casual observer, together they made up the unspoken, unwritten testimony of one man's love for his wife.

How could I explain that?

The tapestry was disintegrating; the structure of my life unravelling before my very eyes, and my friends could only stand by and watch as I struggled to pick up the pieces.

I tried to retain a sense of normality, but every day I was reminded that my life was no longer normal. I took my first solo trip to Tesco's two days after the funeral; the house had been full of people and my larder was now empty. I set off with good intentions, but when I drove home I became so overwrought that I stopped the engine, sat in the car and started to scream. I banged my head on the steering wheel over and over again and cried, 'I can't do this. I can't be alone. I just can't be alone, Charlie.'

As I had been pushing my trolley along the aisles, I realised that I didn't care what I ate any more. I didn't want to cook for myself, I didn't want to shop for myself – I wanted to do it for Charlie. I wanted a shopping list written in Charlie's handwriting. I wanted to look down a neat column of mundane essentials and see 'Things I like' and 'Nice things' written between the ham and jam and Guinness. I wanted to choose scrumptious treats to keep my husband happy and healthy; tomato juice for his Bloody Mary, stock cubes for his gravy, smoked haddock for his rich, creamy kedgeree. But I finished my shopping and left the checkout with a half-empty trolley and a dull ache in the pit of my stomach. Eddie had told me to go by myself and at the time I couldn't understand why; but he knew that it was the first of many psychological hurdles that I had to overcome by myself. The hurdles are hidden from view; you don't see them until you are upon them and then you hit them with such force that they bring you crashing to the floor. Each time you have to pick yourself up, pull yourself together and get ready for the next one.

As I embarked on my solitary steeplechase, my first supper invitation seemed innocuous enough. Three weeks after Charlie's death, Charles and Sally Wace invited me over to their house and with just the three of us it was relaxed, undemanding and thoroughly enjoyable. But when I got in the car to drive home, I suddenly realised that I had nobody to discuss my evening with. There would be no post mortem of the conversation and the company, just a silent journey through the night. The loneliness of widowhood can manifest itself in many different ways, but each time you are reminded that you are half of what you were.

Charlie had gone, but I still needed an outlet for my thoughts, for my humour – black as it was, and for my angst. I needed someone who understood me totally, someone to whom I could say anything, without causing offence. Beth was that person.

My mind was full of scary stuff after Charlie died. There were lions and tigers prowling about in my head, and monstrous black beasts with sharp teeth and bloody claws. Beth was the only person who could go in there. She went in holding a stool out in front of her and cracking a huge whippy whip, and she kept all the beasts at bay. She knew when I needed comforting and she understood when I needed to be alone.

Time alone was a precious commodity in those first weeks, and of all the things that people did for me, taking the girls off my hands was by far the most beneficial. Beth came and took Alice one day whilst Rosie was at nursery school, and I had the luxury of a few hours by myself. I had time to think and time to reflect – but for me reflection was a very dangerous thing. I knew that I couldn't allow myself to dwell on the magnitude of what I had lost and so I blocked it out, but whilst I was alone one solitary thought came into my head. I was in the kitchen making a cup of tea and I suddenly thought, 'I'll never again hear Charlie say, 'I love you'.'

That was it – one notion was all it took to tip me over the edge. I went down, down, down. I stopped trying to be strong and gave in to it. I rang Beth and when she answered I said, 'Just give me five reasons to be alive, because I don't want to be alive any more.' Beth paused for a moment and then gave the answer that only a true friend can give. 'There are only two reasons, Kate.' And she was right. Rosie and Alice – nothing else mattered. They were my reason for being; their need for me acted like a bungee cord that pulled me back up from the suicidal despondency that I had plunged myself into. But at the time I just couldn't see it – I could only see one thing. Beth reminded me of what was important and she would have to keep on doing so, because she was now charged with keeping me alive, just as her husband had been with Charlie.

It was becoming increasingly obvious that I needed to have a complete break from the children, and thankfully my salvation came a few days later when I was invited to stay with friends for the weekend. It was a month after the funeral and it was to be my first proper social outing as a widow. The day started well enough; Rosie and Alice were at home, I felt like a grown up again, and by the evening I was discovering that being alone was turning out to be rather easier than I had envisaged. There was a formal dinner party in the evening. I was sitting amongst four married couples, which is a hellish thing for any widow to have to go through, but as the wine started flowing and the conversation loosened up, I began to feel more and more relaxed. Somebody asked if I had any anecdotes about famous people and I started to reel them off – much to the

amusement of my fellow diners. It was all going so well – I was flying by that
stage. I was funny, I was witty and the other guests were all laughing. It was too
easy. I thought to myself 'Hell, it's not so hard being a widow. I can do this.
Look, I have the whole table hanging on my every word. I can do this. I can be
alone.'

And then I started to run out of anecdotes, but my fellow guest demanded
more, so I began to wrack my brains for a suitable funny story. I could have chosen something safe, I could have chosen something mildly smutty, but instead of
that I chose to take a risk – instead I chose to tell the story that should never
be told...

I thought I had judged the sense of humour of the other people around the
table – and anyway, I knew my hosts would laugh no matter what. So I launched
myself off the precipice, went into free fall and began to tell the 'Licky Dog
Story'. I cannot tell you what the story is about, save that it concerns a little girl
and a dog, which is a very licky dog and ends up making the girl very, very happy.

Well, it started off well enough; my fellow guests were all still laughing and
the mood was buoyant. As I progressed with the story, I could tell they were all
waiting for the punch line; but when I came, it was more of a slap line. Each and
every person around the table looked as if they had just been slapped with a
rather distasteful, three-week old floor cloth. Their look of amusement changed
into one of disgust and even my hosts turned to me and said, 'Oh God, Kate,
that's really horrible.'

I felt the noose tighten around my neck and then they kicked away the stool.

If I had been on the ball I would have come back with a line like, 'Yes, and I've
asked for the dog's phone number.' But my brain was shrivelling, along with
what was left of my ego. I couldn't bear it. I had gone too far and I was left dan-
gling for the rest of the evening. My legs were kicking long into the night but no
one came to cut me down.

Charlie had always been there to give me a look or a nudge when he felt I
might be going to go too far. If he ever thought I was going to tell a story which
might be a little too risqué for polite company, he would pull me up sharp. But
he wasn't with me – I was a speeding train with no breaking mechanism and I
had just run into six stony-faced buffers.

I went up to bed early; woke at 6.00am, packed my bags and left, because I
just couldn't bear to face those people again. As I was driving home along the
M5 south of Bristol, I reached a point where the road splits and there is a steep
drop between one carriageway and another – and I decided that I would drive
through the crash barrier and kill myself. I didn't want to be with people who
didn't care about me anymore. I didn't want to be with people who didn't understand me. I just wanted to be with Charlie. At that moment I thought only of
myself and of my longing for my dead husband. I was so consumed by that longing that I didn't even consider my children and how my death would have affected them. I didn't want to consider what was right and fair – life wasn't right and
fair and I wanted not more part of it.

The barrier flashed past; it would have been over in a split-second but the repercussions would have lasted a lifetime. The urge to do it was very strong, but the love I had for my children was stronger, and so I left the barrier untouched and carried on driving home. And on the way home I decided that I had to go back to work, so that I could learn how to be with adults again, because I realised that alone, I had all the social graces of a chimpanzee with an excess of saliva and a speech impediment. Work would give me something to focus on, and whilst I was there I wouldn't be Charlie's widow or Rosie and Alice's mother, I would just be Kate – Scary Kate, the most fearsome editor in the building.

But I couldn't just skip back to work as if nothing had happened. In my present state it would be futile to even consider working a 10 hour day in a high stress environment. I knew I had to recover my equilibrium and the best place to do that was at home. So I drove back to Ugborough, back to where I felt safe, back to the bosom of my friends. And when I got home I found a casserole dish sitting on my doorstep. It was an unprompted act of kindness from one of my neighbours. She had given me the luxury of a hot meal with no effort; she had taken the onus away from me – I hadn't had to ask for anything.

That stew was worth a thousand words.

Chapter Thirty-Four

When Charlie first died I couldn't eat. I felt like I had a small boulder wedged beneath my breastbone and I couldn't get anything past it. Apparently it is the body's way of preventing the grief exploding out of you; the muscles contract for long enough to allow you to come to terms with what has happened and when you are over the initial shock, the muscles relax once more. That is one advantage, perhaps the only advantage of widowhood – you get to lose weight without even having to try. I had never had to resort to dieting, which I think had something to do with the fact that I had been born without the Chocolate Gene – I had the Mechanical Gene instead.

I am unusual for a girl, in that I eat chocolate but don't crave it. I can take it or leave it. The chocolate gene would have made me desire it; big gloopy vats of it, with nuts and caramel and shiny wrappings, which sweetly entice the unwary into the sordid ways of the Snicker and the Chunky Kit Kat Finger. But I had been born without it – so I would drown in the vat, rather than open my mouth and suck. Charlie was all about food and when he died so did my appetite. The weight fell off me like a margarine mackintosh; I became a walking xylophone and people would come up to me all the time and say, 'Kate, you're looking so thin.' And I would look at them and think, 'Yes, you pea-brain, thank you for pointing out the blindingly obvious – for your information it's called the Dead Husband Diet – very effective, but not one that I would recommend.'

Eating had become a chore, rather than a sensual delight. I wanted nothing more than to keep myself on the chubby side of Kate Moss. I went to the supermarket and stocked my freezer with pre-cooked panaceas for pining people and our previously underused microwave positively pinged with delight every time I came out of the larder. I still made an effort to cook for my children but I had no desire to cook for myself. Walker and Deb made a point of coming over at least once a week to feed me. They sat with me whilst I chased the food around my plate and they would not leave until the plate was empty, but despite their best efforts my healthy appetite had dwindled away to nothing.

It wasn't that I didn't want to eat; the sensation of running my hands over protruding ribs each morning in the shower was distinctly unpleasant and was more than enough to make me want to rush to the fridge and hoover up the entire contents in one go. I knew I had to eat in order to stay healthy; I didn't want to be thin, but grief was feeding on me, both mentally and physically. It also had the effect of rendering all food tasteless – no matter what it was, but it was especially apparent in the food that I cooked for myself in the evenings.

When Charlie was alive my evenings were alive too – alive with conversation, alive with laughter, alive with tastes and smells – alive with touch. But now one evening was indistinguishable from another; I spent each in exactly the same way – cooking something to take away my hunger, drinking something to make me feel relaxed, watching television until I felt too tired to stay awake. And once I was in bed I knew that sleep would overtake me and I could lose consciousness and leave my empty world behind me. Occasionally I would be too exhausted to sleep and would lie awake, staring out into the blackness, and on one such occasion I became aware of a presence in the room. I couldn't see anything but I knew that I wasn't alone, and then I felt a tremendous energy flowing into me. I felt it surge through my body – I was being charged up, just like a battery and I woke up the next morning feeling totally energised. I can't explain what it was, but it happened several times in those first few weeks and has not happened since.

 Somebody upstairs was obviously looking out for me but I also had people around me who were equally committed to my welfare. They told me that I had to go on; they told me that I had to eat, and they looked after my girls and me. Charlie left only a modest amount to me in terms of monetary value – his greatest legacy to me was his friends; they had sustained him throughout his life and now they were comforting me.

The phone rang constantly in the first few weeks after Charlie's death and my evening were filled with talking about Charlie, but gradually the phone rang less often; gradually people loosened their grip. Living in a small village rooted me back to reality; each time I felt that I was alone I would meet an old friend who would restore my faith in human kindness.

Two weeks after I got back from my disastrous weekend away I bumped into Nigel Littleton. I was bringing the girls back from a visit to the village playground when I saw him at the bottom of the square. Nigel had always been special to us, he was the first villager to befriend Charlie and he'd been a true friend ever since. The years had passed and even though I saw him less often, his greeting to me remained the same. He gave me a big soft kiss on the lips and a huge hug and then he asked me how I was. I hadn't had a proper chance to talk to him at the funeral and so he didn't really know the full story regarding Charlie's death. I talked about his illness and of how he'd died and when I felt I had said as much as Nigel could bear to hear, I stood in the middle of the square and let the salty tears of that twenty stone man fall onto my shoulder. Nigel was not ashamed; he just wanted me to know how much he missed his friend.

As we parted he asked if there was anything that I needed and I mentioned that I could do with a couple of loads of wood to stack for the winter. He said he would tell Ilkey the log man the next time he saw him and then he said goodbye and turned for home.

The next morning at 8.30 am I saw Ilkey's truck backing into the lane. He

had come with my wood as soon as he'd heard I needed it. I went out to give him a hand and we stood by his truck, stacking the logs under the trees that ran down the lane. Then, in his rough, gruff voice he said, 'How are you doing?'
I said, 'It's hard, you know Ilkey and I'm still in shock really, but I've got my girls and I think we'll be O.K.'

I talked and he listened – without embarrassment or awkwardness. Ilkey kept asking me questions as we stacked the logs, and when at last his truck was empty we parted on a handshake. I wanted to hug him, but I knew that he would have felt embarrassed at such an open show of affection. Ilkey was a man of few words – but that day, in his gruff, grunting lilt, he spoke volumes to me. Often the simplest of words have the greatest impact and his visit left me with more than just a pile of split oak. He had come to help me when he knew I needed him, and he didn't ask anything in return except his usual payment for a load of logs. The sum of money that changed hands had not altered in the ten years that I'd known Ilkey, and neither had he.

As various people drifted away, I began to discover the strength of the friendship of those who remained. There were many people that we had known as a couple, people who had come to dinner and called round for tea, but Charlie and I were such a self-sufficient partnership that we didn't seek them out as individuals. Even though I was at home all day I avoided the village coffee morning set. I was perfectly happy to see Beth once a week and to potter about on my own for the rest of the time; I had my girls and a husband whom I adored and that was all I needed. I had to reach out to people after Charlie's death; I had to open myself up to them and allow them to see sides of me that I had previously kept hidden. It was incredibly liberating in a way because I was allowing them to see me as an individual, rather than part of a couple. I talked about myself because I could no longer talk about Charlie; I was no longer 'we', I was 'me'. But I was very vulnerable and so suggestible at that time that if somebody had said, 'Kate, I'm going to call round and see you twice a week, just the check you are alright but I need you to give me five thousand pound first.' I would have given them the money. I would have given them anything if I thought they would come round and give me a hug every once in a while.

Physical contact was something that I craved day and night. I had the love of my children and I cuddled them constantly, but I always needed more than that. At first I wanted nothing more than a hug, but as the intensity of my grief built up, so did my longing for a physical release – and the effort of trying to suppress that need only had the effect of intensifying my anger.

My temper was terrifying at the best of times but at weekends my behaviour was totally out of control. I was evil. I positively loathed every second of every minute of every hour of those two endless days. I felt lonely and isolated and I had two active little girls to keep entertained, who fought for my affection and my undivided attention almost continuously. People would often say to me, 'Just ring us up at the weekend and come over, we won't be doing anything.' But I found that very hard to do. Weekends are a special time for families and I remembered that when Charlie was alive I always hated the thought of anyone disturbing our time together. Anyway, what if did ring up and the couple were in the middle of a huge row, or had already invited another family over? What would they say to me and how would I deal with the refusal when it had taken all my courage just to pick up the phone? I didn't call because my need for company was always overshadowed by my constant fear of rejection. As a consequence my friends began to think that I was too proud to ask for help, but it wasn't pride – it was fear.

I grew to hate the sight of happy fathers with happy children, doing fun things in the happy, restful time that is the weekend; because I knew that for Rosie and Alice, spending time with their father meant playing on the mound of grass which marked his grave. I wanted what all my friends had – a husband and a happy life, and being denied them was sometimes too much to bear. I raged against it – but all too often my rage was directed at two little girls who were feeling much the same as I.

I had to vent my anger, I needed a release, but not controlled explosion – my body was crying out for something more.

When Charlie first died, I was numb. But as my senses began to re-awaken and the nerve endings began to spark, so my lower brain began to stir from its slumbers. My higher intelligence was trying to deal with all the madness and the anger and the pain by listening to 'Verdi's Requiem' in a quiet room. But up from the basement came the throb, throb, throb, of 'Push It', by Salt and Pepa. My intelligent side tried to ignore the uncouth music and the vulgar lyrics, but the boys in the basement wanted to play it louder.

And soon the music reached my ears and I too began to get stirrings. That was it. That was the solution to forgetting the terrible, terrible thing that had just happened to me.

I would have sex.

I would have sex; but not nice, gentle, romantic sex – I wanted it long and hard and rough. I wanted a long, hard man to come along and give me rough sex, so I could get rid of all my pent-up pain, all my pent up frustration, all my rage and anger.

But I didn't do it.

It was what I thought I wanted, but it wasn't what I needed. I just needed time. I needed time to heal, and if I had tried to have meaningless sex with a complete stranger I would have hated myself in the morning.

Shame, though.

Chapter Thirty-Five

I went to France on holiday in July. It was something that we had been looking forward to as a family since the winter of the previous year, but now I was doing it on my own with two small children. The flight over was a nightmare in itself, but after a two-hour drive to the house and a trip to the supermarket to get supplies, my nerves were pretty ragged. All I wanted to do was get the girls bathed and into bed – but they had different ideas. They were excited and not a bit sleepy; they wanted to bounce up and down on the bed but I just wanted to get in the car and drive back home. I felt vulnerable being away from my home and my friends, and even though I was staying with Charlie's mother and various members of her family, I felt alone.

After struggling to put my girls to bed for nearly an hour I began to loose my patience. Everybody was outside, enjoying a glass of wine in the early evening sunlight. The sound of laughter was tinkling in through the open window, only to be swept brutally aside by my furious screams, which bounced around the mellow stone walls of the farmhouse, shattering the bucolic calm.

I came very close to physical violence that night. I came as close to a nervous breakdown as I will ever come. I wasn't in the Dordogne – I was in purgatory. I was in a staggeringly beautiful place that Charlie would never see and I hated it. I hated the wooded valley and the rolling hills above. I hated the pretty market town perched on the hilltop. I hated the sparkling water of our heated pool. I hated every mouthful of the wonderful food that we ate every day. I hated everything because he wasn't there to share it with me.
It was too much too soon but I knew I had to do it for my children. They needed a holiday and I couldn't deny them that.

Rosie learned to swim on the second day and that alone made the whole trip worthwhile. She spent the rest of the fortnight cavorting in the crystal waters of the pool like a baby dolphin, whilst Alice bobbed up and down in her floatation suit, screaming encouragement. They were happy – and that was all that mattered to me.

Rosie and Alice deemed our summer holiday a great success, but I was never more relieved than when I pulled up the lane of Cumberland Cottage and walked into my own home once more. I had asked Jeff the builder to do some work whilst we were away; I wanted to redecorate the room where Charlie had died so that I could use it as my study. Jeff had taken the ceiling down, exposed a few inches of the floor joists above and then plaster boarded in between. This, I hoped, would give more height and add a bit of interest to an otherwise unremarkable room. That was the idea, but I was in for a shock when I walked through the door a fortnight later.

The beams were in a terrible state, I nearly wept when I saw them and it was all I could do to stop myself ringing Jeff and asking him to put the ceiling back up. But rather than admit defeat I decided to attack the problem. I began sanding the beams; I worked on them until the rough-hewn timber became smooth and then when I was satisfied, I set about waxing the beams until they were lustrous and golden. They looked fabulous.

I spent the next few nights colour washing the walls and painting the ceiling; I bought new lamps for the bookcase and a Turkish rug for the floor, and then when it was finished I stood back to admire the total effect. But I didn't feel thrilled with my success; I just stood in the doorway and burst into tears. The room looked fantastic but all I could think was, 'What's the point? Charlie's not here to see it.'

I tried to keep life as normal as possible for Rosie and Alice but they were missing Charlie too. Rosie would burst out crying and sob, 'It's not fair, everyone else has got a daddy and all we've got is photographs to look at.' And there was nothing I could say to stem the flow of tears – all I could do was hold her and promise her that I would meet somebody one day, somebody who would look after us and make us all happy again.

But it was an empty promise, because at the time I didn't believe I would ever be happy again.

Sally Wace invited us to come over for the day in early August. It was hot and sultry, and after we had eaten we went for a dip in the pool. Rosie and Alice were happily splashing around with Sally and the children and I went to the deep end and dived under water. But rather than coming to the surface, I stayed underwater. I felt that I could just open my mouth and stay there forever. It was calm underwater; the children's annoying screams had been reduced to muffled irrelevancies. I felt weightless. I felt that the burden of grief that had been pressing down on me had just floated away. I lay face-down and stared at the bottom of the pool. I came up for air and then I dived under again but this time I didn't want to re-surface. The warm water and the feeling of weightlessness had a sweetly soporific effect on me; the voices were getting fainter and I started to drift away. Sally had begun to get worried about the length of time I had been underwater; she swam over to me and stayed by me until I re-surfaced. I had been lying face down and motionless and she wanted to make sure that I was all right – I wasn't all right but I wasn't going to try to kill myself in front of my children.

When Charlie was alive I never imagined what it would be like to have to bring up Rosie and Alice on my own, because that would be like admitting that his death was inevitability, and to me it wasn't. Part of me always believed that he was invincible, and that he would somehow survive for long enough to see his girls grow into adulthood. I had always thought about his funeral, however, but for some reason I never connected it with the reality of his death.

Strange how the mind works.

I had a very romantic ideal of how it would be. I saw myself at the funeral, dressed in black, looking chic and vulnerable with the eyes of all the men upon me. I saw myself sitting at home, sifting through all the dinner party invitations and being besieged by hordes of adoring men who wanted to make it all better. But the reality of my situation was proving to be somewhat different.

I soon discovered that when you're widowed men stay away from you – and in my case it wasn't difficult to see why. I felt like I was a big, black suppurating boil – impossibly tender and liable to burst apart at any moment. I felt that men were afraid to come too near in case they ruptured the thin membrane of sanity that was holding back all the emotional putrefaction inside me. I stopped being a woman and became a grieving, sobbing, inconsolable wreck who craved affection; but had a man been brave enough to give it to me, I wouldn't know what to give him in return because I felt that all that I was was worthless.
I was a boil, just waiting for a dashing knight to come along and lance me.
I waited and waited but nobody came.

In truth, I wasn't ready to meet anyone – after all Charlie was an incredibly hard act to follow – as countless people insisted on telling me (as if that would somehow make me feel better). I began to realise that I would never be ready to meet another man until I had finished grieving for Charlie. And friends kept saying how strong I was and how resilient I had been, but I didn't see myself as strong because I felt all the strength in me ebb away when Charlie died. He was my strength, just as I was his.

So how did I manage to deal with the loss of a man who had been my whole life? Did I seek counselling? Did I go to a self-help group and work through all my angst and anger, sitting on an uncomfortable plastic chair surrounded by other lost souls in need of salvation? Or did I find solace in a daily bottle of vodka and a handful of Valium?

Well, no. I didn't do any of those things. I didn't want to see a counsellor because I had people around me whom I could call upon, day or night. They were my counsellors and I didn't have to see them at a fixed time or on an appointed day – they came when I needed them. Nor did I attend any self-help groups because I knew that I could do exactly that – help myself; and to be perfectly honest the last thing I could cope with at that time was to spend an evening listening to other people's outpourings of grief. Selfish, I know, but I've never done group things very well. If I'm going to become unhinged, then I would rather loosen the screws alone and in the comfort of my own home. If I had wanted to become an alcoholic it would have been ridiculously easy – after all I was now the sole owner of over two hundred bottles of wine and numerous bottles of spirits. But I don't have it in me to become addicted to anything. Now, Charlie would have been very happy to drink himself into oblivion; in fact, shortly before he died we watched the film 'Leaving Las Vegas' in which Nicholas Cage drinks himself to death. I found it to be a disturbing but incredibly moving film but Charlie said he found it 'aspirational' – he was half joking but it didn't surprise me in the slightest.
So I couldn't drown my sorrows – my sorrows were drowning me.

I knew what the problem was but there was no easy way to address it. Bookshops are full of self-help books, there are so many titles to choose from – the list is endless, but I can't be doing with any of them. 'The Little book of Calm', what's that all about? 'Men are from Mars, Women are from Venus'. I can précis that whole book in one line – Women and Men are different and therein lies the attraction. The shelves are stuffed with such books and they all tell you what you already knew but didn't have the conviction to believe.

I didn't need a book to tell me I was mad – it was clear to everybody around me. I walked around all day long with mad staring eyes, with a 'slap me' face; with 'shake me' shoulders, with 'kick me' shins. I walked around all day just waiting for a nice doctor to run up to me, calling for the restraints and the sleepy drug. But I was never restrained and I couldn't sleep.

I wanted to be mad, I needed to be mad, God knows I had every reason to be mad – bonkers, barking, loopy loo, stark staring mad.

It's all part of getting better.

You have to let the madness out, the anger out, the hurt out – otherwise it turns inwards and screws you up for the rest of your life. You can take pills, but that just dulls the pain and the pain is sure to surface later in life, like a big throbbing... Well, like a big throbbing thing that really, really hurts and you can't touch it and it's all red and angry and it just gets bigger and bigger and then it bursts – leaving a big mess on your mirror – leaving you scarred.

So you leave the pills in the bottle.

You need to grieve; because it is only by grieving that you can go forward. I wanted to skip the hard bit and just go forward, but that was not an option – I had to go through it.

At times it felt as if I was standing on my tiptoes in a black sea; and I could see the swell ahead of me. It was hard to stay upright because the current was strong and threatened to pull my legs out from under me, but my friends were there to help me stand. And then I saw it coming towards me and I felt it coming upon me, like a migraine sufferer feels the stirrings of their next bout of cranial torment. I saw the swell rising before me and then I felt it surge over my head and drag me down. Down into the blackness, down I went – but I didn't fight it, I let it envelop me. And I stayed under until the blackness receded and the light began to filter down into the water. And then I rose up once more.

I prompted the swell when I felt it coming. I put on records that made me sad, I looked at all my old photographs; I read the letters that people had written about my beloved boy – I made it come over me.

I made it come.

I made myself feel it and each time I felt it, the swell became smaller. I was gradually using up the dark sea and soon I found myself standing ankle deep in an inky black puddle, and it didn't trouble me any more.

But everyone if different – what worked for me would not necessarily work for another person. There is no definable amount of time or specific method of grieving.

I have a friend who is still in therapy, more than four years after his wife's death. It took him two years just to feel comfortable enough to lie on the therapist's couch – not because he felt uneasy, but because he had a rabid aversion to the Candlewick throw that covered it. Once he had addressed his loathing of tufted bed coverings, so he could go on to address his grief. Everyone recovers in his or her own time, but the single most important thing to learn is that before you can start to get better you have to touch bottom.

Chapter Thirty-Six

I cannot say that there was a specific point when I realised that I had begun to come to terms with Charlie's loss, but I can vividly remember the seminal moment – the lowest point that marked the turning point in my recovery.

It happened six months to the day after Charlie's death. I didn't understand the significance of the six-month marker until I became a widow. It is the time when people drift away because they think you are coping, but it is precisely the time when you need them the most. I felt that I was being buried under the weight of my grief and yet most people assumed that I was over it – that I was over the worst and was beginning to recover. Only I knew that I was far from being over it – in fact I was at breaking point.

I knew that if I were to stand any chance of getting through my ordeal without cracking up completely, I had to try to understand exactly how and why Charlie died. I was extremely fortunate in that I had Chris Burrell to help me. He arrived one Sunday with a pile of folders six inches thick, containing Charlie's very lengthy medical history. He handed them to me and then he and Beth took the children out for the day and I spent a quiet afternoon ploughing through the notes. I read more than I needed to know, but I had to know everything.

I found out how Charlie died and why he died – but initially it didn't help me at all. He died of ventricular fibrillation, which basically means that his heart tripped into a super-fast rhythm of between 300 and 500 beats per minute. Because no blood was being pumped to his brain, loss of consciousness resulted almost immediately, which is why he slumped forward on the sofa. It would have been impossible to get him out of v-fib without the aid of a defibrillator – so I had no chance. Charlie's big old left ventricle had finally given up. He died quickly, painlessly; and he died in my arms and it was the dignity and swiftness of his death that helped me hold onto what was left of my sanity. Charlie could have died anywhere – in his car, at the office or alone in some impersonal hotel room. And I knew that if anybody other than me had tried to resuscitate him, I would have spent the rest of my life wondering if he or she had done enough.

Few people are granted the privilege of seeing what I saw and doing what I did in the last minutes of my husband's life. I wasn't traumatised by it; I was empowered by it. I know that Charlie spent his final moments in the comforting surroundings of his own home. I know that the last few sparks of brain activity in his cerebral cortex were registering the sound of my voice and the sound of his children's laughter; that Rosie's lasting memory of his death is not one of tears and trauma, but of peace. I know because when she asked me about Charlie's death, the question was always the same, 'Why did Daddy fall asleep on the sofa, Mummy?'

I sat and I read each letter of admission, studied each temperature chart and traced Charlie's medical progress through the correspondence of his doctors.

> 'We were all very delighted with his extraordinary post-operative recovery but as you know he is left with significantly impaired ventricular function following these operations and his prolonged illness.'

> 'He is still tiring very easily and is feeling quite exhausted and depressed. There is nothing new to find'

> 'Unfortunately he has gone back into atrial flutter.'

> 'Mentally, this has obviously all come as a major blow.'

> 'Well I never, he is back in sinus rhythm. There must be something in the water up your way.'

> 'He has developed mild mitral regurgitation due to degeneration of his mitral valve and atrial fibrillation'

> 'Cardiac transplantation will quite clearly need to be considered at some stage and I have broached this subject in the past in the gentlest possible way.'

The words pricked me like a hypodermic syringe. I thought I knew everything and yet reading Charlie's medical notes made me realise just how much he had been through in the time that we had been together. I closed the folders and sat in a daze until Rosie and Alice came skipping through the front door. Then later, when they were safely tucked up in bed, I came downstairs, opened a bottle of Rioja and watched *Truly, Madly, Deeply*. Probably the worst film I could have watched under the circumstances – but it was what I wanted to watch.

I went real low that night. I went about as low as I could go without losing it and being carted off screaming to a secure mental institution. I touched bottom, drank the whole bottle of Rioja and then came into the kitchen and walked around the table, shouting, 'Why did he have to go through all that pain? What did he ever do to deserve it? He was such a lovely man – such a kind, gentle man. Why did he have to go through all that torment when so many worthless bastards sail through life without so much as a twisted ankle?
It's not fair. It's not fucking fair.'

And it wasn't fair; after all, rapists, child molesters and wife beaters all seem to live long and untroubled lives. So why did Charlie have to go through hell?

Well, maybe what he endured made him the man he was. Maybe the awful knowledge that he wasn't going to see old age; that he wasn't going to walk his daughters down the aisle or bounce their children on his knee, made him grasp every moment of his short life and live it. Chris Burrell always said that Charlie had a remarkable quality of life for a man with such a severe heart condition – and he did.

And when I had recovered from my night of red wine and rage, I came to realise that I was blessed, because I had been given more joy and love our ten years together than most people get in a lifetime. I began to put it all behind me. I stopped asking, 'Why him?' and started thinking, 'What's done is done, and wishing it hadn't happened the way it did isn't going to bring him back'. You cannot go forward if you are forever looking back, and I wanted to go forward and try to live my life without guilt and without regret – so I did.

Rosie started school in September. She stood by the school gate in her new uniform, clutching her book bag and grinning from ear to ear whilst I took her photograph. I wished for all the world that Charlie could have been with me, but the strange thing was that it was another woman who burst into tears at the sight of the three of us standing alone together. I no longer felt sad; I had begun to accept it. I was becoming stronger.

Shortly afterwards, at the beginning of October, I decided to take my first positive step towards starting my new life. I placed a small advert in the local paper and after interviewing several distinctly unsuitable types, I found what I had been searching for. An angel with a Geordie accent turned up on my doorstep one afternoon – my prayers had been answered. Nanny Pat was an instant success with Rosie and Alice, and her presence in our lives heralded a fundamental change in my outlook on life. I was now able to go away for the weekend; I could return to work, I could begin to recover my sanity. She was the best thing that could have happened to us.

My old boss, Duncan welcomed me back to work with open arms. It was hard at first; my old colleagues would come in to my edit suite and inevitably the conversation would turn to the subject of Charlie's death. I would not be able to speak for long without breaking down; it didn't seem to matter how reconciled I thought I had become to his loss, every time somebody came up to me and said something nice about Charlie, the wound would open up again. I felt the need to talk about him constantly but gradually, over time, I found that I could hold a conversation without bursting into tears at the very mention of his name. And when I started to talk about the future and not about the past I knew that I was beginning to heal.

As winter drew on my recovery plan was well under way. I had begun to eat normally again but I still couldn't make myself cook Sunday lunch. Poor Rosie and Alice only got roast beef when they went out for lunch because I couldn't bear the thought of cooking it myself. I had decided to block out an event that had a particular significance – it was Charlie's favourite meal and the thought of eating it without him seemed like an act of betrayal.

I had tried to carry on as if nothing had happened once before, by going to the Anchor on a Friday night and bringing home fish and chips for myself. It was fine until I put the fish and chips on the table, but as soon as the first mouthful reached my lips I was filled with all the happy memories of how it used to be and I couldn't eat it. I just sat at the end of an empty expanse of table and cried. Deb Lapthorne had been in the pub that night and was well aware of the significance of what I was attempting. She rang shortly afterwards, and when I had finished speaking to her I no longer felt sorry for myself. I stopped crying, poured myself a Guinness and spent the rest of the evening thinking how amazingly lucky I was to have such a true friend as her.

But there was still the problem of 'that meal'. Sunday was a special day for Charlie and me, and Sunday evenings were always sacrosanct. Charlie enjoyed cooking, but on a Sunday he really went to town. I didn't venture into the kitchen at all; I simply waited to be summoned to the table, whereupon I would eat huge quantities of whatever was put in front of me. My job was washing up afterwards, which always struck me as a very good deal indeed.

The Sunday roast was only a meal – at least that's what I tried to tell myself, but it seemed that cooking it was reaffirmation of the fact that Charlie was never coming back. I started with lamb. I was alone every Sunday evening, but every Sunday evening my table groaned with enough food to feed several hungry people. Eventually, as Alice and Rosie got older, I moved the meal to Sunday lunchtime, so that we could all eat together. Rosie has developed into quite a carnivore and adores crispy roast potatoes and lots of rich brown gravy, and Alice loves roast chicken, lots of stuffing and as many vegetables as I can squeeze on her plate.

It took me quite a while to summon up the courage to tackle roast beef. I made a special trip to see Mr. Wilkinson in Modbury and he found me a fabulous piece of rolled rib, which I cooked for Eddie and Bubble the very next evening. The Yorkshire puddings were light and crispy, the meat was deliciously rare and the gravy was perfect. I think my husband would have approved.

I had overcome many obstacles in the eight months since Charlie's death and my final test was to be New Year's Eve. I had got through Eddie and Bubble's wedding, Rosie and Alice's birthday and our first Christmas alone. I had got through each painful reminder of Charlie's absence but the end of the year was the goal that I had been longing to reach. Bubble had once said to me, 'If you can get through this year, then you can get through anything.' And I held on to those words as a drowning woman holds onto a piece of driftwood.

I hated 1998 – it was a bastard of a year. It had given me no joy, only heartbreak and I couldn't wait to see the back of it. I wanted to spend the evening on my own because the thought of being with a load of drunken, happy people, kissing and laughing, was too horrible to contemplate. Walker and Deb came up to see me and left me a curry for my supper. They were like a couple of zookeepers visiting some rabid, slavering beast. They all but pushed the plate through the door with a stick because they knew how evil was feeling.

I sat alone at the end of the table and ate my supper in silence. Then, when I had digested my food, I poured myself a large glass of Madeira and went up onto the roof. It is a flat roof and from it you can see the whole of Ugborough square. I went up there because I had one duty to fulfil before the year was out. I had promised Charlie that he could have a cigar on New Year's Eve 1999. He was very excited at the prospect of his first nicotine 'hit' for a decade, but he never got to have his cigar, and so I decided that I would smoke it for him.

I sat on the window ledge, lit my fat Cuban cigar and began puffing away. As I sipped my Madeira I could see the lights of the village below, and I could see people come and go from the Anchor, but nobody saw me. I was totally invisible, save for the glow of my Monte Cristo in the blustery darkness. I sat and waited for the church bell to strike twelve, and on the last strike of the bell, I shouted 'Fuck off 1998, I hope I never see your like again.'
I had done it. It was over and now I could begin again. I watched the last puff of smoke drift skywards and then came inside.

As the awful spectre of 1998 floated off into the ether, I went into 1999 with a renewed sense of optimism. Life was getting better. I was taking small steps, one at a time. I was moving on. Nobody can tell you when to take each step; each decision is yours and yours alone. But it is not always easy, because even the simple act of emptying a wardrobe takes on a monumental significance when you know that you are divesting yourself of part of your husband's identity. There is no time limit on undertaking such a painful task. Some people feel the need to do it right away, some take months or years and some people leave cupboards bulging and rooms untouched because they need to retain some tangible evidence of their partner's existence. Somehow the feel of a jumper or the smell of a shirt is a wholly more powerful reminder than a simple photograph. When I could no longer touch Charlie's skin, I could still touch the clothes that had come into contact with his skin. I took one of his shirts to bed with me at night because it still smelt of him, and when I closed my eyes I could imagine that he was lying in bed beside me, and not buried beneath the cold, dark earth. I needed to smell him because I could no longer see him; but in time the smell faded – along with my other sensory memories. I started to forget the unforgettable. I struggled to remember the exact sound of his voice and the sight of his beaming face. I was losing him all over again. I found myself faced with a choice. I could recharge my memory banks by endlessly watching home videos. I could leave our bedroom as an untouched and untouchable shrine to my late husband – or I could gradually let him go.

In the end the decision was taken out of my hands. Rosie started the process of letting go, by taking Charlie's shaving brush one evening and running it around the inside of his wooden shaving bowl. I was getting ready to go to out and failed to notice what she was doing; she had unwittingly destroyed the signature swirl of pink soapy bubbles, which her Daddy had left on the last morning he would ever need to shave and which I had carefully preserved ever since. When I saw what she had done I became almost hysterical with rage. I screamed at her, and then pushed her out of my bedroom, because I was

Chris Burrell, with his daughter Jessica and Rosie

frightened I might injure her if she stayed.

But it was only soap.

Soap meant nothing to Rosie, but my angry words meant a great deal, and I was left feeling deeply ashamed. I knew that what I had done was wrong. I could not preserve the memory of Charlie by saving every scrap of everything he'd ever touched – for that way lies madness. It was a bit of dried lather and nothing more.

I will keep Charlie's memory alive – not in a turned wooden bowl, but in the minds of my children. Recollections of Charlie's life will swirl around their heads for as long as I have breath in my body, but his clothes and clutter will gradually disappear. Rosie and Alice will always have the things that Charlie held most dear, like his pocket knife and his fountain pen, but his tatty old jeans and baggy jumpers are long gone. I still have a few items in his wardrobe which I cannot bring myself to part with. I could take them to a charity shop, but the thought that I might one day see a man walking through Plymouth dressed in Farrah slack, slip-on shoes and Charlie's beloved keeper tweed jacket is just too horrible to contemplate. The clothes that are left don't take up much room, and anyway, there can't be much call for button fly trousers nowadays, can there?

Chapter Thirty-Seven

I used to consider myself a lucky person, but the events of the past few months had given me a somewhat jaundiced view of the surprises that life might hold in store for me.

It had been rough year. No only had I lost my husband, I had taken a stressful holiday in the Dordogne which ended with me crashing my hire car into three other cars on the way to Bordeaux airport. After I returned home some boys from the village school kicked a football over the fence, which smashed through my greenhouse. And if that wasn't enough, during a particularly violent thunderstorm, my house was struck by lightening, which blew up my computer and various other electrical items too numerous to mention. My mother came to see me just afterwards to survey the damage, and as she walked into the kitchen she caught sight of a vase of flowers and said, 'Kate, you shouldn't bring lilac into the house, don't you know it's unlucky?' I paused for a moment, looked at her and said, 'Mother, my husband has just dropped dead, I've had a car crash, a lightening strike and my greenhouse is history. How much more bad luck do you think I can possibly have? Please, bring in more lilac. It's not the lilac that's unlucky, it's me!'

I seemed to be having a hell of a run of bad luck, but just when I thought that things couldn't possibly get any worse – they did. I found a large lump in my left breast. I remember the moment clearly. I couldn't quite believe that it could happen to me – not after everything else – but it was real enough. I rang Beth straight away and she told me not to worry and said that I should see a doctor as soon as possible. And then I realised that something had fundamentally altered in the way I was reacting. I was praying that I didn't have breast cancer; I was praying that I wouldn't die and leave my two little girls behind.

I was praying for my life.

Up to that point it had been easy to think about death and to casually contemplate taking my own life. I had taken my girls shopping a few weeks before and Alice had run off as I was unfolding her pushchair. I couldn't find her anywhere but I didn't panic, I just thought to myself, 'If anything has happened to her then I'm going to go home and shoot myself.' I was perfectly calm and rational about it; Rosie and Alice were all I had left and I knew that if any harm were to befall them then I would finally snap. I had taken a lot but I couldn't take that. Luckily I found Alice; she was sitting on the floor of the shoe shop next door, trying on men's shoes. I picked her up, took her home and never thought about killing myself again.

Suicide is a selfish option but one that is easy to contemplate when depression overwhelms you. But when you are faced with the reality of death, when it is taken out of your hands – then it becomes truly frightening. When I found the lump I knew I was no longer in control of my fate. I began to dread what the specialist would say to me. I made myself sick with worry, conjuring up visions of a tumour that was turning my healthy breast tissue into a grey amorphous mass – a carcinogenic carbuncle, blighting the most visible symbol of my womanhood.

When I eventually got to see the consultant the examination was over in a matter of minutes. To my great relief the lump turned out to be harmless – but not nameless. The doctor sat me down and solemnly informed me that I had a 'breast mouse' – so called because it runs away from your fingers when you press it. I began to giggle, partly from relief and partly because of the visual image that I had in my mind – not of a terrible tumour, but of a furry little creature scampering about beneath my bra. If it needed removing would they employ a surgical technique or would they simply try to entice it out with a piece of cheese? I know a breast lump is nothing to joke about, but I couldn't help myself – and the poor consultant had no idea why I was laughing.

I was laughing because for the first time since Charlie's death, I felt glad to be alive.

As winter gave way to spring I began to mellow. I took my girls out at weekends; we went swimming or shopping and I began to enjoy what I had previously loathed. I became less angry and more forgiving. I became a better mother. Rosie and Alice coped with my volatility remarkably well; they could see that I was struggling to deal with being alone and they began to help me. I stopped shouting and started talking. I had been at pains to explain everything about their father's death and the events that had led up to it; but they had gained their own understanding of what had happened and expressed it with a simple eloquence that often left me speechless.

One day I was pushing Rosie on the swing and she said, 'Mummy, Daddy is like a woodlice. Daddy is like a woodlice because his body is just an empty shell, and his soul is up in heaven.' What can you say? What do you say? She was right, of course. Alice came out with her own version one day when we were visiting Beth. She asked to go outside and play with Dodi Rabbit, but there was one problem – a dog had killed Dodi Rabbit a few days before. Beth looked at me and said, 'Shall I tell her, or do you want to do it?' I decided to break the news in as gentle a way as possible, so I said, 'Dodi Rabbit has gone to heaven to be with Daddy.' Alice just turned to me and said, 'Is Daddy a rabbit, Mummy?'

My children were and are my priority. Alice cannot really remember Charlie and so she doesn't really miss him as much as her sister, but Rosie can vividly remember him and those memories can sometimes be acutely painful. A friend once told me a perfect analogy for describing the grief of a child. She said that grief for adults is overwhelming and all consuming, but grief for a child is like a black puddle, which they can jump into one day and jump out of the next. When they are in it they feel desperately sad, but the next day the sadness is all but forgotten.

Because I had begun to recover, I thought that Rosie too was over the worst, but as she matured, so her perception of death altered; and one day it hit her – hard. The catalyst for Rosie's outpouring of grief was a visit to her father's grave. We had been many times before, but for some reason that particular visit provoked an extreme reaction. Rosie started to become increasingly introspective and withdrawn. She began to bombard me with questions about Charlie and became overtly morbid and repeatedly drew pictures of the headstone and the epitaph. We went away for the weekend and I caught her stealing, which was totally out of character for Rosie. When I confronted her about it she lied, and then accused our hostess of hitting her. I initially reacted in entirely the wrong way; instead of remaining calm and trying to understand what had prompted such antisocial behaviour, I was very hard on her and told her that I would not tolerate stealing or lying under any circumstances.

We arrived home late on Sunday. I unpacked the car and went into the kitchen to begin cooking supper. As I breezed about the kitchen Rosie turned to me and said, ' I want to die so that I can be with Daddy.' Hearing my own daughter saying that she wished she were dead was one of the most heart-rending things I have ever experienced. I was so shocked that I couldn't speak for a moment and then all I could say was,' Daddy would be very upset if he thought you wanted to be in heaven with him. You have the whole of your life ahead of you and as long as I'm around I'm not going to let any harm come to you.' And then Alice ran up to me and flung her arms around my neck and said, 'I don't want to die, mummy. I don't have to die as well do I?'

Things seemed to be spiralling out of my control but I knew I had to act quickly when a few days later Rosie's nanny caught her putting a ribbon over her light until it began to smoke. When questioned about it, Rosie innocently explained that if the house caught on fire then we could all go up to heaven and be with Daddy again. When I found out what she'd said it put the fear of God into me. I had wrongly presumed that because I had accepted Charlie's death, then Rosie would automatically feel the same way. But she didn't feel the same. It had taken her a long time to realise that Charlie wasn't away in some faraway land called heaven – a place that he could just walk out of at any time and appear at the door as if nothing had happened. He was dead, and he was never coming back. And it was hard for her to accept that she was the only girl in school whose daddy had died. She would try and talk about it to her friends, but they would just tease her, and the childish taunts of the playground can be far more wounding than most adults would care to admit. She was going through hell and I had no idea how to help her, so I sought advice from a friend who had also lost her father at a young age and who had since become a counsellor – and only then did I begin to understand.

I saw that I was the one who was at fault, and that I was the only person who could help her. Rosie needed time alone with me – not stressful weekends spent fighting for my attention with her sister, but quiet time with just the two of us – time that would make her feel grown-up and special. She needed to hold onto me when she went to bed because that was the time when her thoughts turned to her daddy. But I had got into the habit of coming home from work, reading her a story and putting her quickly to bed because I wanted to go down-stairs and relax. I knew that she wanted me to stay with her, but I was often too tired and distracted to see why. Rosie needed me to understand that stealing and lying were simply ways of getting my attention. Rosie needed me – and was telling me in the only way she knew how, and as soon as I put my friend's advice into practice, Rosie became a different girl. I took her 'girlie shopping', which she adored. We tried on clothes together, we eat in a proper restaurant- we had fun. And at bedtime I stayed with her, cuddling her until she fell asleep. I made time to listen and when she asked me why her daddy had to die so young, I explained what had caused his death and told her that it was better that he died when he did, than have his beloved girls see him getting weaker and weaker. I told her over and over again, but ultimately, no amount of explanation can make a little girl understand why she has lost her daddy.

Thankfully Rosie and Alice are now both growing into happy, well-adjust-ed children. They are totally different in terms of looks and personality, but have each inherited their father's bravery and incredible strength of will. Rosie is a very self-reliant little girl, thoughtful and quiet, and always very measured in her actions. She is long-limbed and graceful with startlingly blue eyes and freckles on her nose. She is very bright and asks about her father constantly; is totally open and honest and will talk about him whenever she feels the need, to who-ever is nearby at the time. Sometimes people find it a little difficult to know what to say to her, but occasionally a person will respond to her in an altogeth-er different way, as happened whilst we were visiting my parents in Sidmouth, the year after Charlie died.

It was a sunny day and I was watching Rosie playing happily on the beach, when she suddenly walked over to a lady, sat down on the towel beside her and said, 'It's Father's Day today and I'm feeling very sad because my daddy's died.' I watched them chatting for a few minutes and then the lady came over to me and said, 'Your little girl has just opened her heart to me and if it's alright with you, I'd like to sit and talk to her for a while.'
I told her I was more than happy for her to sit with Rosie for as long as she liked. The lady probably didn't realise it at the time, but I knew that she was giving my daughter the best kind of counselling there is – unsolicited, unprompted and freely given, and for that small act of kindness she will have my eternal gratitude. Rosie is now dealing with the death of her father with amazing maturity for such a young girl, but then I would expect nothing less because she is Charlie's daugh-ter, through and through.

Alice Boydell is quite a girl. She was nicknamed 'Tonka' as a toddler, because of her ability to cannon off objects and get up without a word of com-plaint and she is, according to my parents, exactly like me when I was a child. Her hair and skin are darker than Rosie's is, and she has piercing green eyes, big dimples and a winning smile. She is as robust as her sister is slight, and she has her mother's temper – but she also has the ability to charm almost anybody that she comes across.

My girls, as they are today

Even as a baby, she would sit in the trolley as I wheeled it around the super-market and attract admiring glances and smiles from every passer-by. Now though, she attracts stares of disbelief, because she will happily sit and munch her way through a whole red pepper as we go about our shopping.

She is sadly not old enough to remember her father, because she was only 20 months old when he died, but I know he would adore her and find her as end-lessly amusing as I do. She is really quite a character and my only sadness is that Charlie died before he got to see her develop into what she is today.

I am blessed to have two such wonderful children.

They are my joy and my life.

Chapter Thirty-Eight

I don't see ghosts, I don't see auras, or pixies or little green men flying about in U.F.O.'s, but I have experienced one or two strange things since Charlie died, which I find very hard to explain.

When everybody went home after the funeral, I was left in the house on my own for the first time. I was upstairs bathing, and the television was on in our bedroom. The BBC were showing Victoria Wood in concert, and I listened to it as I got out of the bath and towelled myself dry. I was only half-paying attention, but I did hear her say, 'The three worst things that can happen to you in your life are, divorce...' And then all the lights began to flicker and the T.V. screen went blank. It lasted for a few seconds, and I said, 'I know, Charlie, I know.' And then the lights came once again and Victoria Wood said, 'and moving house.' And carried on with her monologue. I found out the next day that nobody else in the village had experienced a loss of picture, and when Pixie called me on the phone, I asked her what the missing word had been. She paused for a moment and said, 'Death'.

I feel Charlie's presence around me all the time and I feel wafts of air going past my face when I am standing in the kitchen. I'm sure it can all be explained away, but other people feel it too. I found a book lying on the spare bed which didn't have its dust jacket on, so I began put it on and as I did so I looked at the title – it was called 'When Disaster Strikes'. I chuckled to myself and turned the book over but I stopped chuckling when I read what was on the back. It said, 'Another book in this series, 'The Anatomy of Bereavement'.

Just before Christmas, I was invited to the annual Two Four Christmas party. Charlie and I had always loved going, but that year I went with my parents, which isn't quite the same; nonetheless, I had an excellent evening. The following morning I was lying in bed, in that half-awake, half-asleep state which one is loathed to come out of, and I was suddenly aware that Charlie was laying beside me. I couldn't see his face clearly, but he was reaching out his hand to me and making the same noise that he made when he was dying. It is a noise which I could never forget but which I cannot remember – my brain denies me access to it because it is too painful to hear again. I looked over and just said, 'Charlie, Charlie, Charlie, Charlie.' And then I woke up.

It was a very vivid dream and it stayed in my mind until that afternoon, when I had to go and see Walker and Deb. I was baking cakes with my girls and I needed an egg, so I called round to get one off the Cakemeister General. I walked into the kitchen and said, 'I had a dream about Charlie this morning.'

And Deb just looked at me and said, 'I saw Charlie at the end of my bed last night.'

I picked myself up off the floor, and she went on to tell me that she was just drifting off to sleep, when she saw Charlie, standing at the end of her bed, shimmering like Captain Kirk on a bad transporter day. He was wearing ripped jeans and a holey jumper, but she couldn't see his face clearly. He spoke to her and said, 'I'm trying to hold Kate. I want to hold her in my arms, and let her know I'm there, but I can't touch her.' And then Deb got an image in her mind of Charlie in a huge transparent bubble. He was pushing out on the walls of the bubble, but he couldn't break through it. He then said, 'I want to hold Kate in a way that she'll know that it's me, and nobody else. I want her to know that I'm with her. They've let me stay and I'm with her.' And then he vanished from the end of the bed. Now, you can say what you like about the coincidence of two people dreaming of the same person, after all, it's not that unusual. But to have Deb seeing Charlie, and hearing him expressing the need to hold me, and then to have me dream of him the following morning reaching out to me, is, it has to be said, rather more than a coincidence.

I have only had one other dream in which the intensity of my feelings and the vividness of the images within the dream stayed with me in such a way. It happened shortly before Charlie and I first met, and I can still remember every detail of it to this day. I never told Charlie about it; I don't begin to understand what it means – I will leave you to draw your own conclusions.

The dream began in a huge Roman amphitheatre. I was sitting in the audience and next to me sat my husband, who was grossly overweight and balding. There was a game being played out in the arena below us, involving a large ball, which bounced down onto the floor of the arena and then back up into the stands, and if it happened to hit a member of the audience they would fall down dead. The ball bounced around for a while; striking down people all around us, and then it suddenly bounced up high and hit my husband. He fell forward, clutching his chest as if he were suffering a heart attack and then dropped down dead.

I calmly got up from my seat, walked out of the arena and into a Roman villa. I came upon a couple in one of the rooms; they were lying on a day bed making love. I watched them for a while and then walked away, passing out of some French doors and into lush green countryside beyond. I saw a pair of fox cubs playing in the long grass but I couldn't see their mother. I could hear the sound of a hunting horn and then I saw a pack of hounds approaching, so I hid the cubs. We stayed hidden until the huntsmen had ridden past and then the mother of the cubs came back and thanked me for saving them.

My attention was then drawn to the noise of people singing. I looked down the hill to see a group of American puritans wearing black hats and black robes with starched white collars. They were carrying long staffs and walking in a procession along the lane that ran along the bottom of the field. I asked the vixen who they were and she said, 'They are the sea trout singers and they've come to sing to the sea trout.'

I left the vixen and her cubs and followed after the puritans, but I didn't let them see me. They walked over a bridge and down into a tiny medieval hamlet. The houses were all crowded on top of each other and lanes than ran between were very narrow. I found myself alone in a small alleyway, I could hear a noise coming from one of the buildings and so I went to investigate. I walked into a small workshop and there stood a young man, bending over a lathe. He was making something out of wood and when I tapped him on the shoulder he stopped the lathe and turned around to look at me. He had an incredibly handsome face and he smiled at me as if he knew me. I asked him what he was making and he said, ' I'm making a wedding ring.' I asked him who it was for and he said, 'It's for you, you're going to be my wife.'

Chapter Thirty-Nine

In February I flew to New York with Eddie and Bubble. We were going ostensibly to shop, but we also had tickets to the hottest show on Broadway, namely 'The Blue Room', starring Nicole Kidman and Ian Glen, a fine Shakespearean actor who would be appearing on stage naked. Naked! I could hardly contain my excitement.

We took our seats on the plane. I was sitting by the aisle, but I could just as easily have been in the hold, it wouldn't have mattered to me. Just the thought of a week of being a grown-up, without having to worry about the girls, and without having to talk about Barbies and Coco Pops, was a truly thrilling prospect. I would be able to drink and smoke and swear – well not smoke, but I could make up for that by drinking and swearing even more. I would be an adult and do adult things, I would stay out late and lie-in in the mornings, until I felt the need to get up and spend more money. It would be a blast.

I ate my lunch, watched the film and then pulled on my sleepy mask and gently dozed of to the drone of the engines. I was busily dreaming about Ian Glenn, cartwheeling starkers across an empty stage, when there was a terrific crash. I sat up and pulled off my eye mask, and watched in amazement as a lady picked herself off the floor by my seat. She had tripped and fallen, cracking her head on the armrest of the annoying American man in front of me. There was a lot of rushing about and then she was helped to the back of the plane so that she could lie down.

I picked up a magazine and was toying with the idea of resuming my dream about Ian Glenn, when I heard the lady across the aisle from me call for a stewardess. She said, 'My husband is feeling a little faint, can he have the oxygen mask?' I didn't want to appear as rude as the annoying American man, who was craning round his seat, asking the stewardess what was the matter. But I did sneak a look. I sneaked a look, and a look was all I needed to tell me that the man was in big trouble.

He was in heart failure.

There was a grey pallor to his skin that was unmistakable. I had seen it in Charlie's face so many times. It was etched into my memory. It was impossible to mistake for anything else. I sat back in my seat and wondered what to do next. I could see that the lady had no idea what was wrong and I didn't want to alarm her, but at the same time I felt that I had to do something.

I got out of my seat, knelt down by her side and said, 'I'm not a doctor, but I know a bit about the heart because my husband had heart disease. Do you mind if I take your husband's pulse?'

217

She told me to go right ahead and so I took her husband's wrist and measured his pulse. It was way-low – about 40 beats per minute, which was why he
was feeling faint. I told her that he was feeling faint because he wasn't getting
enough oxygenated blood to his brain, but I didn't mention the heart failure,
because people panic when you say heart failure and think you mean a heart
attack. The man perked up a little thanks to the oxygen and his wife told me
that he'd had chest pains the previous year, but that he was taking tablets for it.

I went back to my seat and left them alone. The annoying American was
still asking the stewardess to tell him what was wrong with the man, but she just
ignored him. I began to feel grateful that we were flying with Virgin, because
they were one of only two airlines at the time that carried defibrillators on every
flight. And then the man suddenly slumped back in his seat and the stewardess
immediately paged for a doctor. The doctor examined him and he was quickly
taken to the front of the plane, and stretchered straight to hospital as soon as
we landed. Eddie and Bubble didn't know what to say to me; after all it wasn't
exactly the best way to start my holiday. But as I watched the woman being comforted by the stewardess, as I watched her trying to make light of it, as I
watched the fear in her eyes, I knew I wasn't that woman any more. I sat back
and thought, 'It's gone from me now.'
I knew that her worry was no longer my worry. I was free of it and so was
Charlie.

And when I think back on that flight, I wonder what the odds are against
being on a plane where somebody goes into heart failure. And then I wonder
what the odds are against sitting right next to somebody who goes into heart
failure on that plane. And then I wonder what the odds are against a woman
tripping up and knocking herself out, right next to the person who is about to
go into heart failure, and making so much noise that it wakes me up from a deep
sleep. There are just too many coincidences for my liking.

I had a week – such a week in New York. I got to see the sensational Nicole
Kidman acting her body stocking off, and a rather fine Shakespearean actor
'tackle out'. I got to spend money on myself. I was loud and outrageous but I
was with people who loved me and who didn't give a damn what I did, as long
as I was happy doing it. I had the best time.

When Eddie and Bubble flew home I went over to New Jersey to see Jenny
and David Dally, who were now living in Princeton. I told them about my event-
ful flight and they decided to take me to Philadelphia for the day, to take my
mind off it. We visited a science museum, went into the first exhibit and I was
immediately confronted with a twenty foot high model of a heart. It was hollow
and you could walk around whilst listening to the sound of blood being circu-
lated; I thought it was very funny, but David and Jenny were a tad bit embarrassed to say the least.

We went for lunch in a huge food hall and once we'd eaten we strolled
around the stalls. David and Jenny stopped at a chocolate stand and there was a
lot of muttering and furtive glancing in my direction, so I went to investigate.
In pride of place, at the front of the stall, was a display featuring anatomically

correct chocolate hearts. I had to laugh, but I thought to myself, 'O.K, I get the idea, but I think we've done with the heart thing now. Enough of the heart thing, already!' I bought a particularly fine specimen in milk chocolate and took it home as a present for Chris Burrell – who pronounced it correct in every detail, before Beth devoured it – aorta and all.

On my return I made an appointment to have an aromatherapy massage and a session in a floatation tank. I had been given the treatments as a Christmas present and I thought that a massage would be a very good way to try and release some of the tension that had built up over the past few months. I wasn't sure about the floatation tank but I decided to go with an open mind and see what happened.

The treatment centre was situated in a pretty market town called Totnes, which is the home of all things alternative and spiritual in the South Hams. I arrived in good time and was shown around by a charming middle aged woman who was dressed in the standard Totnesian attire of Conker shoes (easy on the feet, hard on the eye) and loose fitting ethnic clothing in a multitude of colours. She took me into the floatation room, gave me an explanation of what was about to happen and left me to it.

The bath was filled with a solution of water and Epsom salts heated to blood temperature. It was very shallow and only just large enough for me to recline fully, but once I had closed the door and manoeuvred myself into posi-tion I had no sensation of being in the water at all. It was as if I was suspended in the midst of a warm, black void. I closed my eyes and tried to relax, and soon the effort of relaxing caused me to drift off into a totally altered state. I had no perception of time or space, of touch or smell; I was only aware of the soft music that drifted around the tank and of my own slow, rhythmic breathing. I found the experience of being totally deprived of external stimuli incredibly liberating; I was free to explore the inner-workings of my brain; I was free to feel; free to drift. I tried very hard to conjure up a vision of Charlie from the blackness. I felt that if he were ever going to appear to me than this would be an ideal place – my mind was open, all he had to do was walk inside. I was convinced that he would materialise but all that I saw was blackness, nothingness – space.

The hour passed in a matter of moments and after I'd showered I went next door for a massage. The massage was initially not as relaxing as I had hoped. It had nothing to do with the skill of the masseuse – she was extremely good at her job – it was all down to me. The sensation of having someone touch-ing my bare skin for the first time in nearly a year was extremely disconcerting. I was tensing up as she was trying to relax me; in fact I was secretly wishing that she would take her big, chapped paws off me and leave me the hell alone. But then she started to work on my upper arm and all the tension left me. The feel-ing was both relaxing and energising but it was nothing compared to the exqui-site sensation that would follow. She picked up my hand and began to knead my palm. I didn't know what pressure points she was stimulating but the bells were ringing all at once. She took each finger in turn and worked her way from one end to the other, flicking the fingertips as she reached them to expel all the bad energy. I was totally helpless and it was all I could do to stop myself groaning with the pleasure of it.

When it was over she sat me down and asked me a few questions. Her opening gambit of 'How have you been?' was rather a tricky one. I decided to be honest and told her that I hadn't been that great, as my husband had just died. She seemed completely unfazed and told me that she could see that I was like a bubbling pot, whose lid was banging up and down. She said that I needed to lift the lid right off and get rid of all my steam and then she looked over her glasses and solemnly said, 'Have you tried a scream?'

Well, I laughed so much that I nearly fell off my chair. I don't think she had been expecting that particular reaction, and on reflection I feel that I might have tried to appear a little more earnest, but at that moment I was too spaced out to care. Anyway, she told me what to do and I promised her, albeit with a hint of scepticism, that I would give it a try.

I did try it a few nights later. I put on a pumping C.D. that I could get really worked up over, I walked around for a bit until I could feel the scream building up inside me and then I let it out. The lid lifted, the steam came whistling out and the resulting headache lasted for most of the next day.

I have concluded that screaming therapy is not for me. I prefer laughing – after all, laughter is much easier on the ears and is far less frightening for the neighbours.

Chapter Forty

I had seen death. I had witnessed the destruction of everything I held dear. I had lost Charlie but in the aftermath of his death I had re-discovered myself and had redefined the way I wanted to live. I had been mad, but now I just wanted to be bad and dangerous to know.

The changes that took place were not confined to my state of mind; they also affected the way I looked. My face lost the strained expression that had so often betrayed my hidden worries in the last years of Charlie's life; my sad eyes began to twinkle again and I looked younger and felt fitter than I had done for years. I went to the gym every week and worked out all my aggression on inanimate objects, rather than storing it up and exploding at my children. But the gym is a dangerous place for a young widow. The gym is a place where you look at other bodies and begin to admire your own. The gym should have been the place to work off my sexual tension, but in my case it only served to heighten it.

I used to walk around the supermarket on my way home in my cycling shorts and t-shirt, feeling all pumped-up and super fit. I started to pay an unnatural amount of attention to the root vegetables – admiring their form and handling them with rather more enthusiasm than was absolutely necessary. I would look at men as I passed them in the aisles with a gaze that could have melted all the butter in the chilled cabinet.

I needed sex, but in terms of sexual gratification, widowhood sucks.

My friends were aware of my needs and suggested that I might like to invest in a device to help me alleviate my deep-felt want. I have to say that I did investigate a few girlie toy sites on the Internet, but what they had on offer didn't really measure up. Twelve inches of pulsating, gyrating, foul smelling rubber seemed less than appealing so I decided that what I needed was a different kind of pleasure-giver.

What I had in mind was an awesome little number in silver and black leather. Twelve feet of pure sex, it took me from 'Mmm...' to 'Oh my God!' in just over seven seconds. And when people asked why I looked so happy, I could tell them without embarrassment that it was my Audi A3 T Sport that had put the smile back on my face, and not a Jiggly Wiggly Jelly Giant or a Thrustmaster Big-Boy Bouncy Stick.

I loved my car and it made me very happy, but not in the way I needed. I was at my sexual peak, but it wasn't only sex that wanted – there was something that I desired more than anything else.

A kiss.

Kissing is something that you take for granted when you're married. It is the most intimate of acts; you cannot make a person kiss you – they have to want to. I longed for a kiss above all else – the kind of kiss that takes you deep; the kind of kiss that takes you so deep that you can feel your head turning inside out with the shear pleasure of it. But as time passed I began to grow increasingly despondent about my chances of ever being kissed again. The adoring men and endless dinner parties had not materialised. I wasn't a suppurating boil any longer but still that elusive gentleman failed to appear. I felt I was ready to be with a man again, but looking good and feeling confident were not enough.

To my great disappointment I had only received one invitation to a dinner party where an available man had been present. I was so grateful to the couple for inviting me to dinner that I arrived on their doorstep bearing two bottles of wine, flowers and chocolates. They had prepared me – I knew what to expect. I expected a strapping Royal Marine, thick of neck and firm of thigh. I expected him to find me irresistible, after all I had invested in a new thong, I was dressed in tight black trousers and a cream v-neck – I looked hot and I was ready for anything. If there was instant chemistry – I was ready; if he gave me smouldering looks across the dinner table – I was ready; if he walked me home and then asked to come inside and teach me the basics of unarmed combat – I was definitely ready.

I knocked on the door and waited for it to open, and then I knew that I was not ready. I was not ready to meet a man who resembled a shy curate – thin of neck and weak of thigh. I was expecting a rufty-tufty Action Man but this one didn't come with gripping hands, eagle eyes and real hair – mine came with matching thermos and note from his mother saying that he couldn't go out on manoeuvres because of a nasty head cold. I wanted to cry, but I had cried enough, so I decided to get drunk instead.

Eventually it was time to leave. I felt perfectly sober whilst sitting on the sofa, but when the time came to get up and make my way to the door, I realised that the large gin and tonic that I had started the evening with had suddenly caught up with the four glasses of wine and two glasses of port that followed. They mixed themselves into a potent cocktail as I got to my feet, and effected a temporary loss of motor function, which made my progress from sofa to hall a less than graceful affair. My hostess was patiently waiting at the door for me; she was holding up an object; and I looked at it and thought, 'She's holding a coat, and I can see that it's my coat, but I have no idea how to put it on.'

As I struggled with the effort of locating my decidedly uncooperative arms into the sleeves of my coat, my dinner companion stepped forward and asked to walk me home. I declined his offer, choosing instead an unaccompanied stagger up the hill.

And that was it. That was my big chance – gone.

And once again I walked home alone.

A few days later I was sitting in the spring sunshine with a friend and she was telling me how she had met her husband on a blind date. I looked at her and said, 'I would love to go on a blind date, but no one has ever asked me. I might as well face it, no eligible man is going to walk up the lane, knock on the door and say, 'Hello, I'm an attractive single man, would you like to come out on a date with me?' And then I knew what I had to do. I suddenly realised that I could sit at home forever, waiting for a man who would never appear. I had to take control of my life. So I went home, turned on my computer and took a trip to Planet Sad.

Planet Sad is the loneliest planet in cyberspace. It is a place so lonely that The Lonely Planet Guide doesn't even bother to write about it. It is the final destination for all those unfortunate people for whom conventional dating has failed, and for others who find comfort in the virtual anonymity of an e-mail romance. It is safe, sterile and guilt- free; you can dump and be dumped at the touch of the button without fear of recrimination, because in cyberspace, no one can hear you scream.

I blame Beth for my first mouse-encounter. She decided that the place to meet a man would be a chat room. I was rather reluctant but she refused to leave my house until I had entered the realms of anorakdom and so I agreed to try it – just once.

It was a strange experience. I chose the nickname 'T-Sport', after my car, because that was rather more anonymous than Desperate Widow. I talked to some person called Paul or Peter for a while and then someone butted in on our conversation, using the term LOL, which I found out later, is geekspeak for 'laughs out loud'. I began to feel a little uncomfortable at the thought of having a real-time conversation with a complete stranger and so I exited the chat room. But later that evening I went in again.

I tried to use the same nickname but it was taken, as were Kate, KateB and every other variation of my name. In desperation I chose a name that I believed no one else would have thought of. I entered the chat room as 'Mrs Miggin's Pie Shop' – but very soon wished that I hadn't.

I looked down the list of chatsters, pausing at names like 'Throbber' 'Sexkitten', 'Ten- incher' and 'Pussy Galore' and realised that this was the ulti- mate in safe sex. Any twelve-year-old boy can become a super stud from behind the safety of his keyboard, and the chances are that the svelte, blond sex kitten that he's talking dirty to, is a bored, overweight housewife whose husband is snoring happily on the sofa in the next room. You can be anybody you want to be in cyberspace, but I didn't want to be anybody else and I certainly didn't want to spend my evenings talking to a spotty teenager with a personality disorder and a junior hard-on, so I left the chat room and never went back.

My next cunning plan was to post an advert in an Internet dating agency. I scanned in a photograph, wrote a very tongue-in-cheek ad and sent it winging off into cyberspace. Just to be on the safe side, I also enrolled with another agency, but this time I was required to fill in a very lengthy form. I started off with good intentions, but got a little bored towards the end. The last question asked me to describe my best feature. It was very late, I was very tired and so I wrote a brief description of my best asset and sent off the form.

I awoke the next morning with the same feeling that you get when you wake up with a dreadful hangover – I knew that I'd done something very bad the night before but I couldn't quite remember what it was. It took me a few moments – and then the full horror of what I'd written suddenly hit me. I had submitted a form to a respectable dating agency, which ended with the words; 'I've got a bottom like a peach – only not as furry.'

I didn't know what to do with myself for the rest of the day; all I could do was hope that there weren't too many sad perverts out there, waiting to reply to my ad.

How wrong I was.

My first reply came from a man called Malcolm. Malcolm – I should have stopped right there, but curiosity got the better of me. I read on, the warning signs were all there – he was clearly a swinger and by the end of the letter the swingometer was banging off the end of the scale. Then came the killer sentence; 'I'm not God's gift to women' (as if I hadn't already guessed) 'My best bits are my legs, bum and Tongue – I greatly enjoy giving women oral pleasure'.

I couldn't quite believe what I had read but I couldn't bring myself to read it again. I felt dirty and desperate and I could see Charlie leaning over his cloud, looking down at me and saying, 'You sad old widow. Just look at what you've reduced yourself to.'

But still they came – dozens of replies from all over the world. I couldn't stop them and I didn't delete my ad because I still believed that one decent man might look at my picture and send me a reply.

And then one day he did. Just as I was about to remove my advert I got a reply that made me sit up and take notice. It was genuinely funny – the first reply that had a modicum of wit. He told me that he was fit, he told me how he dressed and what kind of shoes he wore. He had me right there, hanging on his every word.

I sent him this reply:

> I have had so many weird losers replying to my desperate lonely heart ad that I hardly bother to read them any more. Your e-mail stands out like a beacon of wit in a sea of mediocrity. It's 8.00pm on Sunday night and I was just about to put my computer to bed for the night, when I decided to check my In Box. I'm glad I did.
>
> My name is Kate and you already know a bit about me, although I do think my ad is a trifle misleading in that I omitted to mention the facial hair and prosthetic limb.
>
> I had lunch with friends today and I was telling them about my trip to planet sad, and concluded that I would never meet anyone remotely suitable (or normal for that matter) by trawling through cyberspace. Lonely hearts are for losers aren't they?
>
> Well, in the most part I think they are – judging by some of the responses that I've had so far. Your response was perfect, but I have to know why a chap who sounds as nice as you do, was looking at an obscure U.S-run lonely hearts club web site in the first place?

Are you a swinger/bored married man/confused gay man/librarian? If so I'm afraid our relationship is at an end. If you are none of the above then I'm glad.

You sound very active; I'm surprised I haven't seen you tramping through my village, which strangely enough, lies nestled on the edge of south Dartmoor. (I'm not giving too much away at this stage in case you turn out to be a psychotic fruitcake with a prosthetic limb fetish).

Nick, I like the way you dress, I like your name, I think your wit is razor sharp – you didn't mention the fact that you have a sense of humour, but you didn't need to, it's written all over the page.

I hope you will e-mail me back,

Kate

And then came his reply:

Read Me! Read Me! Read Me! Read M! Read Me! Read Me! Rea.......

Ok, I hope that got your attention. (I didn't want you to miss it amongst the endless lists of losers. So. You've sussed my ruse, but being a bored, confused bi-curious, swinging librarian doesn't make me a bad person.

How did I end up at the Net's most obscure lonely hearts web site? I just happened to be surfing some of my favourite, exotic Continental and Far East sites (www.limblessluvclub.se, www.stumps&stuff.com etc. When I arrived at the most desperate quadrant of Planet Lonely a number of 'choices' were offered. One had a photo! I went for it like a rainbow trout goes for a gold-haired Hare's Ear (a fly fishing metaphor – not just a pretty face you know). There you were. That was weeks ago and I couldn't put the ad out of my mind. The rest is history.

Have you ever read the lonely hearts column of Private Eye? I used to be addicted, not least because they were extremely amusing. (I did, of course, read the rest of the periodical as well – I'm not completely sad). That said, lonely hearts net browsing is not my preferred area. (No, that's www.limblessluvclub.se....).

Still enjoying this? Please be bored enough...

Nick.

'Please be bored enough' – that was the clincher.

And so it went on. I began to look forward to getting home each night just in case there was another message in my In Box. He was funny and clever but I had no idea what he looked like so I asked for a photo. Eventually, after considerable prevarication he sent me a picture of a man in a wetsuit, mask and snorkel, which I presumed to be him – although it could have been anyone. It made me laugh – he made me laugh, and for the first time since Charlie's death I knew that there was a man who was thinking about me. I was flattered, I felt wanted, it all seemed too good to be true. And so it turned out to be.

He was married.

I asked him outright about the exact nature of his marital status when I felt that he was trying a little to hard to avoid the question. I knew I had to find out before I became too attached to him; I suppose I always had my suspicions but when he eventually came clean I felt totally crushed. He'd chosen to deliberately deceive me; he knew that I was a widow and he knew from my ad exactly what I was looking for in a man. I had been honest and up-front right from the start and he had not.

It was clear to me that all he wanted was a casual flirtation. I had given him a guilt-free ego- boost and an excuse to stay late at the office. It was easy and completely safe. But in return he had given me something very dangerous – he had given me hope. He sounded so perfect but I had learned to my cost that nice shoes, a good suit and a dry wit do not make an honourable man. I suppose I was an easy target but even though I was hurt, I still wanted to meet him face to face. He had awakened something in me that I couldn't ignore. I wanted to look him in the eye and see for myself what kind of man could make me laugh and cry at the same time – was he potentially the second love of my life or simply a bored married man who could no longer communicate with his wife?

We met one evening at a safe venue and I when I caught my first glimpse of him I was rather disappointed. He looked like a slighter version of Charlie, but he had none of the charisma and worryingly small hands. We spent the evening not talking about each other and he wouldn't look me in the eye. We parted on a handshake and I drove home knowing that I had my answer. I sent him a final e-mail, thanking him for taking me out and I never contacted him again.

But my search for a man was not over. Strangely enough my e-joke about having a prosthetic limb would come back to haunt me a few months later. During the school holidays I took the girls to stay with Eddie and Bubble on the Isle of Wight. We went to the beach and toured around the island, and for a treat I was given a day off to go racing on board a friend's yacht. It was the last day of Cowes week and after the race my friend Kate and I decided to go ashore for a sundowner. We walked up Cowes high street and much to our delight we were engulfed by wave upon wave of fit, attractive sailors. Kate was asking me about the qualities that I looked for in a man and I was pointing them out in the bronzed hunks that passed us by. There is something about a man with salt spray in his hair that I find irresistible, and that night I was spoilt for choice. Eventually we stopped at an off licence to buy some wine. I spotted a pleasant-looking man dressed in shorts and a t-shirt in the queue beside me and said to Kate, 'Now look, this is the sort of man we need.' He smiled at me and as he did so I looked down and said jokingly, 'Yes, but I'm not too sure about that strapping around his leg.' He stopped smiling and muttered, 'That's not strapping.'

Admittedly it was dark and I wasn't wearing my glasses, but that was no excuse for failing to notice that he had a false leg, and that the strapping that I had so pointedly referred to was there to hide the join. I didn't know where to look and I couldn't hide behind Kate because by that stage she had completely disowned me, so I had to stand by the man that I had insulted until it was my turn to be served. I tried to smile at him but to no avail – he hated me and who could blame him?

What is it with me? I really have nothing against men with disabilities; after all Charlie wasn't exactly a perfect physical specimen and that didn't stop me falling in love with him. But it did strike me as typical, that of all the beefy bipeds that thronged through the town that night, the man I chose to try and engage in a spot of flirtatious banter was lacking a vital limb. Somebody upstairs must have been having a big celestial joke at my expense – either that or they had misheard me – admittedly I had been praying for a strapping bloke – just not that kind of strapping.

Chapter Forty-One

How do you know when you are over it? How do you tell when you have finally come to terms with death? I knew the day I bought an album by Radiohead called 'The Bends'. I played it as I was driving home from a shopping expedition, and when the third track began I experienced a strange feeling of deja vu. 'High and Low' was the song that was playing as I pulled up the lane after my first solo shopping trip, and it was the track that prompted me to break down and start banging my head on the steering wheel of my car -Radiohead can do that to you sometimes.

But when I listened to the same song a year later I didn't feel like breaking down, I just sat back and enjoyed the music; and I thought to myself how much Charlie would have liked it.

And that is the difference between grief and acceptance.

I wish that he'd lived long enough to sit in bed with me and laugh out loud at 'Ali McBeal' and 'Sex and the City'. I wish that he could have experienced the 'Big Brother' phenomenon. I wish that he could have seen Alice in the humble role of a sheep, stealing the show at her playgroup nativity, and heard Rosie at the tender age of six, reeling off lines from 'Blackadder'. I wish for so many things, but wishing won't bring Charlie back.

There are friends who think about me every day; people who loved Charlie and who get angry that a couple who shared such joy should have been parted and denied the happiness that they so rightly deserved. But I don't think like that. I cannot think like that. Charlie and I shared ten blissful years together – but I do not wish that he had lived any longer. To wish that would be selfish, because his quality of life was deteriorating by the day. He died a dignified death. He didn't languish in hospital for weeks on end and pass away under the detached gaze of some overworked junior doctor.

He died in my arms.

My breath was the last breath in his body and when he died I felt that I never wanted to inhale again.

But I did.

I had to – for the sake of my children.

And when Rosie comes back at me with a funny one-liner, as she so often does, I think of her father. When Alice sits in the bath, looks up at me in all innocence and says, 'Mummy, I can't stop thinking about melons.' I think of her father. I think of Charlie when I look into their faces and he shines back at me out of their eyes. I haven't lost Charlie – I see him every day in my daughters.

228

I only wish that they could see him too.

And what of the future?

Well, last night I was reading Alice one of her favourite books – *Green Eggs and Ham* by Dr. Seuss – and as I got into the rhythm of the book,

> 'I do not like them with a fox,
> I do not like them in a box,
> I do not like green eggs and ham, I do not like them Sam I am.'

I realised that I have exactly the same problem – only with men...

> 'I do not like his slip-on shoes,
> I do not like his liberal views,
> I do not like his golfing slacks,
> I do not like his hairy back,
>
> I wouldn't if he drove a Mini,
> I couldn't if his legs were skinny,
> His nasal hair is far too long,
> His taste in music is all wrong,
> I do not like this gentleman,
> I do not like him, Sam I am.

My problem is that I want it all; I want good looking and smart, I want funny and well-educated – I want what I had in Charlie. I sometimes feel that I am being far too judgmental and too picky, but maybe it's just that I'm scared.

Apart from my Internet disaster, I haven't been taken out by a single man since Charlie's death, which I'm sure you'll agree is a pretty pitiful record. It's not that I have been turning men away at the door; it's just that the opportunity has not yet presented itself. I am perfectly capable of looking after myself. I can service my lawnmower, hang shelves and build a Wendy house without needing any assistance – but a cordless hammer drill is no replacement for a man. I am equipped for a life of self-sufficiency but all I want is for a big strong chap to come and take care of me. Call me old fashioned, but that's the way I am.

Rosie and Alice need a father and they try to encourage me in my efforts at securing a mate. As I leave the house for work, Rosie will follow me out of the door and shout words of encouragement like, 'Mummy, I don't like what you're wearing, you'll never catch a man's eye looking like that.' And sometimes Alice will sit in the back of the car and call out, 'Mummy, you look really foxy today.' And suddenly I feel like a million dollars again.

I want to be loved again – to be in love again. I want the spark in me to be re-ignited. And I want so much for my girls. I cannot hope to replace Charlie because he is irreplaceable, but I will do everything in my power to find the right man to care for my children.

And when I find him I'm going to put away my cordless drill and make him the happiest man alive.

Epilogue

The anniversary of Charlie's death dawned clear and bright, as I knew it would. Beth came over with some flowers and we had a cup of coffee and then walked down Donkey Lane towards the burial ground.

I felt elated.

Beth and I were joking and laughing and I knew that if anybody saw us, they would think that we weren't showing a due amount of reverence on such a sad and solemn day. But I didn't feel sad or solemn – I felt like it was the first day of my new life.

I had done it. I had survived a year so hellish that Satan himself would have looked at it, shaken his horny head and said, 'Nah, that's too heavy duty for me, I think I'll go and have a cuppa with Doreen in her lovely wool shop.'

We arrived at the graveside and I showed Beth the headstone that marked where my love lay. It was perfect in every detail – it had to be, it was my last obligation to my husband. Made from a plain slab of Cornish slate, it had lettering which had been hand-cut by a Cornish stonemason with a grip of granite and a heart as soft as soapstone. I had first spotted him when he was doing some restoration work in Ugborough church – I met him quite by chance and I'm glad I did, because he was a gentleman and a craftsman. His work is truly superb, and I know Charlie would have looked at the headstone and then said in true Devon fashion, 'Proper job.'

I chose a particular type of lettering in the Arts and Crafts style and wrote a simple epitaph, which I felt would explain to people why Charlie had died so young, and also what kind of man he had been.

The epitaph read:

> They said his heart was weak
> No heart was ever stronger

I knelt down by the grave and I ran my fingers along each letter of the words I had chosen to mark the life of a brave and honourable man. The edge of the lettering was razor sharp, but the slate was soft and warm to the touch. The grave was covered in a rich carpet of crocuses and narcissi, which my girls and I had planted the winter before. The flowers were turning their faces to the sun, but when the flowers had gone, the words would remain – sharp and deep on the smooth, warm slate. Sharp and deep like the scar across my heart – but

just as time will soften and fade the words, so time will heal the scar.
I felt that my life had lain dormant like the bulbs we had planted in the soil; but now I was blossoming – I was strong again and I was turning my face to the sun.

Charlie was up on his cloud watching me, swinging his legs and watching me turn my face towards the sun. And he will stay on his cloud as the years pass, and watch patiently as I fall in love again and live out a long and happy life. He will watch his girls grow into adulthood and he will be by their side when they walk down the aisle on their wedding day. He will watch as I grow old and feeble and then he will get up from his cloud and stroll over to the pub, because it's Friday night and they're serving fish and chips. But every night is Friday night in heaven, just as every morning is Sunday morning.

And he will walk into the bar and see his Granny and Grandpa Charles, sitting in the snug with his Daddy, and they will wave to him as he goes to the counter to order his pint of Bass. And then he will stand and chat to Anson and Trevor and they won't let him leave until they've bought him another pint or two. And then he'll take his leave and his fish and chips and make his way home.

When he gets home he will sit and wait for me; and when I walk through the door I won't be old and feeble, I will be as young and vibrant as the day he first met me. Charlie will hold out his hand to me, his strong gentle hand to me and I will join him at the table.

But I shan't worry that my fish has gone cold, because in heaven, cod moves in a mysterious way in an effort to stay warm.

And we will eat our fish and chips and we will talk about our week, and plan what we are going to do at the weekend. And we'll be excited because we have the house all to ourselves, for the girls are outside playing and it will be many years before they are ready to come home.

And the sound of our laughter will drift out of the room; out across the yard, out over Pimple the Gloucester Old Spot, and Daisy the house cow. It will float like thistledown past the little grey Fergy and out across the Elysian field which Charlie can at last call his own. And the sound of our laughter will drift slowly down and mingle with the woodsmoke drifting lazily up from the chimneys of the village below.

The End

Did I do good, Charlie?

Acknowledgements

It has taken four years to get this book into print. At times I thought I would have to give up on it, but every time my resolve faltered there were people saying 'You have to get the book published, the world needs stories like yours.' And I carried on, and thanks to the love and support and of my friends and family I am now a published author. Hurrah!

I have so many people to thank: in the first instance, my parents, Terry and Eileen Dobson, who gave me such a great start in life. Secondly, I have to thank Walker and Deb Lapthorne, who gave me the copper-bound notebook in which to start writing my story, and have supported me ever since. I am indebted to my sister-in-law Christobel de Cruz, who carefully read through each section as I wrote it and gave a critical assessment. She was very patient with me, despite my rather cavalier attitude to punctuation. I call her the apostrophe Nazi, because of her fanatical loathing of the mis-use of that particular punctuation mark – so this is for you Bubble, Thank's!

Sallie Coolidge, is a woman who has shown me endless patience. She and I have become friends since she first undertook to edit the manuscript, and it is her implicit faith in me and her continued belief in the merits of this book that have kept me going after each and every set back.
I owe her a great deal more than I can ever say with tennis balls.

My best friend, Beth Burrell, has been my saviour. She is unfailingly good-humoured, honest, funny, kind and true. She is the finest example of a human being that I will ever know, and I thank God for her love and support.

I am grateful for the help of Chris Burrell MB, BS, FRCP, in checking the medical accuracy of this book and also for helping me to understand Charlie's very complicated medical history. Chris epitomises all that is best about the medical profession; he is an outstanding cardiac physician, with more skill and a greater concern for the well being of his patients than he will ever be given credit for. He is a true humanitarian and a wonderful man.

To my other friends and family, whose love has helped to fill the terrible void that Charlie's death left in my life, I have only gratitude and eternal thanks. You have backed me every step of the way, fed me, nagged me, read my work and given me the belief in its validity. You will see your name below, you know who you are, and I couldn't have written this book without you.

Edward Boydell, Jane Edwardes, Victoria Boydell, Alex Schoch, Charles and Sally Wace, Linda Gibson, Julie Benson, Alex and Sarah Ashworth, David and Jenny Dally, Tim and Joan Gorrell, Jo and Alex Mackie, Graeme and Liz Mackie, Philip and Kate Robert-Tissot, David and Susan Leyland, Adam Leyland, Rob and Sara Wormald, Tim and Charlotte Chicken, Pat Whitelaw and John Allan, James and Annie Hill, Charlotte and Izzy Bircher, Ruth Langsford, Chris Sutton-Scott-Tucker, Michael and Juliet Sutton- Scott- Tucker, Nick Irving, Nigel and Angie Littleton, Tim Long, Ilkey, Derek and Christine Wilkinson, Charles and Charlotte Style, Julia Runnagal, Kent Upshon, Amanda Jedynak, Neil Connery, Alison Ronnie, Liz Hughes, Lane and Margie Moore, Lydia North, Amy Bingham, Annette Richman, Wendy Shaw and Rosemary Good.

My thanks also go to Charlie's cardiac surgeon Mr. Alan Wood; Mr. Michael Marrinan, Dr. John Halliday, the late Professor Ronnie Campbell, Marie Cooper, Susan Orchard and every member of the medical profession who cared for Charlie during his lifetime.

Personal letters and e-mails included in this book are reproduced with the kind permission of Alex Ashworth, Charles Wace and Simon Berry.

Photo: Libbi Pedder

Kate Boydell was born in Devon in 1964. For the last 21 years she has worked in various jobs in television, starting as a film camera assistant and currently as a video news editor.

Kate decided to write *Big Hearted Man* following the untimely death of her husband Charlie. She decided to write a practical guide to widowhood, and published it on the Internet. The unexpected response to the site, www.merrywidow.me.uk, was immediate and overwhelming. Kate has since been featured on Radio Four *Woman's Hour*, Nicky Campbell's Breakfast Show on Radio Five Live, *This Morning* and *Kilroy*. She has been featured in articles in *The Mail On Sunday 'You' Magazine, The Observer Magazine* and *Reader's Digest*.

Kate lives in Devon with her two daughters, Rosie aged 9, and Alice aged 7.